CORRIGENDUM

Ref: Sales No. E.05.II.E.1
ISBN 92-1-116915-1
ECE/CEP/125

March 2005
Geneva

ENVIRONMENTAL PERFORMANCE REVIEWS

BOSNIA AND HERZEGOVINA

Environmental Performance Reviews Series No. 20

<u>Corrigendum</u>

For pages vi, vii, viii, and ix, <u>read</u>

ECE/CEP/125/Corr.1
English only

GE. * 2 0 0 5 0 3 0 6 7 9 *

ENG

LIST OF CONTRIBUTORS

State of Bosnia and Herzegovina

Mr. Reuf Hadzibegic Assistant Minister	Ministry of Foreign Trade and Economic Relations
Mr. Ibro Čengić	Ministry of Foreign Trade and Economic Relations
Mr. Zlatko Hurtić	Ministry of Foreign Trade and Economic Relations
Mr. Haris Mešinović	Ministry of Foreign Trade and Economic Relations
Mr. Hamdo Tinjak	Ministry of Foreign Trade and Economic Relations
Mr. Sahrudin Sarajcic	State Agency for Statistics
Mr. Hasan Zolić	State Agency for Statistics
Ms.Nada Bojanic	Directorate for EU Integration
Dr. Jozo Bagarić	State Veterinary Administration, Sarajevo

Federation of Bosnia and Herzegovina

Mr. Cero Mehmed Assistant Minister	Federal Ministry of Physical Planning and Environment
Ms. Andja Hadziabdic	Federal Ministry of Physical Planning and Environment
Ms. Azra Kora-Mehmedovac	Federal Ministry of Physical Planning and Environment
Mr. Mladen Rudez	Federal Ministry of Physical Planning and Environment
Mr. Hilmo Sehovic Assistant Minister	Federal Ministry of Energy, Mining and Industry
Mr. Nedzad Brankovic Minister	Federal Ministry of Transport and Communications
Mr. Fuad Bahtanovic	Federal Ministry of Agriculture, Water Management and Forestry
Mr. Peskovic Bajram	Federal Ministry of Agriculture, Water Management and Forestry
Mr. Ahmed Duranovic	Federal Ministry of Agriculture, Water Management and Forestry
Ms. Hazima Hadzovic	Federal Ministry of Agriculture, Water Management and Forestry
Mr. Pasalic Omer	Federal Ministry of Agriculture, Water Management and Forestry
Ms. Hasena Rovćanin	Federal Ministry of Agriculture, Water Management and Forestry
Mr. Jure Sesar	Federal Ministry of Agriculture, Water Management and Forestry
Ms. Velinka Topalović	Federal Ministry of Agriculture, Water Management and Forestry
Mr. Mladen Vasić	Federal Ministry of Agriculture, Water Management and Forestry
Ms. Vesna Veljancic	Federal Ministry of Agriculture, Water Management and Forestry
Mr. Dalibor Vrhovac	Federal Ministry of Agriculture, Water Management and Forestry
Dr. Slavenko Sehovic	Federal Ministry of Health
Mr. Niaz Uzunovic	Federal Ministry of Health
Mr. Zaim Heco	Federal Ministry of Transport and Communications

Mr. Zlatan Dedić	Agency for Privatization in the Federation of Bosnia and Herzegovina
Mr. Safet Husanovic	Office for Reconstruction and International Relations
Mr. Martin Tais	Federal Meteorological Institute, Environmental Section
Ms Esena Kupusovic	Federal Meteorological Institute, Hydrological department
Mr. Rasim Amzić Assistant to the Minister	Mostar Canton
Ms. Zijada Krvavac Assistant Minister	Ministry of Physical Planning and Environment, Sarajevo Canton
Mr. Abid Saric Minister	Ministry of Economy, Sarajevo Canton
Mr. Musair Veledar	Department for Agriculture, Municipality Stari Grad Mostar
Mr. Drekovic Jakub	Water Supply and Sanitation, Sarajevo
Ms. Sabina Begić	Department of Planning, Development and Environmental Protection, Tuzla Municipality
Ms. Jasminka Dzinic	Director of Public Enterprise Tuzla Forests
Mr. Izet Delalić	Thermal Power Plant "Tuzla"
Mr. Mehmed Lacic	Forester Tuzla
Doc. Dr. Sabahudin Bajramović	University of Sarajevo, Agricultural Faculty Sarajevo
Prof. Dr. Hamir Čustović	University of Sarajevo, Agricultural Faculty Sarajevo
Prof. Dr. Vjekoslav Selak	University of Sarajevo, Agricultural Faculty Sarajevo
Dr. Esma Velagić	University of Sarajevo, Agricultural Faculty Sarajevo
Mr. Mustafa Omanović	Professor Emeritus, University of Sarajevo
Doc. Dr. Nezir Tanović	Agicultural Institute Butmir, Sarajevo
Ms. Ramiza Alić	Hydro-Engineering Institute, Sarajevo
Mr. Tarik Kupusovic	Hydro-Engineering Institute
Mr. Branko Vucijak	Hydro Engineering Institute
Ms. Aida Pilav	Institute for Public Health
Ms. Aida Vilic	Institute for Public Health
Ms. Alma Gusinac-Skopo	Institute for Public Health
Mr. Abdulfetah Hadzic	Institute for Public Health of Canton Sarajevo
Mr. Jadranko Prlić	South East Institute for Strategic International Studies
Mr. Mehmed Buturovic	Public Enterprise "Vodno Podrucje Slivova Rijeke Save", Sarajevo
Ms. Naida Andelic	Public Enterprise "Vodno Podrucje Slivova Rijeke Save", Sarajevo
Mr. Stjepan Matic	Public Company "Natural Park Hutovo Blato"
Ms. Eldina Muftić	ECON, Sarajevo, Company for organic farming

Republika Srpksa

Prof. Jaksic Borislav Vice-Minister	Ministry of Spatial Planning, Civil Engineering and Ecology
Mr. Mihajlo Stevanović Assistant Minister for Water Management	Ministry of Agriculture, Forestry and Water Management
Mr. Mirsad Pekic Assistant Minister	Ministry of Economy and Coordination

Mr. Zoran Stjepanović Assistant Minister	Ministry of Economic Affairs (Relations) and Coordination
Mr. Ljubo Glamocic Assistant Minister	Ministry of Industry and Technology
Ms.Bilijana Markovic Assistant Minister	Ministry of Spatial planning, Civil Engineering and Ecology
Mr. Brane Milosevic Assistant Minister	Ministry of Trade and Tourism
Mr. Marinko Biljanović Assistant Minister for Air, Water and Railway Traffic	Ministry of Transport and Communications
Mr. Rajko Djorojevic	Ministry of Spatial Planning, Civil Engineering and Ecology
Mr. Petar Jankovic	Ministry of Spatial Planning, Civil Engineering and Ecology
Ms. Radmila Kostic	Ministry of Spatial Planning, Civil Engineering and Ecology
Mr. Ozren Laganin	Ministry of Spatial Planning, Civil Engineering and Ecology
Mr. Gojko Miljanic	Ministry of Spatial Planning, Civil Engineering and Ecology
Ms. Radojka Popović	Ministry of Spatial Planning, Civil Engineering and Ecology
Ms. Svjetlana Radusin	Ministry of Spatial Planning, Civil Engineering and Ecology
Ms. Ljiljana Stanisljevic	Ministry of Spatial Planning, Civil Engineering and Ecology
Mr. Dušan Nešković	Ministry of Agriculture, Forestry and Water management
Mr. Milan Ninčić	Ministry of Agriculture, Forestry and Water management
Mr. Mladen Stojanvić	Ministry of Agriculture, Forestry and Water management
Mr. Igor Jokanovic	Ministry of Transport and Communication
Mr. Zoran Došen	Directorate for Privatization
Mr. Ragoljub Davidovic	Mayor of Banja Luka, Banja Luka Municipality
Mr. Branco Lasic	Banja Luka Municipality
Mr. Radovanovic	Banja Luka Municipality
Mr. Djordje Danojevic	Banja Luka Municipality
Prof. dr. Nikola Mičić	University of Banja Luka, Agricultural Faculty
Prof. dr. Mile Dardić	University of Banja Luka, Agricultural Faculty
Mr. Đurić	University of Banja Luka, Agricultural Faculty
Prof. Dr. Petar Durman	University of Banja Luka, Agricultural Faculty
Doc. Dr. Mihajlo Marković	University of Banja Luka, Agricultural Faculty
Mr. Lazo Roljić	University of Banja Luka, Faculty of Economics
Mr. Ratko Comic	Professor, Faculty of Forestry
Mr. Petar M. Gvero	Faculty of Mechanical Engineering
Mr. Drago Trkulja	Hydromet. Institute
Mr. Mirolad Balaban	Public Health Institute

Ms. Dusanka Danojevic	Public Health Institute
Mr. Marko Lalic	Public Health Institute
Ms. Sladjana Petkovic	Public Health Institute
Ms. Jelena Kadic	Republic Institute for Protection of Cultural, Historical and Natural Heritage
Mr. Miladin Trbic	Institute of protection, ecology and informatics
Mr. Zoran Lukač	Institution for Urban Planning, Banja Luka
Mr. Dragan Milojčić	Institute of Urbanism
Mr Radivoje Bratic	Institute for Water Management

Brčko District

Mr. Goroljub Jovanovic	Department of Utilities Brčko District Government
Ms. Suada Ćatović	Department of Utilities Brčko District Government

Regional Environmental Centre for Central and Eastern Europe

Mr. Jasna Draganic	Country office
Mr. Zoran Mateljak	Office Mostar
Mr. Nešad Šeremet	Country Office
Mr. Djordje Stefanovic	Office Banja Luka

Non-governmental organisations

Dr. Aleksandar Knezevic	President CETEOR
Ms. Azra Jaganjac	Associate Professor, University of Sarajevo

Miscellaneous

Ms. Sanda Midzic	Centre for Environmentally Sustainable Development
Dr. Hajrudin Simicic	Associate Professor

List of International Contributors

Mr. Moises Venancio	UNDP, Deputy Resident Representative
Ms. Paulien van Noort	UNDP, Programme Officer Environment
Mr. Armin Klockhar	Project on Forestry, World Bank
Mr Stuart Thompson	Legal Advisor for Natural Resources Office of High Representative
Mr. Haris Hajrulahovic	WHO Liaison Office for Bosnia and Herzegovina
Ms. Dubravka Trivic	WHO Liaison Office for Bosnia and Herzegovina Office Banja Luka

Printed at United Nations, Geneva
GE.05-30112-February 2005 – 2,380

ECONOMIC COMMISSION FOR EUROPE
Committee on Environmental Policy

ENVIRONMENTAL PERFORMANCE REVIEWS

BOSNIA AND HERZEGOVINA

UNITED NATIONS
New York and Geneva, 2004

Environmental Performance Reviews Series No.20

NOTE

Symbols of United Nations documents are composed of capital letters combined with figures. Mention of such a symbol indicates a reference to a United Nations document.

The designations employed and the presentation of the material in this publication do not imply the expression of any opinion whatsoever on the part of the Secretariat of the United Nations concerning the legal status of any country, territory, city or area, or of its authorities, or concerning the delimitation of its frontiers or boundaries.

UNITED NATIONS PUBLICATION
Sales No. E.05.II.E.1
ISBN 92-1-116915-1
ISSN 1020-4563

APR 2 6 2005

Foreword

Environmental Performance Reviews for countries-in-transition were initiated by Environment Ministers at the second "Environment for Europe" Conference in Lucerne, Switzerland, in 1993. As a result, the UNECE Committee on Environmental Policy decided to make the Environmental Performance Reviews a part of its regular programme.

Ten years later, at the Fifth Ministerial Conference "Environment for Europe (Kiev, 21-23 May 2003), the Ministers confirmed that the UNECE programme of environmental performance reviews (EPR) had made it possible to assess the effectiveness of the efforts of countries with economies in transition to manage the environment, and to offer the Governments concerned tailor-made recommendations on improving environmental management to reduce their pollution load, to better integrate environmental policies into sectoral policies and to strengthen cooperation with the international community. They also reaffirmed their support for the EPR programme as an important instrument for countries with economies in transition, and decided that the programme should continue.

Through the Peer Review process, Environmental Performance Reviews also promote dialogue among UNECE member countries and harmonization of environmental conditions and policies throughout the region. As a voluntary exercise, the Environmental Performance Review is undertaken only at the request of the country itself.

The studies are carried out by international teams of experts from the region, working closely with national experts from the reviewed country. The teams also benefit from close cooperation with other organizations in the United Nations system, including the United Nations Development Programme, the United Nations Environment Programme, the World Bank and the World Health Organization, as well as with the Organization for Economic Cooperation and Development.

The Environmental Performance Review of Bosnia and Herzegovina is the twentieth in the series published by the United Nations Economic Commission for Europe. I hope that this Review will be useful to all countries in the region, to intergovernmental and non-governmental organizations alike and, especially, to Bosnia and Herzegovina, its Government and its people.

Brigita Schmögnerová
Executive Secretary

Preface

The Environmental Performance Review (EPR) of Bosnia and Herzegovina began in September 2003, with the first preparatory mission, during which the final structure of the report was established. Thereafter, the review team of international experts was constituted. It included experts from Belgium, Bulgaria, Italy, Norway, Slovenia, Sweden and the former Yugoslav Republic of Macedonia, together with experts from the secretariats of the United Nations Economic Commission for Europe (UNECE) and the European Centre for Environment and Health of the World Health Organization (WHO/ECEH).

The review mission took place from 2 to 14 November 2003. A draft of the conclusions and recommendations as well the draft EPR report were submitted to Bosnia and Herzegovina for comment in April 2004. In September 2004, the draft was submitted for consideration to the Ad Hoc Expert Group on Environmental Performance. During this meeting, the Expert Group discussed the report in detail with expert representatives of the State of Bosnia and Herzegovina and of the two entitles -- the Federation of Bosnia and Herzegovina and Republika Srpska, focusing in particular on the conclusions and recommendations made by the international experts.

The EPR report, with suggested amendments from the Expert Group, was then submitted for peer review to the UNECE Committee on Environmental Policy at its eleventh session in October 2004. A high-level delegation from the Government of Bosnia and Herzegovina participated in the peer review. The Committee adopted the recommendations as set out in this report.

The report covers twelve issues of importance to Bosnia and Herzegovina, divided into three sections, including the framework for environmental policy, management of pollution and natural resources and economic and sectoral integration. Among the issues receiving special attention during the reviews were the policy, legal and institutional framework, public participation in decision-making and access to information; the use and supply of water resources, including drinking water; land use, agriculture and biodiversity; management of waste and contaminated sites, eco-tourism and energy.

The UNECE Committee on Environmental Policy and the UNECE review team would like to thank the Governments of Bosnia and Herzegovina, of the Federation of Bosnia and Herzegovina of Republika Srpska and of Brčko District, and the many excellent national experts who worked with the international experts and contributed with their knowledge and assistance. UNECE wishes the Government of Bosnia and Herzegovina further success in carrying out the tasks before it to meet its environmental objectives and policy, including the implementation of the recommendations to support and promote environmental protection, to improve overall national living standards, and to strengthen international cooperation.

UNECE would also like to express its deep appreciation to the Governments of Germany, Hungary, Italy, Norway, the Netherlands, Sweden, Switzerland and the United Kingdom for their support to the Environmental Performance Review Programme, to the European Centre for Environment and Health of the World Health Organization for its participation in the Review, and to the United Nations Development Programme and the World Bank for their contributions to the work in Bosnia and Herzegovina and the preparation of this report.

LIST OF TEAM MEMBERS

Ms. Mary Pat SILVEIRA	ECE secretariat	Team Leader
Mr. Antoine NUNES	ECE secretariat	Project Coordinator
Mr. Jyrki HIRVONEN	ECE secretariat	Introduction
Ms. Vanya GRIGOROVA	Bulgaria	Chapter 1
Mr. Oleg DZIOUBINSKI	ECE secretariat	Chapter 2
Mr. Mikhail KOKINE	ECE secretariat	Chapter 3
Mr. Metodija DIMOVSKI	The former Yugoslav Republic of Macedonia	Chapter 4
Mr. Michel HOUSSIAU	Belgium	Chapter 5
Mr. Ivan NARKEVITCH	ECE secretariat	Chapter 6
Mr. Jon OPEM	Norway	Chapter 7
Mr. Ljupco MELOVSKI	The former Yugoslav Republic of Macedonia	Chapter 8
Ms. Laura SUSANI	Italy	Chapter 9
Mrs. Marta HRUSTEL-MAJCEN	Slovenia	Chapter 10
Mr. Mats JOHANSSON	Sweden	Chapter 11
Dr. Plamen DIMITROV Dr. Bettina MENNE	Bulgaria WHO/ECEH	Chapter 12

The designations employed and the presentation of the material in this publication do not imply the expression of any opinion whatsoever on the part of the Secretariat of the United Nations concerning the legal status of any country, territory, city or area or of its authorities, or concerning the delimitation of its frontiers or boundaries. In particular, the boundaries shown on the maps do not imply official endorsement or acceptance by the United Nations.

UNECE Information Unit
Palais des Nations
CH-1211 Geneva 10
Switzerland

Phone: +41 (0)22 917 44 44
Fax: +41 (0)22 917 05 05
E-mail: info.ece@unece.org
Website: http://www.unece.org

The mission for the project took place from 2 November to 14 November 2003.

LIST OF CONTRIBUTORS

State of Bosnia and Herzegovina

Mr. Reuf Hadzibegic Assistant Minister	Ministry of Foreign Trade and Economic Relations
Mr. Ibro Čengić	Ministry of Foreign Trade and Economic Relations
Mr. Zlatko Hurtić	Ministry of Foreign Trade and Economic Relations
Mr. Haris Mešinović	Ministry of Foreign Trade and Economic Relations
Mr. Hamdo Tinjak	Ministry of Foreign Trade and Economic Relations
Mr. Sahrudin Sarajcic	State Agency for Statistics
Mr. Hasan Zolić	State Agency for Statistics
Ms.Nada Bojanic	Directorate for EU Integration
Dr. Jozo Bagarić	State Veterinary Administration, Sarajevo
Mrs. Andja Hadziabdic	EIA Department

Federation of Bosnia and Herzegovina

Mr. Cero Mehmed Assistant Minister	Federal Ministry of Physical Planning and Environment
Mrs. Azra Kora-Mehmedovac	Federal Ministry of Physical Planning and Environment
Mr. Hilmo Sehovic Assistant Minister	Federal Ministry of Energy, Mining and Industry
Mr. Nedzad Brankovic Minister	Federal Ministry of Transport and Communications
Mr. Fuad Bahtanovic	Federal Ministry of Agriculture, Water Management and Forestry
Mr. Peskovic Bajram	Federal Ministry of Agriculture, Water Management and Forestry
Mr. Ahmed Duranovic	Federal Ministry of Agriculture, Water Management and Forestry
Ms. Hazima Hadzovic	Federal Ministry of Agriculture, Water Management and Forestry
Mr. Pasalic Omer	Federal Ministry of Agriculture, Water Management and Forestry
Mrs. Hasena Rovćanin	Federal Ministry of Agriculture, Water Management and Forestry
Mr. Jure Sesar	Federal Ministry of Agriculture, Water Management and Forestry
Mr. Mladen Vasić	Federal Ministry of Agriculture, Water Management and Forestry
Dr. Slavenko Sehovic	Federal Ministry of Health
Mr. Niaz Uzunovic	Federal Ministry of Health
Mr. Zaim Heco	Federal Ministry of Transport and Communications
Mr. Zlatan Dedić	Agency for Privatization in the Federation of Bosnia and Herzegovina
Mr. Safet Husanovic	Office for Reconstruction and International Relations
Mr. Martin Tais	Federal Meteorological Institute, Environmental Section
Ms Esena Kupusovic	Federal Meteorological Institute, Hydrological department

Mr. Rasim Amzić Assistant to the Minister	Mostar Canton
Ms. Zijada Krvavac Assistant Minister	Ministry of Physical Planning and Environment, Sarajevo Canton
Mr Abid Saric Minister	Ministry of Economy, Sarajevo Canton
Mr. Musair Veledar	Dept. for Agriculture, Municipiality Stari Grad Mostar
Mr. Drekovic Jakub	Water Supply and Sanitation, Sarajevo
Ms. Sabina Begić	Department of Planning, Development and Environmental Protection, Tuzla Municipality
Mrs. Jasminka Dzinic	Director of Public Enterprise Tuzla Forests
Mr. Izet Delalić	Thermal Power Plant "Tuzla"
Mr. Mehmed Lacic	Forester Tuzla
Dr. Sabahudin Bajramović	University of Sarajevo, Agricultural Faculty Sarajevo
Prof. Dr. Hamir Čustović	University of Sarajevo, Agricultural Faculty Sarajevo
Prof. Dr. Vjekoslav Selak	University of Sarajevo, Agricultural Faculty Sarajevo
Dr. Esma Velagić	University of Sarajevo, Agricultural Faculty Sarajevo
Mr. Mustafa Omanović	Professor Emeritus, University of Sarajevo
Doc. Dr. Nezir Tanović	Agicultural Institute Butmir, Sarajevo
Ms. Ramiza Alić	Hydro-Engineering Institute, Sarajevo
Mr. Tarik Kupusovic	Hydro-engineering institute
Mr. Branko Vucijak	Hydro engineering Institute
Ms. Aida Pilav	Institute for Public Health
Ms. Aida Vilic	Institute for Public Health
Ms. Alma Gusinac-Skopo	Institute for Public Health
Mr. Abdulfetah Hadzic	Institute for Public Health of Canton Sarajevo
Mr. Jadranko Prlić	South East Institute for Strategic International Studies
Mr. Mehmed Buturovic Director,	Public Enterprise "Vodno Podrucje Slivova Rijeke Save", Sarajevo
Ms. Naida Andelic	Public Enterprise "Vodno Podrucje Slivova Rijeke Save", Sarajevo
Mr. Stjepan Matic	Public Company "Natural Park Hutovo Blato"
Mrs. Eldina Muftić	ECON, Sarajevo, Company for organic farming

Republika Srpksa

Prof. Jaksic Borislav Vice-Minister	Ministry of Spatial Planning, Civil Engineering and Ecology
Mr. Mihajlo Stevanović Assistant Minister for Water Management	Ministry of Agriculture, Forestry and Water Management
Mr. Mirsad Pekic Assistant Minister	Ministry of Economy and Coordination
Mr. Zoran Stjepanović Assistant Minister,	Ministry of Economic Affairs (Relations) and Coordination
Mr. Ljubo Glamocic Assistant Minister	Ministry of Industry and Technology
Mrs.Bilijana Markovic Assistant Minister	Ministry of Physical planning, Civil and Ecology
Mr. Brane Milosevic Assistant Minister	Ministry of Trade and Tourism

Mr. Marinko Biljanović Assistant Minister for Air, Water and Railway Traffic	Ministry of Transport and Communications
Mr. Rajko Djorojevic	Ministry of Spatial Planning, Civil Engineering and Ecology
Mr. Petar Jankovic	Ministry of Spatial Planning, Civil Engineering and Ecology
Mrs. Radmila Kostic	Ministry of Spatial Planning, Civil Engineering and Ecology
Mr. Ozren Laganin	Ministry of Spatial Planning, Civil Engineering and Ecology
Mr. Gojko Miljanic	Ministry of Spatial Planning, Civil Engineering and Ecology
Ms. Radojka Popović	Ministry of Spatial Planning, Civil Engineering and Ecology
Mrs. Svjetlana Radusin	Ministry of Spatial Planning, Civil Engineering and Ecology
Mr. Dušan Nešković	Ministry of Agriculture, Forestry and Water management
Mr. Milan Ninčić	Ministry of Agriculture, Forestry and Water management
Mr. Mladen Stojanvić	Ministry of Agriculture, Forestry and Water management
Ms. Velinka Topalović	Federal Ministry of Agriculture, Forestry and Water Management
Mrs. Vesna Veljancic	Federal Ministry of Agriculture, Forestry and Water Management
Mr. Dalibor Vrhovac	Federal Ministry of Agriculture, Forestry and Water Management
Mr. Igor Jokanovic	Ministry of Transport and Communication
Mr. Mladen Rudez	Federal Ministry of Urban Planning and Environment
Mrs. Ljiljana Stanisljevic	Ministry of the Urbanism, Civil Engineering and Ecology
Mr. Zoran Došen	Directorate for Privatization
Mr. Ragoljub Davidovic	Mayor of Banja Luka, *Banja Luka Municipality*
Mr. Branco Lasic	*Banja Luka Municipality*
Mr. Radovanovic	*Banja Luka Municipality*
Mr. Djordje Danojevic	*Banja Luka Municipality*
Prof. dr. Nikola Mičić,	University of Banja Luka, Agricultural Faculty
Prof. dr. Mile Dardić	University of Banja Luka, Agricultural Faculty
Mr. Đurić	University of Banja Luka, Agricultural Faculty
Prof. Dr. Petar Durman	University of Banja Luka, Agricultural Faculty
Dr. Mihajlo Marković	University of Banja Luka, Agricultural Faculty
Mr. Lazo Roljić	University of Banja Luka, Faculty of Economics
Mr. Ratko Comic	Professor, Faculty of Forestry
Mr. Petar M. Gvero	WG on Air, Faculty of Mechanical Engineering
Mr. Drago Trkulja	Hydromet. Institute
Mr. Mirolad Balaban	Public Health Institute
Ms. Dusanka Danojevic	Public Health Institute
Mr. Marko Lalic	Public Health Institute
Ms. Sladjana Petkovic	Public Health Institute

Mrs. Jelena Kadic	Republic Institute for Protection of Cultural-Historical and Natural Heritage
Mr. Miladin Trbic	Institute of protection, ecology and informatics
Mr. Zoran Lukač	Institution for Urban Planning, Banja Luka
Mr. Dragan Milojčić	Institute of Urbanism
Mr Radivoje Bratic	Institute for Water Management

Brčko District

Mr. Goroljub Jovanovic	Department of Utilities Brčko District Government
Mrs. Suada Ćatović	Department of Utilities Brčko District Government

Regional Environmental Centre for Central and Eastern Europe

Mr. Jasna Draganic	Country office B&H
Mr. Zoran Mateljak	Office Mostar
Mr. Nešad Šeremet	Country Office, Bosnia and Herzegovina
Mr. Djordje Stefanovic	Office Banja Luka

Non-governmental organisations

Dr. Aleksandar Knezevic	President CETEOR
Ms. Azra Jaganjac	Associate Professor, University of Sarajevo

Miscellaneous

Ms. Sanda Midzic	Centre for Environmentally Sustainable Development
Dr. Hajrudin Simicic	University of Tuzla

List of International Contributors

Mr. Moises Venancio	UNDP, Deputy Resident Representative
Mrs. Paulien van Noort	UNDP, Programme Officer Environment
Mr. Armin Klockhar	Project on Forestry, World Bank
Mr. Stuart Thompson	Legal Advisor for Natural Resources Office of High Representative
Mr. Haris Hajrulahovic	WHO Liaison Office for Bosnia and Herzegovina
Ms. Dubravka Trivic	WHO Liaison Office for Bosnia and Herzegovina Office Banja Luka

TABLE OF CONTENTS

LIST OF FIGURES

LIST OF TABLES

LIST OF BOXES

ACRONYMS AND ABBREVIATIONS

BAT	Best Available Technique
BiH	Bosnia and Herzegovina
BOD	Biological oxygen demand
CARDS	Community, Assistance, Reconstruction, Development and Stabilisation
CEPRES	Centre on Ecology and Natural Resources of the Sarajevo University
CFCs	Chlorofluorocarbons
CITES	Convention on International Trade in Endangered Species of Wild Fauna and Flora
COD	Chemical Oxygen Demand
CORINAIR	COoRdinated INformation AIR
CORINE	CO-oRdination of INformation on the Environment
CPI	Consumer price index
DDT	DichloroDiphenylTrichloroethane
EBRD	European Bank for Reconstruction and Development
EC	European Commission
EEA	European Environment Agency
EIA	Environmental Impact Assessment
EIB	European Investment Bank
EIONET	European Environment Information and Observation Network
EME	Environmental Management in Enterprises
EMEP	Cooperative Programme for Monitoring and Evaluation of the Long-range Transmission of Air Pollutants in Europe
EMS	Environmental Management System
EPR	Environmental Performance Review
EQO	Environmental Quality Objective
EQS	Environmental Quality Standard
EU	European Union
FAO	Food and Agriculture Organization of the United Nations
FBiH	Federation of Bosnia and Herzegovina
FDI	Foreign Direct Investment
GDP	Gross Domestic Product
GEF	Global Environmental Facility
GHGs	Greenhouse gases
GIS	Geographic Information System
GMO	Genetically Modified Organisms
GTZ	Gesellschaft für Technische Zusammenarbeit GmbH
HACCP	Hazard Analysis and Critical Control Point
HCFCs	Hydrochlorofluorocarbons
HDI	Human Development Index
HESME	Health, Environment and Safety Management in Enterprises
HMs	Heavy Metals
HPP	HydroPower Plant
IAEA	International Atomic Energy Agency
ICTY	International Criminal Tribunal for the Former Yugoslavia
IDB	Islamic Development Bank
IDPs	Internally Displaced Persons
IFI	International Financing Institution
IFOAM	International Federation of Organic Agricultural Movements
I-FOR	NATO Implementation Force
ILO	International Labour Organisation
IMF	International Monetary Fund
IPCC	Intergovernmental Panel on Climate Change
IPPC	Integrated Pollution Prevention and Control
ISCE	Inter-Entity Steering Committee for Environment
ISO	International Standardization Organization

IUCN	World Conservation Union
JICA	Japan International Cooperation Agency
KM	Konvertibilna Marka or Marka
LEAPs	Local Environmental Action Plans
LIFE	Financial Instrument for the Environment
MAB	Man and Biosphere Programme of UNESCO
MAC	Maximum Allowable Concentration
MAD	Maximum Allowable Discharge
MAFWM	Ministry of Agriculture, Forestry and Water Management
MAP	Mediterranean Action Plan
MEAs	Multilateral environmental agreements
MOFTER	Ministry of Foreign Trade and Economic Relations
MSPCEE	Ministry of Spatial Planning, Civil Engineering and Ecology
MoU	Memorandum of Understanding
NATO	North Atlantic Treaty Organisation
NEAP	National Environmental Action Plan (Program)
NEHAP	National Environmental Health Action Plan
NGOs	Non–Governmental Organizations
NMVOC	Non-Methane Volatile Organic Compounds
ODS	Ozone-Depleting Substances
OECD	Organisation for Economic Co-operation and Development
OHR	Office of the High Representative
OSCE	Organization for Security and Co-operation in Europe
PAH	PolyAromatic Hydrocarbon
PCA	Partnership and Co-operation Agreement
PCB	PolyChlorinated Biphenyl
PHARE	Assistance for Economic Restructuring in the countries of Central and Eastern Europe
PIC	Prior Informed Consent
POPs	Persistent Organic Pollutants
PPI	Producer Price Index
PPP	Purchasing Power Parity
PRPS	Poverty Reduction Strategy Paper
PRTR	Pollution Release and Transfer Registry
R BiH	State of Bosnia and Herzegovina
REC	Regional Environmental Center
REReP	Regional Environmental Reconstruction Programme
RS	Republika Srpska
SDC	Swiss Agency for Development and Cooperation
SEA	Strategic Environmental Assessment
SFOR	Stabilisation Force
SFRY	Socialist Federal Republic of Yugoslavia
SME	Small and Medium Enterprises
SPM	Suspended Particulate Matter
SR BiH	Socialist republic of Bosnia and Herzegovina
UEIP	Urgent Environmental Investment Projects
UNDP	UN Development Programme
UNECE	United Nations Economic Commission for Europe
UNEP	United Nations Environment Programme
UNESCO	United Nations Educational, Scientific and Cultural Organization
UNFPA	United Nations Population Fund
UNHCR	UN High Commissioner for Refugees
UNICEF	United Nations Children's Fund
UNIDO	United Nations Industrial Development Organization
USAID	United States Agency for International Development
USD	US Dollars
VAT	Value-Added Tax

VOCs	Volatile Organic Compounds
WB	World Bank
WHO	World Health Organisation
WWF	World Wide Fund for the Nature

SIGNS AND MEASURES

..	not available
-	nil or negligible
.	decimal point
ha	hectare
kt	kiloton
g	gram
kg	kilogram
mg	milligram
mm	millimetre
cm^2	square centimetre
m^3	cubic metre
km	kilometre
km^2	square kilometre
toe	Tons of oil equivalent
l	litre
ml	millilitre
min	minute
s	second
m	metre
°C	degree Celsius
GJ	gigajoule
kW_{el}	kilowatt (electric)
kWh	kilowatt-hour
kWh_{el}	kilowatt-hour (electric)
kW_{th}	kilowatt (thermal)
MW_{el}	megawatt (electric)
MW_{th}	megawatt (thermal)
MWh	megawatt-hour
GWh	gigawatt-hour
TWh	terawatt-hour
Bq	becquerel
Ci	curie
mSv	millisievert
Cap	Capita
Eq	equivalent
h	hour
kV	kilovolt
MW	megawatt
Gcal	gigacalorie
Hz	hertz

Currency

Monetary unit: Konvertibilna Marka (KM)

Exchange rates: IM F

Year	Konvertibilna Marka / US $
1995	1.43
1996	1.50
1997	1.73
1998	1.76
1999	1.84
2000	2.12
2001	2.19
2002	2.08
2003	1.73

Source : IM F. International Financial Statistics, A pril 2004.

INTRODUCTION

I.1   The physical context

Bosnia and Herzegovina has a land area of 51,209 km^2 (Statistical yearbook 2002) and is situated on the Balkan Peninsula in South-eastern Europe. The country is bounded to the north, west, and southwest by Croatia (border length 932 km) and to the east and southeast by Serbia and Montenegro (total border length 606 km, of which 249 km with Montenegro and 357 km with Serbia). The country also has a 13-km-long coastline along the Adriatic Sea around the town of Neum.

Bosnia and Herzegovina is a mountainous country with 62% of the land more than 700 m above sea level. The Dinaric Alps cross the country from its western border with Croatia to the southeast. The highest peak is Mount Maglic, rising to 2,387 m (7,831 ft) on the border with Serbia and Montenegro. The country also has 10 other mountain peaks higher than 2000 m and 40 peaks between 1500 m and 2000 m. The north is heavily forested, while the south has flatter areas of fertile soil used primarily as farmland.

The country is situated between the continental and Mediterranean climatic zones, which creates three local climatic areas. The northern inland territory has a moderate continental climate with warm summers and cold, snowy winters. The mountain areas above 700 m have a mountain climate with short, cool summers and long, severe winters with snow. The annual precipitation in the inland and Alpine region is between 1,500 to 2,500 mm. The south has an Adriatic-Mediterranean climate with sunny, warm summers and short, mild, rainy winters, and an average annual precipitation of 600 to 800 mm. The average temperature in Sarajevo, in the continental zone, is -1°C in January and 20°C in July.

The main river is the Sava (331 km within Bosnia and Herzegovina), which runs along the northern border. The Sava and its tributaries, the Bosna (271 km) crossing through Sarajevo, the Una, the Drina and the Vrbas all flow to the north. Few rivers, notably the Neretva (218 km), flow towards the Adriatic Sea. Rivers also define the country's two historical provinces; Bosnia lies in the Sava river valley and Herzegovina is situated in the Neretva river basin and the upper reaches of the Drina.

Forest and woodland cover 39% of the country, meadows and pastures 20%. About 14% of the land is arable, with 5% under permanent crops. Before the war Bosnia and Herzegovina produced specialty agricultural products, such as fruit and tobacco, but it had to import more than half its food, including essential staples. Its natural resources include deposits of minerals such as salt, manganese, silver, lead, copper, iron ore, chromium and coal.

Figure I.1: Land use

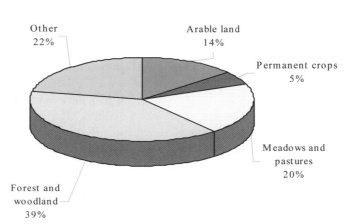

Source: USA Department of Defence 1993.

Figure I.2: GDP by sector in 1999 and 2000 (per cent of total GDP)

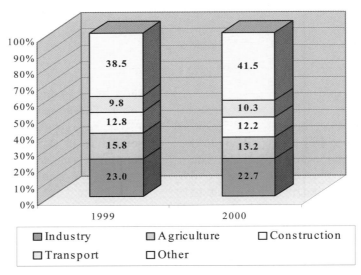

Source: UNECE common statistical database, 2003.

I.2   The human context

In the latest census (1991), Bosnia and Herzegovina had 4,377,033 inhabitants and the population density was 85.5 inhabitants/km^2. Current population figures vary significantly depending on the source. According to Bosnia and Herzegovina's Agency for Statistics, the permanent population in 2001 stood at 3,798,000 (Statistical Bulletin 2, 2003). The largest cities include the capital Sarajevo, which is also an important cultural and commercial centre (population 380,000), Banja Luka (pop. 250,000), Mostar (pop. 140,000) and Zenica (pop. 135,000) (source: estimation of OHR-2002). Between 1991 and 2002 the population movement from the countryside to the towns increased the urban population from 40 to 60%.

The population peaked in 1991. Since then hundreds of thousands have died in the war or were forced to flee their homes. Most of those who fled went to Serbia and Montenegro, Germany, Croatia and Sweden. This emigration has not only reduced the population but also caused a permanent brain drain.

In addition to the emigration out of the country, there are still up to 350,000 internally displaced persons (IDPs) within Bosnia and Herzegovina (source: United Nations High Commissioner for Refugees (UNHCR), In July 2003). The return of IDPs and refugees to their place of origin was mandated by the 1995 Dayton Peace Agreement, but has not happened yet. Especially the return of people to areas where their ethnic group is a minority has been difficult.

Bosnia and Herzegovina has three major population ethnic groups: Bosniaks, Serbs and Croats. All are Slavs and the primary difference among them is their religion. Serbs are traditionally Orthodox Christians, Croats Roman Catholics and Bosniaks, descendants of ethnic Slavs who converted to Islam in the 15th and 16th centuries during the Ottoman period, are generally Sunni Muslims. No single ethnic group comprises a majority. In the 1991 census, prior to independence, Muslims represented 43.5% of the population, Serbs 31.2%, Croats 17.4%, Yugoslavs (people of mixed Muslim, Serb and Croat ancestry) 5.6%, and others (Montenegrins, Albanians, Roma, Jews) 2.3%. The 'Yugoslav' identity used in 1991 was abandoned after the break-up of Yugoslavia (Statistical Yearbook).

The largest cities had mixed populations in 1991, but the war made them almost homogeneous. Sarajevo, located in the Federation of Bosnia and Herzegovina near the boundary of Republika Srpska, is a united city. However, the city's population was 90% Bosniak by 1996. Mostar had by 1995 been divided into a Croat western part and a Bosniak eastern part, with very few Serbs or "others" left in either. Banja Luka, the largest town of Republika Srpska, was almost 100% Serb already by 1993.

The country's fertility rate decreased from 1.6 in 1991 to 1.4 in 2001, which is lower than the European Union average of 1.5 in 2000. The birth rate decreased as well, from 14.4 (per 1000) in 1991 to 9.9 in 2001. The infant mortality rate of 7.6 (per 1000) in 2001 was only a little over half of the

1991 figure of 14.6. Unfortunately, the mortality rate increased from 6.7 per 1000 in 1991 to 8 in 2001. The latest available pre-war 1991 figures gave a life expectancy of 76 years for women and 69.5 years for men.

In 2001 the country's human development index, measured by the United Nations Development Programme (UNDP), was 0.777 (on the scale of 0.0 to 1.0). Bosnia and Herzegovina was 66th out of 175 countries reviewed, which puts it in the group of countries with medium human development.

Primary education is compulsory for all children from age 7 to age 15 and both primary and secondary education are free of charge. The country has seven universities: Banja Luka, Bihac, two in Mostar (by one in East and West Mostar), two in Sarajevo (Sarajevo and Srpsko Sarajevo) and Tuzla. According to the UNDP Human Development Index Report (2003) the adult literacy rate in 2001 was 93%.

The country has three official languages: Bosnian, Croatian and Serb. These three languages are basically South-Slavic languages with minor differences. Two different alphabets are in use; Latin script and the Cyrillic alphabet.

I.3   The historical and economic context

History

In November 1943, a partisan congress in Jajce, proclaimed a new federal Yugoslavia of South Slav peoples, naming Josip Broz Tito its marshal and prime minister. Bosnia and Herzegovina with its mixed multi-ethnic Serb, Bosniak (Muslim) and Croat populations was established as one of six constituent republics of Yugoslavia.

The economic problems and rise of nationalism accelerated Yugoslavia's disintegration, which had begun after Josip Broz Tito's death, in 1980. His successors could not bring together their political views or interests, nor agree on economic policies.

Acceptance of the common institutions and finally even the federalism declined, and tensions and disputes among the republics and among their ethnic groups became unmanageable.

The disintegration of Yugoslavia's ruling party, the League of Communists, in January 1990 led to multiparty parliamentary elections in all six republics by the end of the year. These elections produced absolute or relative majorities for nationalist parties in all the republics. As a result, Slovenia and Croatia declared their independence in June 1991. The Socialist Republic of Bosnia and Herzegovina and the Socialist Republic of Macedonia soon followed suit.

In March 1992, the Government of the Socialist Republic of Bosnia and Herzegovina held a referendum on independence; 67% voted in favour. Bosnia and Herzegovina declared independence on 5 April, and the Serbian Democratic Party formally proclaimed a separate independent Republika Srpska. The United States and the European Union recognized the independence of the country on 6 April 1992, but a war erupted the same week, escalating to a conflict in which all three ethnic groups tried to consolidate their control over the country.

To achieve a ceasefire, several international conferences, attended by all the parties, were held in Lisbon, London and Geneva in 1992-1993. The United Nations began imposing economic sanctions on the Federal Republic of Yugoslavia in 1993 and co-sponsored with the European Union a series of peace plans that one or more Bosnian fractions rejected.

The war continued throughout 1994 and until late 1995. Then a combination of efforts finally led to negotiations and the adoption of an agreement at a United States Air Force base near Dayton, Ohio, signed on 21 November 1995. The war ended with the final version of Dayton Peace Agreement being signed on 14 December 1995 in Paris.

Table I.1: Demography and health indices, 1990-2001

	1990	1991	1992	1993	1994	1995	1996	1997	1998	1999	2000	2001	2002
Birth rate (per 1000)	15.0	14.3	...	...	...	...	12.8	12.9	12.3	11.4	10.5	9.9	...
Fertility rate	...	1.6	1.6	...	...	...	1.6	1.7	1.6	1.4	1.3	1.4	...
Mortality rate (per 1000)	6.5	6.7	...	...	...	...	6.9	7.5	7.9	7.7	8.1	8.0	...
Infant mortality rate (per 1000)	14.8	14.6	...	24.7	...	...	14.0	12.4	11.0	10.1	9.7	7.6	...

Sources: WHO. Health for All database. www.who.dk on 21.10.2003

Table I.2: Selected economic indicators, 1995-2002

	1995	1996	1997	1998	1999	2000	2001	2002
GDP (change, 1995=100)	100.0	154.2	210.7	243.1	266.3	280.7	293.3	304.3
GDP (% change over previous year)	..	54.2	36.6	15.4	9.5	5.4	4.5	3.7
GDP in current prices (million KM)	2,860	4,125	6,562	7,439	8,604	9,433	10,217	10,694.4
GDP in current prices (million US$)	1,995.6	2,740.9	3,783.9	4,227.7	4,686.7	4,449.9	4,675.9	5,142.7
GDP per capita (US$ PPP per capita)	896.1	1,398.6	1,934.5	2,243.7	2,477.4	2,682.8	2,841.2	2,960.0
Share of agriculture in GDP (%)	37.6	40.4	44.2	45.8	15.8	13.2	..	..
Industrial output (annual 1989=100)	..	..	..	..	35.2	39.2	39.2	39.9
Agricultural output (% change over previous year)	..	..	115.4	..	96.3	..	..	..
Labour productivity in industry (% change over previous year)	-22.1	59.8	11.3	15.0	10.4	8.8	17.9	11.7
CPI (% change over the preceding year, annual average)	-14.5	-20.3	8.6	6.8	-0.7	1.4	2.1	1.0
PPI (% change over the preceding year, annual average)	68.7	-4.8	4.5	3.6	4.3	0.9	2.4	0.7
Registered unemployment (% of labour force, end of period)	..	..	39.0	38.7	39.0	39.4	39.9	42.7
Balance of trade in goods and non-factor services (million US$)	-930.0	-1,546.0	-1,758.2	-3,115.6	-3,296.9	-2,626.0	-2,961.1	-3,401.6
Current account balance (million US$)	-193.0	-748.0	-1,060.2	-1,093.2	-1,385.5	-1,086.6	-1,305.3	-1,728.9
" (as % of GDP)	-9.7	-27.3	-28.0	-25.9	-29.6	-24.4	-27.9	-33.6
Net FDI inflows (million US$)	0.0	0.0	0.0	66.7	176.8	146.3	125.4	293.1
Net FDI flows (as % of GDP)	..	..	..	1.6	3.8	3.3	2.7	5.7
Cumulative FDI (million US$)	0.0	0.0	0.0	66.7	243.5	389.8	515.2	808.3
Foreign exchange reserves (million US$)	207.0	235.0	80.4	174.5	452.3	496.6	1,221.2	1,321.4
(as months of imports)	2.30	1.50	0.41	0.55	1.31	1.57	3.58	3.51
Total net external debt (million US$)	3,361.0	3,620.0	4,330.0	2,800.0	3,200.0	2,950.0	2,600.0	2,407.0
Exports of goods (million US$)	152.0	336.0	575.0	663.8	831.8	1,175.3	1,131.6	1,114.4
Imports of goods (million US$)	1,082.0	1,882.0	2,333.2	3,779.4	4,128.7	3,801.3	4,092.7	4,515.9
Ratio of net debt to exports (%)	2,211.2	1,077.4	753.0	421.8	384.7	251.0	229.8	216.0
Ratio of net debt to GDP (%)	168.4	132.1	114.4	66.2	68.3	66.3	55.6	46.8
Exchange rates: annual averages (KM/US$)	1.43	1.50	1.73	1.76	1.84	2.12	2.19	2.08
Population (1000)	4,140.5	4,170.1	4,199.8	4,229.8	4,256.4	4,229.7	4,272.3	4,302.7

Source: UNECE Common statistical database and National Statistics, 2003.

The Dayton Peace Agreement established a new constitution for Bosnia and Herzegovina and internationally organized elections. It also established a united Bosnia and Herzegovina made up of two entities, the Federation of Bosnia and Herzegovina and Republika Srpska.

In 1995-1996 a multinational implementation force (I-FOR) of 60,000 troops was deployed to Bosnia and Herzegovina to keep the peace and implement the Dayton Peace Agreement. I-FOR was succeeded in 1997 by a smaller, stabilization force (SFOR) whose mission is to deter renewed hostilities. The United Nations International Police Task Force in Bosnia and Herzegovina was replaced at the end of 2002 by the European Union Police Mission, the first such police training and monitoring task force from the European Union. As of February 2004, SFOR still remains in the country.

Economy

Before the war Bosnia and Herzegovina had a diversified economic structure. Industrial production (43 %), Agriculture and Forestry (18 %) and Mining (14%) were important and produced the main part of the GDP. Tourism was also well developed. Yugoslavia's military industries were heavily concentrated there, and the defence industry, producing about 40% of Yugoslavia's armaments and was a significant part of the economy.

The war devastated the country's infrastructure. Bosnia and Herzegovina is the second poorest country of the former Yugoslav republics just after the former Yugoslav Republic of Macedonia. During the war about 45% of its industrial plants, including about 75% of its oil refineries, were destroyed, damaged or plundered. The transport infrastructure suffered similar destruction and approximately 35% of the main roads and 40% of the bridges were damaged or destroyed.

In 1991, just before the war, annual inflation was already at 116%, but the outbreak of the war brought about massive hyperinflation and the consumer price index (CPI) shot up to 83,327% in 1992. The Central Bank of Bosnia and Herzegovina was established in 1997 and the introduction of the new national currency, the konvertibilna marka, or marka (KM), in January 1998 finally brought inflation down. The konvertibilna marka was pegged originally to the deutsche mark and now to the euro. Since 1997 inflation has been single-digit and the latest CPI figure for 2002 was 1%.

The war caused industrial production to plunge, and in 1993 it was only about 20% of the 1989, pre-war level. Neither the end of the war nor international lending or aid has helped industry to regain its former production levels. Industrial output grew at high annual percentage rates from 1995 to 2000 and slowed down after that to 1.7% (2002), but the original starting point was so low that production still remains at 39.9% of its 1989 level.

As a consequence of the war, inflation and industrial decline, unemployment soared to an estimated 70-80% in 1995. The economic recovery began after the 1995 Dayton Peace Agreement. The end of the hostilities and the very low level of economic activity during the war caused GDP to grow 54.2% in 1996. The fast growth continued until 1999 but slowed to 3.7% in 2002. GDP growth has eased unemployment markedly, although registered unemployment in 2002 was still 42.7%.

The war and economic blockades severely disrupted Bosnia and Herzegovina's external trade with both the Federal Republic of Yugoslavia (now Serbia and Montenegro) and Croatia. In 1990 Bosnia and Herzegovina's imports totalled about $1.9 billion and exports about $2.1 billion. In 1996 imports were at the same level, $1.9 billion, but exports totalled only $171 million. The huge trade deficit was covered by foreign aid and reflects the degree of Bosnia and Herzegovina's dependence on financial assistance.

The big industrial conglomerates that dominated Bosnia and Herzegovina's pre-war economic life remain largely un-restructured and are operating at a fraction of their production capacity. While 90% of registered companies are in private hands, the big conglomerates remain under State ownership. Comprehensive privatization legislation is now in place, but the political obstacles to privatization remain impressive.

I.4 The institutions

Bosnia and Herzegovina is composed of two entities, the Federation of Bosnia and Herzegovina and Republika Srpska and the District Brčko, which is under direct jurisdiction of the administration of the State. The country has a three-member joint presidency comprising one Bosniak, one Croat and one Serb elected by popular vote – two from the Federation of Bosnia and Herzegovina and one from Republika Srpska. All three have equal rights. They serve for four years. The chairmanship of the Presidency rotates every eight months.

The Presidency appoints and the House of Representatives approves and confirms the appointment of the Council of Ministers for a period of four years. Currently, the Council of Ministers is composed of the Chair and nine ministers, all appointed on ethnic lines. Each minister has one deputy from a different ethnic group.

The Parliamentary Assembly has two chambers, the House of Representatives and the House of Peoples. The House of Representatives has 42 directly elected members. Two thirds of them are elected from the entity of Federation of Bosnia and Herzegovina and one third from the entity of Republika Srpska. The latter has 15 members, five Croats, five Serbs and five Bosniaks, elected by the parliaments of the entities. The Parliamentary Assembly adopts laws and decides on the budget of the State institutions. The Presidency ratifies international treaties after approval of the Parliamentary Assembly. All legislation requires the approval of both houses. The Presidency is responsible for the foreign policy of the country and the Council of Ministers has power over foreign trade and foreign affairs, but in general all government functions not expressly given to it lie with the entities.

The Federation of Bosnia and Herzegovina has its own constitution, a bicameral parliament and a government headed by a Prime Minister, who is nominated by parliament. The significant centres of political power in the Federation are the ten cantons, which have their own parliaments and governments.

Republika Srpska has a unified governmental structure, a unicameral People's Assembly and a directly elected president.

In some cases, like refugees and IDP matters, where the policy is set by the State but administrated by the entities, the lack of a unified administration hinders the State in attaining consistent policies. In 2003 the customs administration (Custom Office) was established at State.

Table I.3: Ministries of Bosnia and Herzegovina

Ministry of Foreign Affairs
Ministry of Foreign Trade and Economic Relations
Ministry of Communications and Transport
Ministry of Finance and Treasury
Ministry of Human Rights and Refugees
Ministry of Justice
Ministry of Security
Ministry of Defence
Ministry of Civil Affairs

Table I.4: Ministries of the Federation of Bosnia and Herzegovina

Ministry of Defence
Ministry of Internal Affairs
Ministry of Justice
Ministry of Finance
Ministry of Energy, Mining and Industry
Ministry of Transport and Communications
Ministry of Labour and Social Policy
Ministry of Displaced Persons and Refugees
Ministry of Protection of War Veterans and Disabled Veterans Issues
Ministry of Health
Ministry of Science, Education, Culture and Sports
Ministry of Trade
Ministry of Physical Planning and Environment
Ministry of Agriculture, Water Management and Forestry
Ministry of Development and Entrepreneurship

The highest judicial authority in Bosnia and Herzegovina is the Constitutional Court. It has nine judges, four elected by the Federation's House of Representatives, two by Republika Srpska's People's Assembly and three non-Bosnian citizens appointed by the President of the European Court of Human Rights. The new State Court deals with inter-entity legal issues such as passports, identity cards and illegal immigration. In addition, both entities have their Supreme Courts supplemented by cantonal and municipal courts in the Federation of Bosnia and Herzegovina and municipal courts in Republika Srpska.

The Office of the High Representative (OHR) was established as a result of the Dayton Peace Agreement to oversee the implementation of its civilian aspects and to coordinate the activities of the civilian organizations and agencies operating in Bosnia and Herzegovina.

At the beginning of the peace process, OHR acted as a bridge builder between the war-time parties. Currently, its main task is to ensure that the institutions function effectively and responsibly. The High Representative has substantial political power and can remove public officials from office if they violate legal commitments or the Dayton Peace Agreement. The High Representative can also impose laws as he/she sees fit if Bosnia and Herzegovina's legislative bodies fail to do so.

OHR is focusing its efforts on three priorities: economic reform, the effective functioning of the institutions of State and refugee return.

Table I.5: Ministries of Republika Srpska

Ministry of Economy, Energy and Development
Ministry of Finance
Ministry of Education and Culture
Ministry of Justice
Ministry of Defence
Ministry of Interior
Ministry of Administration and Local Government
Ministry of Health and Social Welfare
Ministry of Agriculture, Forestry and Water Management
Ministry of Transport and Communications
Ministry of Trade and Tourism
Ministry of Spatial Planning, Civil Engineering and Ecology
Ministry of Labour and Protection of the Veterans
Ministry of Economic Affairs and Coordination
Ministry of Refugees and Displaced Persons
Ministry of Science and Technology

Table I.6: Departments of Brčko District

Department of Administrative Support
Department of Budget and Finance
Department of Public Works
Department of Utilities
    Logistics Unit is responsible for environmental protection
Department of Urbanism, Real Estate Affairs and Economic Development
Department of Health, Public Safety and Municipal Services
Department of Education
Department of Agriculture and Forestry
Department of Public Records

I.5   The environmental context

The management of water resources and waste water is an environmental priority. Poor water management is wasting otherwise abundant water resources. The lack of protection of water sources as well as the release of untreated waste water to surface waters contaminate raw water, making the quality of the water in the supply network unsatisfactory.

The sustainable development of rural areas is threatened by intensive industrialization and accelerated urbanization, which are exerting pressure on natural resources through unplanned construction on agricultural land, indiscriminate forest harvesting and inadequate waste disposal. At the same time rural areas suffer from landmines and the small size of the agricultural plots hinders food production.

Biological and landscape diversity suffers from unbalanced spatial management and the unplanned exploitation of natural resources. There is no institutional framework for the management of bio- and geo-diversity or the natural and cultural heritage. Legislation is applied inefficiently and only small areas are adequately protected.

Social attitudes to waste disposal and the lack of harmonization and organization combined with insufficient economic measures and legislation have led to fly-tipping throughout the country. In addition, few functioning landfills are sanitary. The country has no hazardous waste handling, management or disposal system. The approximately 1000 tons of expired pharmaceuticals left over from wartime donations are a particular waste problem.

The use of outdated technologies exacerbates the environmental problems. Poverty caused by the dismal performance of the economy combined with poor water quality, food safety and waste management harm public health. The country needs a universal health-care policy and strategy.

Minefields cover about 8% of Bosnia and Herzegovina, endangering human life and preventing agricultural exploitation of the land. A de-mining strategy and intensive de-mining are crucial for human health and security as well as the development of agriculture and forestry.

At the same time, the country is now moving rapidly to establish a sound institutional, legal and policy base for environmental protection and the management of natural resources, both in the entities, especially through the Inter-Entity Steering Committee for the Environment, set up in 1998, and at the State level, through, for instance, the National Steering Committee for Environment and Sustainable Development created in 2002, which brings together all the stakeholders from the two entities, Brčko District and the State for the first time.

Figure I.3: Map of Bosnia and Herzegovina

The boundaries and names shown on this map do not imply official endorsement or acceptance by the United Nations.

Figure I.4: Map of the Cantons and regions in Bosnia and Herzegovina

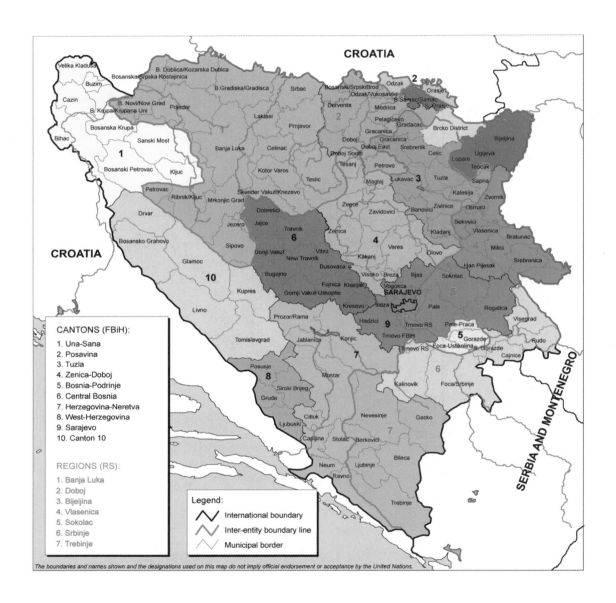

CANTONS (FBiH):

1. Una-Sana
2. Posavina
3. Tuzla
4. Zenica-Doboj
5. Bosnia-Podrinje
6. Central Bosnia
7. Herzegovina-Neretva
8. West-Herzegovina
9. Sarajevo
10. Canton 10

REGIONS (RS):

1. Banja Luka
2. Doboj
3. Bijeljina
4. Vlasenica
5. Sokolac
6. Srbinje
7. Trebinje

Legend:

/\/ International boundary
/\/ Inter-entity boundary line
/\/ Municipal border

The boundaries and names shown and the designations used on this map do not imply official endorsement or acceptance by the United Nations.

PART I: THE FRAMEWORK FOR ENVIRONMENTAL POLICY AND MANAGEMENT

Chapter 1

POLICY, LEGAL AND INSTITUTIONAL FRAMEWORK

1.1 Introduction

Since the end of the war, Bosnia and Herzegovina has made considerable progress, particularly in maintaining the peace, creating new institutions and establishing a legal structure. It now needs to move beyond peace implementation to applying the standards of the European Community and realizing its place among European countries.

Other challenges reflect deeper underlying issues of socio-economic and political transition. Serious environmental problems that date back to pre-war years combined with a general unawareness of environmental issues, a very complicated institutional base and a lack of implementation of the legislation are the main obstacles to the sustainable development of the country.

The internationally brokered Dayton Peace Agreement, which ended the war, established Bosnia and Herzegovina as a State comprising two entities, Republika Srpska and the Federation of Bosnia and Herzegovina, each with a high degree of autonomy. Brčko District was established as a separate, self-governing administrative unit.

As the State Constitution, adopted on 1 December 1995, contains no provisions for the environment, it is understood that environmental law is a responsibility of the entities unless they agree otherwise.

The Constitution of the Federation of Bosnia and Herzegovina contains only one reference to environmental responsibilities: article 2 in part III states that both the Federation and the Cantons are responsible for environmental policy. The Constitution of Republika Srpska states that "everyone shall have the right to a healthy environment …[and] shall be bound, in accordance with the law and with his possibilities, to protect and improve the environment" (art. 35). It also notes that the entity "shall protect and encourage … the rational use of natural resources with a view to protecting and improving the quality of life and protecting and reviving the environment to the

general benefit" (art. 64). Article 9 of the 2000 Statute of Brčko District of Bosnia and Herzegovina (Official Gazette BiH, 9/00; Official Gazette RS, 9/00) prescribes the district's functions and powers, which include the environment.

There is, however, currently a push towards strengthening the State in many areas, including the environment. Cooperation between the State and the entities in environmental matters is being strengthened.

1.2 Institutional framework

The Office of the High Representative is the chief civilian peace implementation agency in Bosnia and Herzegovina. The 1995 Dayton Peace Agreement designated the High Representative to oversee the implementation of its civilian aspects on behalf of the international community. The mandate of the High Representative is set out in annex 10 to the Agreement, which declares the High Representative to be the final authority in theatre to interpret the Agreement on the civilian implementation of the peace settlement. The Peace Implementation Council, a group of 55 countries and international organizations that sponsor and direct the peace implementation process, has subsequently elaborated on his mandate. The High Representative has no authority over the military Stabilisation Force led by the North Atlantic Treaty Organisation.

The High Representative oversees economic reconstruction, governmental institution-building and the promotion of a stable market economy. Until the State establishes or strengthens its own environmental institutions, the Office of the High Representative continues to work with the entities to support legal and political solutions to the country's environmental problems.

At the State level

Article 9 of the Law on the Ministries and Other Administrative Bodies of Bosnia and Herzegovina (Official Gazette BiH 2003), enacted in March

2003, assigns responsibilities for environmental protection to the Ministry of Foreign Trade and Economic Relations. Specifically, it gives it "responsibility for operations and tasks within the jurisdiction of Bosnia and Herzegovina relating to the definition of policy, fundamental principles, coordination of activities and harmonizing the plans of the entities' governmental bodies and institutions at the international level" in agriculture, energy, environmental protection, and the development and the exploitation of natural resources.

The Ministry's Sector of Natural Resources, Energy and Environmental Protection consists of three departments: the Department for Coordination of the Management of Natural Resources, the Department for Energy and the Department for Environmental Protection.

The Ministry has plans to build up a staff of around 20 in the environment and natural resources sector, but, at present, there are only two. The State and the entities are also discussing the possibility of establishing an environment agency, but no firm decision has been made.

The Ministry of Foreign Affairs, which is responsible for international agreements and conventions, the Ministry of Transport and Communication and the Directorate for European Integration also carry out work related to the environment. In addition, some independent institutions, such as the Institute for Standardization, Metrology and Intellectual Property and the Agency for Statistics, gather and publish environmental information.

To coordinate environmental matters at the State level the National Steering Committee for Environment and Sustainable Development was established in 2002 with broad participation from the State and the entities, Brčko District, non-governmental stakeholders and independent experts. Its main purpose is to facilitate work on projects and international agreements.

At the entity level

The organization and responsibilities of environment-related ministries in the two entities are similar and prescribed by law: the Law on Federal Ministries and Other Administrative Bodies in the Federation of Bosnia and Herzegovina (Official Gazette F BiH 19/2003); and the Law on

Ministries in Republika Srpska (Official Gazette RS 70/2002).

Federation of Bosnia and Herzegovina

In the Federation, these institutions are the Ministry of Physical Planning and Environment and the Ministry of Agriculture, Water Management and Forestry. The former comprises the Environment Sector. It has three departments: the Department of Ecology and Environmental Impact Assessment, the Department of Biodiversity and Natural Ecosystems Conservation, and the Department of Protection of Air, Water, Soil and of Waste Management. It has a total staff of nine, including the Assistant Minister and the Heads of the three departments.

In addition to the two above-mentioned ministries, many other authorities in the Federation of Bosnia and Herzegovina deal with environmental issues indirectly, as prescribed by law. These include other ministries, independent administrative offices and institutions, and institutions related to the ministries. They are listed in tables 1.1 and 1.2.

Their overall responsibilities are also defined in the Law on Federal Ministries and Other Administrative Bodies, but they are not further specified in by-laws or regulations. This leads to a lack of clarity and a potential overlap and duplication of functions. Furthermore, there is no mechanism to coordinate the environmental work of all of these bodies, although individual staff do work together case by case. The Ministry of Transport and Communications has taken the first steps to establish a special environmental unit for major infrastructure projects with environmental implications.

The Federation is divided into ten cantons (see table 1.3) with 84 municipalities. According to chapter III of its Constitution, the Federation and the cantons are jointly responsible for the "policy of environmental protection" and for the "use of natural resources" (art. 2). These responsibilities, according to article 3, may be exercised jointly or separately, or by the canton as coordinated by the Federation. Each canton has its own constitution and government. The cantons' environmental authorities are their ministries of civil engineering, physical planning and environmental protection and their ministries of agriculture, water management and forestry.

Table 1.1: Institutions with significant environmental responsibilities

Ministries	Related institutions
Ministry of Physical Planning and Environment	
Ministry of Agriculture, Water Management and Forestry	Institute for Crop Protection in Agriculture
Ministry of Health	Administration Office for Protection from Radiation and for Radiation Safety
Ministry of Education and Science	
Ministry of Culture and Sports	Institute for the Protection of the Cultural, Historical and Natural Heritage
Ministry of Energy, Mining and Industry	Institute for Metrology Institute for Geology - (is being set up)
Ministry of Transport and Communications	

Source: Law on Federation Ministries and Other Bodies of Federation Administration 58/02.

Their other ministries with environmental responsibilities are usually the ones dealing with health, industry, energy and mining (or the economy in general), labour and public welfare. They are listed below.

The cantons' constitutions provide for the establishment of a council of cantons to coordinate and harmonize policies and activities of common interest. There is, however, no evidence that such a council has ever met.

According to the Law on Physical Planning, the municipalities are self-governing. As a result, they may issue permits for new developments without the approval of the cantonal ministry. However, the inspectorates (for noise, air and waste) are based with the cantonal ministries. There are some good examples of coordination between the cantonal authorities and the municipalities for such activities as site inspections and permitting.

Republika Srpska

In Republika Srpska, the relevant institutions are the Ministry of Physical Planning, Civil Engineering and Ecology, and the Ministry of Agriculture, Forestry and Water Management.

The Ecology Sector of the former is made up of seven people, including the Assistant Minister. Administration is more centralized in this entity, which has no cantons, although there is a local administration in the entity's 65 municipalities.

In Republika Srpska, some other ministries and independent administrative offices and institutions also have environmental responsibilities. They are listed in tables 1.4 and 1.5.

The entity is responsible, with the municipalities, for ensuring environmental protection in accordance with the law. It is also supposed to meet the specific environmental protection needs of its citizens in accordance with article 102.5 of its Constitution. Here, too, the lack of a regulatory framework that specifies the functions of the various bodies with environmental responsibilities creates the potential for overlap and duplication. Since power is more centralized and there are direct links between the entity's authorities and the municipalities, there is less likelihood of misunderstanding. Nonetheless, good coordination is still desirable.

The larger municipalities have units for the control of construction, water and waste management and, more recently, environmental inspection.

Table 1.2: Independent institutions with environmental responsibilities

Institute of Statistics
Meteorological Institute
Administration Office for Geodesy and Property: Legal Proceedings
Administration Office for Civil Protection

Source: Law on Federation Ministries and other Bodies of Federation Administration 58/02.

Table 1.3: Cantonal ministries with environmental responsibilities

Canton	Ministries
Una-Sana	Ministry of Economy Ministry of Health
Posavina	Ministry of Industry, Energy and Physical Planning Ministry of Health
Tuzla	Ministry of Industry, Energy and Mining Ministry of Health
Zenica-Doboj	Ministry of Economy Ministry of Health
Bosna-Podrinje	Ministry of Labour, Health, Social Policy and Displaced Persons
Central Bosnia	Ministry of Economy Ministry of Health
Herzegovina-Neretva	Ministry of Economy, Entrepreneurship and Agriculture Ministry of Health, Labour and Public Welfare
West Herzegovina	Ministry of Economy Ministry of Health
Sarajevo	Ministry of Economy (agriculture, water management and forestry) Ministry of Health
Canton 10	Ministry of Economy Ministry of Labour, Health, Public Welfare and Refugees

Source: Law on Federation Ministries and other Bodies of Federation Administration 58/02.

Brčko District

According to the 2000 Statute of Brčko District, its Government consists of nine departments (art. 47). The Department of Utilities has a logistics unit, with one environmental specialist, directly responsible for environmental protection.

The other departments that are partially involved in environmental issues are:
- The Department of Public Works;
- The Department of Urbanism, Real Estate Affairs and Economic Development;
- The Department of Health, Public Safety and Community Services;
- The Department of Education; and
- The Department of Agriculture and Forestry.

The environmental authorities in both entities are significantly understaffed. The situation does not appear to be any better at cantonal or municipal levels. The cantonal ministries have one to three environmental specialists, and the municipalities are only now developing environmental units, starting with one environmental inspector.

Coordination

The Office of the High Representative and other international organizations have supported close coordination between the two entities, inter alia, in harmonizing their environmental legislation and adopting a joint approach to the implementation of environmental rules. For example, in June 1998, the entities' Governments signed a memorandum of understanding, brokered by the Office of the High Representative, to create an Inter-entity Commission for water. One month later, through a similar process, a memorandum of understanding was signed to create an inter-entity environmental steering committee.

Table 1.4: Ministries with significant environmental responsibilities

Ministry of Physical Planning, Civil Engineering and Ecology
Ministry of Agriculture, Forestry and Water Management
Ministry of Economy, Energy and Development
Ministry of Education and Culture
Ministry of Health and Social Welfare
Ministry of Transport and Communications
Ministry of Trade and Tourism
Ministry of Science and Technology

Source: Law on Ministries and other Bodies of Administration of Republika Srpska.

Table 1.5: Independent bodies with environmental responsibilities

Institute of Statistics
Hydro-Meteorological Institute
Institute for the Spatial Planning
Institute for the Protection of the Cultural, Historical and Natural Heritage
Institute for Standardization and Metrology
Institute for Geological Survey
Directorate for Water

Source: Law on Ministries and other Bodies of Administration of Republika Srpska.

Inter-entity Steering Committee for the Environment

The Inter-entity Steering Committee for the Environment was established in 1998 specifically to deal with environmental issues delegated to it by the entities. The Committee consists of eight members. Its secretariat services are provided by the local office of the Regional Environmental Center (REC). The Committee's purview includes:

• International environmental agreements;
• International environmental programmes;
• Cooperation with the European Environment Agency (EEA);
• Harmonization of existing and future environmental legislation and regulations;
• Harmonization and monitoring of environmental standards;
• Harmonization of environmental action plans with physical planning in both entities;
• Harmonization of environmental databases and information systems;
• Information collection and exchange (inter-entity and international); and
• Harmonization of contingency plans for emergencies.

Over a five-year period (1998-2003) the Committee organized approximately 40 meetings, especially to coordinate issues related to international cooperation, including participation at events, development of projects and reporting to international environmental organizations. It reviewed and helped to harmonize a package of new environmental laws before their final adoption in both entities. The Committee is acknowledged as the competent inter-entity body for the environment.

Inter-entity Commission for Water

The Inter-entity Commission for Water is responsible for cooperation on all water management issues among the relevant ministries of both entities. Its goal is to prevent potential disputes in water management. The Commission includes both government officials and private citizens from the two entities, as well as representatives from the donor community and the Office of the High Representative. Its responsibilities include:

• International waterways;
• International water-management projects;
• Cooperation with neighbouring countries (Croatia, and Serbia and Montenegro);
• Harmonization of regulations in water management;
• Harmonization of water-quality issues and monitoring of water quality;
• Water resources protection through control of solid waste disposal;
• Oversight of laboratories that monitor water quality;
• Construction and reconstruction of water management facilities important to both entities;
• Water facilities that straddle the border between both entities;
• Collection and exchange of information (inter-entity and international); and
• Harmonization of emergency response plans.

The goals of this Commission and the expectations of its results are similar to those of the above-mentioned Committee. It meets frequently, once a month, to solve current water management problems and its tasks are practical. It pays special attention to cooperation with neighbouring countries, to the preparation and approval of a new water management act, to facilitating the development of a pilot project to establish water basin districts, and to solving some contradictions between the existing water permit regime and the new environmental legislation.

National Steering Committee for Environment and Sustainable Development

By decision of the Council of Ministers of 16 May 2002, the National Steering Committee for Environment and Sustainable Development was established at the State level. It has 54 members, including non-governmental organizations, scientists, universities and other stakeholders, in addition to representatives from the two entities and Brčko District. Its secretariat is located in the Ministry of Foreign Trade and Economic Relations. Its work is largely carried out through eight subcommittees on: the protection of the ozone layer, climate change, long-range transboundary air pollution, persistent organic pollutants, biodiversity, land degradation, transboundary waters and transboundary movements of hazardous waste.

The work of this Committee is improving cooperation among the State, the entities, the district and the non-governmental sector.

1.3   Policy framework

Although neither the State nor the entities have an environmental policy, some important programmes for environmental action have been prepared and adopted in recent years. The Global Framework Strategy for Economic Development in Bosnia and Herzegovina for 2001-2004 touched on some related issues. And, in Republika Srpska, pursuant to its new Law on Environmental Protection, work has begun on drafting an environmental protection strategy.

The National Environmental Action Plan (NEAP) was the first document specifically oriented to environmental problems. It was prepared with the support of the World Bank in both entities in parallel and with the participation of representatives from ministries, scientists from research institutes and academic institutions, and NGOs.

The intended output of the process is an environmental action plan for the whole country that would outline long-term priorities, provide assistance to environmental officials to participate in ongoing international processes, give guidance in drafting laws and policies, and support institution-

building. The eight priorities identified in NEAP are: water resource management and waste-water treatment; sustainable development in rural areas; environmental management (information system, integral planning and education); protection of biological and landscape diversity; waste and waste management; economy and sustainable development; public health; and demining. About 450 projects have already been initiated under NEAP and 50-60 of them have been selected and are under preparation.

NEAP was adopted at the beginning of 2003 by the entities' Governments after open public discussion. It has not yet, however, been adopted by the Assembly of Brčko District, nor has it been debated, let alone adopted, in any State body or institution.

Much attention has recently been given to the finalization and approval of the Poverty Reduction Strategy Paper or Mid-term Development Strategy of Bosnia and Herzegovina (2004-2007), which was adopted on 5 February 2004. The Paper gives a broad overview of the national economic and social situation in all sectors, including the environment and water. The priorities of the environment sector identified in the Paper, including in its Action Plan, generally follow those set out in NEAP. Most of the measures envisaged in the Paper, however, are short-term. The Paper is considered by the Environment Ministries in both entities as the environmental strategy paper and the expectation is that it will play this role for a certain time. However, according to some observers, there are differences of opinion between the two entities on the role of the State in environmental protection, and the Paper does not provide sufficient arguments in favour of environmental protection and sustainable development.

The Council of Ministers has adopted an initiative of the Ministry of Foreign Trade and Economic Relations to draft a strategy for environmental protection and sustainable development. This has also received the support of the National Steering Committee for Environment and Sustainable Development. In 2002 both chambers of the Parliamentary Assembly supported the drafting of this document, and the House of Peoples of the Parliamentary Assembly also required the Council of Ministers urgently to prepare an action plan for drafting the strategy.

Other environmental policy-making documents are the Mediterranean Action Plan (MAP), prepared under the Global Environment Facility and approved in December 1999, and the State Strategy for Solid Waste Management, prepared under the European Union (EU) PHARE Programme and adopted in 2000-2001 by the Governments of both entities but not yet by the Assembly of Brčko District.

MAP is intended to promote the implementation of the Barcelona Convention and its Protocols. A review of issues related to this objective has been undertaken, and the National Action Plan was drafted in January 2000.

Information on the country's Strategy for Solid Waste Management is contained in chapter 6, on the management of waste and contaminated sites.

A biodiversity strategy and a nature protection strategy are planned. There is no policy for water management and water protection. Some strategic documents prepared in the former Yugoslavia such as the Water Management Master Plan (published in 1994) are still followed in both entities. (See chapter 7, on water management.)

There are also some local initiatives to develop local environmental action plans (LEAPs) in both entities.

1.4   Legal framework

The former Yugoslavia issued a number of legislative documents that deal with natural resource management and the environment. Even today there are over 70 such legislative acts that are still valid in both entities. Despite this impressive work, there was little public awareness of the importance of applying environmental policy and legislation because there were no transparent procedures for environmental decision-making.

State level

There are no laws or other regulations on the environment at the State level. However, the Council of Ministers has charged the Ministry of Foreign Trade and Economic Relations with coordinating the drafting of an environmental protection bill. There is agreement with the Environment Ministries of both entities and the Government of Brčko District that they will take part in drafting the law, as will independent expert and non-governmental organizations.

Entity level

Annex 2 to the new State Constitution stipulates that all laws that were in force in Bosnia and Herzegovina when the Constitution comes into effect and that are not inconsistent with it may remain in force. For the period 1996-2002, before new legislation was passed, this was important for the environment because it confirmed the standing in both entities of the Law on Physical Planning, passed in September 1987 (Official Gazette SR BIH 9/87). This Law was general and covered all major components of the environment. It dealt with the overall issues of urban planning, physical planning, the environment and building.

The Federation of Bosnia and Herzegovina's new Laws on Physical Planning (Official Gazette F BiH 52/2002) and on Construction (Official Gazette F BiH 55/2002) go farther and include, for example, requirements for strategic environmental assessment "to protect the environment adequately spatial planning documentation is being prepared" (art. 8) and environmental assessment or environmental permits for new construction (art. 27, para. 4, and art. 41, para. 6).

Environmental protection in Republika Srpska has been regulated in a similar manner. Its new Law on Physical Planning was issued in 1996, but has since been amended several times (Official Gazette RS 19/1996, 25/1996, 10/1998 and 53/2002).

Separate laws on the environment and environmental media were drafted after 1998 for each of the entities, with financial support from the EU Community Assistance, Reconstruction, Development and Stabilisation Programme (CARDS). Considerable effort was made to harmonize them in order to avoid future difficulties with implementation. Both packages of laws have been discussed and approved by the Inter-Entity Steering Committee for the Environment. The contents of these laws are not identical, but are very similar and there are no differences as far as technical issues and goals are concerned. That is important to prevent unfair competition, but also for Bosnia and Herzegovina's possible accession to the EU.

These laws are:
- The Law on Environmental Protection;
- The Law on Air Protection;
- The Law on Water Protection;
- The Law on Waste Management;

- The Law on Nature Protection; and
- The Law on the Environmental Fund.

The new laws reflect European practice. They are to a large extent harmonized with the goals and the principles of EU environmental legislation.

For example, the Law on Environmental Protection lays down the principles of sustainable development, precaution and prevention, substitution, integration, cooperation and responsibility-sharing, public participation, access to information and the polluter pays. It includes the most effective and advanced tools for environmental management, such as environmental impact assessment, strategic environmental assessment, environmental permitting (integrated pollution prevention and control (IPPC) permits), major accident prevention, environmental quality standards, eco-labelling, voluntary environmental management systems, and civil liability for environmental damage.

The Law on Air Protection requires monitoring, using general and particular emission limit values, setting air quality standards, measuring air quality in particularly polluted areas and informing the public. EU air quality standards and emission limit values will be adopted.

The Law on Water Protection sets the provisions for water protection planning and establishes the river basins and sub-basins, and, to protect the water ecosystems, determines limit values for pollution as well as general and particular water protection measures.

The Law on Waste Management determines the activities and responsibilities in waste management including those of the producers, sellers, and waste collection systems. It sets special provisions for household waste, waste treatment and waste transport, including the movement of transboundary waste, waste disposal, waste incineration, general rules for hazardous waste, and waste disposal sites registration.

The Law on Nature Protection is also based on the principles of cooperation, precaution, prevention, and the polluters pays. It calls for capacity-building, the regulation of nature protection planning and the determination of the joint responsibilities of the entities. General and special measures are provided for the protection of landscapes, wild animals and plants, and the development of protected areas under Natura 2000. Under this Law an inter-entity

or State body should be established to, inter alia, act as an advisory body, create a red list for the country, set guidelines for the introduction of species and for transboundary cooperation and develop a nature protection strategy.

The Law on the Environmental Fund establishes a fund and determines its activities, the preparation of a financial plan, the management structure and management tools.

The six laws were adopted in Republika Srpska in 2002 (Official Gazette of RS 50, 51, 53/2002) and in the Federation of Bosnia and Herzegovina in 2003 (Official Gazette F BiH 33/2003).

Republika Srpska has also adopted other specialized environmental laws, such as the Law on Hunting (Official Gazette RS 4/2002) and the Law on Forests (Official Gazette RS 66/2003). The Federation is preparing similar laws.

Brčko District will submit its environmental framework legislation for adoption by its Assembly in December 2003. According to article 70 of its Statute, all laws and regulations from both entities shall remain in force in the district if they do not contradict the provisions of the Statute and provided that the district has not adopted its own laws.

It is expected that the cantons will prepare their own environmental legislation following the framework laws adopted recently by the Federation. Some of them, like Tuzla, Zenica-Doboj, Posavina and West Herzegovina, have already adopted laws on environmental protection.

The cantonal ministries have the right to develop their own legislation consistent with and within the framework of the Federation's acts. This implies that the Federation's legislation is adopted first. However, given the slow speed at which this is happening (up to four years in some cases), the cantons often prepare their legislation on the basis of the Federation's draft laws. As a consequence, the cantonal legislation and the Federation's final, adopted legislation may not be fully consistent, thereby further complicating implementation. The cantons also have the option of delegating their environmental responsibilities either downwards, i.e. to the municipalities, or upwards, i.e. to the Federation.

The adoption of this set of advanced environmental laws is a great step forward, but without the secondary legislation, implementation is impossible. In Republika Srpska the environmental legislation has been in force since mid-2002, but so far no by-laws or regulations have been approved. The only exception is the "Rule on conditions for performing environmental activities", regulating the conditions for legal persons to perform specific environment-related activities, such as preparing environmental impact studies.

The Law on the Procedure for Concluding and Implementing International Agreements establishes the State's official procedure for the ratification of international legal instruments. It was adopted by the Parliamentary Assembly in 2000 (Official Gazette of BiH 29/00).

1.5 Implementation of the legislation and enforcement

Environmental impact assessment

Under the general provisions of the Laws on Physical Planning and Laws on Construction, both entities have been taking environmental impacts into account before the final adoption of projects. This has meant that the environmental authorities issue environmental permits on the basis of project documentation. Depending on the size of the proposed activity, an environmental impact study could be prepared by external, licensed experts. The process is one of environmental expertise, not environmental impact assessment (EIA) as commonly defined. For instance, there are no provisions in these laws regarding public participation and public access to information related to environmental impacts.

Water permits are granted by water management authorities at the Ministry of Agriculture, Forestry and Water Management in both entities. There are three types of permits: for design, for a new activity for a period of five years and for existing facilities. Under pressure from the international financial institutions and non-governmental organizations, environmental impact studies have been prepared by licensed experts, and discussed with the public concerned public in specific cases, such as flood protection.

The new Laws on Environmental Protection require all steps of a formal environmental impact assessment, including early notification, screening and scoping, public participation, and access to information and decision-making. These are very advanced procedures that will demand a lot from all

participants: the developer, the environmental authorities, the competent authority for the final approval, and the public concerned – in fact, from society as a whole. Implementation of the laws needs very transparent and precise regulations as well as broad public awareness campaigns to inform stakeholders of their opportunities for involvement in the EIA procedure. There are no such regulations at present, although the respective ministries in the two entities are drafting them.

Some cantons in the Federation have adopted their own laws on environmental protection, physical planning and water, with provisions on EIA. These laws follow the general EIA requirements set out in the Laws on Environmental Protection. Some have also already adopted their own EIA regulations, raising the question of consistency between their legislation and that of the Federation. To ensure effective implementation, the cantons should await the entity's EIA regulations. These will determine the activities subject to mandatory EIA and the competencies of the Federation's and the cantons' environmental authorities.

The Laws on Environmental Protection adopted in both entities also contain strategic environmental assessment (SEA) requirements. According to the Federation's Law on Environmental Protection, SEA is required for actions that "involve detrimental regional impacts" and "regulations intended to introduce regulatory instruments for environmental protection." In Republika Srpska, SEA should be carried out "in the course of adopting regulations and decisions that are passed by the Government or municipal or town assemblies." However, procedural issues, such as public access to information and public participation in decision-making, have not been addressed in the Laws. Without such procedures, implementation is not possible.

Permitting

Federation of Bosnia and Herzegovina

Because of the lack of appropriate regulations, there is no environmental permitting system, such as integrated permitting. At present, according to the Law on Physical Planning, the Ministry of Physical Planning and Environment licenses large installations, but it needs the help of specialized institutes to determine licensing requirements. Under the current procedure, it receives advice from the Ministry of Agriculture, Water Management and Forestry and the Ministry of

Energy, Mining and Industry. Licences are issued in three steps: the Ministry's Physical Planning Sector issues the urban *concordance* (licence for the location of the installation) and the building permit (licence for building); and its Environment Sector issues the resource-use permit.

During the licensing process, a commission must be established by the Minister or Assistant Minister and paid for by the applicant. This commission consists of specialists from the Ministry, and its task is to check the data provided by the applicant and the quality of the equipment (or installation). The Ministry issues the licence and, where appropriate, specifies additional conditions, for example, the carrying out of an environmental impact study.

According to the provisions of the Law on Water Protection, water management agreements and water management permits are issued to regulate the water use and waste-water discharge of large installations.

There is a conflicting situation concerning licensing legislation with the cantons. The licensing of smaller installations should be done by the cantons or by the municipalities. The Ministry of Physical Planning and Environment sees itself as the central environmental licensing body. However, the cantons with large industrial installations have their own environmental laws and their ministries see themselves as the environmental licensing bodies. This causes confusion for applicants for large installations.

As with the EIA procedure, the Law on Environmental Protection sets the general requirements for integrated permitting (IPPC), which in practice will replace the current licensing. It is expected that the IPPC regulations will bring clarity to the environmental permitting of large installations. Again, deciding which body should issue the permits is a matter of priority.

Republika Srpska

Although Republika Srpska adopted the Law on Environmental Protection in the middle of 2002, the situation there with respect to integrated permitting is the same as that already described for the Federation of Bosnia and Herzegovina. The Ministry of Physical Planning, Civil Engineering and Ecology oversees the licensing of large industrial installations following the requirements

of the Law on Physical Planning. Public concerns related to water quality are considered by the Ministry of Agriculture, Forestry and Water Management and the Ministry of Economy, Energy and Development.

To obtain urban *concordance* and building permits for buildings and other facilities, the applicant is obliged to obtain an expert opinion on the special conditions of construction and the consequences of the development's operation. A recognized institution appointed by the Ministry of Physical Planning, Civil Engineering and Ecology reviews the documentation.

For large installations the procedure starts in the Ministry. According to article 77 of the Law on Physical Planning, a request for permits for buildings and activities identified in article 76, paragraph 2, of the same Law must be submitted to the Ministry via the municipal administrative body for urban affairs. The Ministry takes a decision after consultation with the municipality or municipalities involved.

The licensing of smaller installations is done by municipalities. According to article 77 of the Law on Physical Planning, a request for an urban *concordance* should be filed at the municipal administrative body for urban affairs. The procedure is the same as that for larger projects. The applicant must obtain an urban *concordance* covering the location, construction and operation of the facility.

Environmental inspections

There are no environmental inspectorates at the State level. However, the two entities have recently recruited environmental inspectors (one person) at their Environment Ministries. The inspectors carry out inspections at the request of members of the public. In some cases the inspection is integrated, i.e. representatives from the entities' other inspectorates (e.g. health, construction, water and forest), inspectors from the cantonal ministries and municipal inspectors are included. As a result of the site inspection, the different inspectors impose fines and other penalties according to the specific regulations that they are obliged to enforce.

Both entities are preparing laws related to inspections. According to the draft laws, environmental inspectors will be centralized in each of the entities to strengthen enforcement.

1.6   Conclusions and Recommendations

With the structure established by the Dayton Peace Agreement, it is difficult to streamline environmental legislation, policies and activities or make them consistent. The division of responsibilities among the different authorities is not always clear. This further complicates the situation and has a negative impact on implementation and enforcement. Considerable progress has been made through the establishment of, first, two inter-entity bodies – the Inter-entity Commission for Water and the Inter-entity Steering Committee for the Environment – and, more recently, the National Steering Committee for Environment and Sustainable Development. There appears to be a movement towards strengthening the role of the State in environmental matters, as evidenced by the creation of this National Committee and the decision of the Council of Ministers that the Ministry of Foreign Trade and Economic Relations should draft both a State-level environmental protection bill and a strategy for environmental protection and sustainable development. This could be extremely helpful in rationalizing environmental management in the country.

Under the ReREP programme, a feasibility study is examining the possible establishment of a national environment agency with the support of the European Commission Delegation to Bosnia and Herzegovina. However, much work remains to be done to reach consensus about such an agency and define its role, structure, scope and jurisdiction. It seems clear that the need is growing for a coordinating body for international agreements and programmes for environmental protection and the use of natural resources in Bosnia and Herzegovina. Mechanisms must be found to allow the State to play an appropriate role in environmental affairs, enabling Bosnia and Herzegovina to participate regionally and globally, as well as to maintain a level of consistency between the entities and Brčko District in developing national environmental policy and management.

Recommendation 1.1:
The Council of Ministers should establish an environment agency, which should:
(a) Provide advisory services to the authorities and institutions on both State and entity level in creation of strategy of sustainable development, environmental policy and management and protection of environment, natural resources and natural heritage;

(b) Collect environmental monitoring data and report, as appropriate, to international bodies, convention-governing bodies and the European Environment Agency;
(c) Manage, supervise and coordinate the implementation of the entities' plans for management and protection of waters, air, land, forests, as well as management of waste and chemicals (POPs, ODS, transboundary pollutants and dangerous pesticides);
(d) Develop methodologies to facilitate a common approach to environmental management; and
(e) Provide training, capacity building and awareness rising.

The environment agency should rely on and assist the inter-entity bodies.

Because of the war in 1992-1995, Bosnia and Herzegovina could not take part in many of the activities under Agenda 21, which resulted from the 1992 United Nations Conference on Environment and Development in Rio de Janeiro (Brazil). Its National Environmental Action Plan was the first comprehensive document about the environmental problems in the country and their prioritization. The proposals of the NEAP provided a basis for the assessment of needs for environment and water management in the Mid-term Development Strategy of Bosnia and Herzegovina. The NEAP, however, has not been adopted at the State level. In any case, these documents cannot substitute for a national strategy for both sustainable development and protection and management of the environment.

Recommendation 1.2:
Pursuant to the decision of the Council of Ministers, the Ministry of Foreign Trade and Economic Relations should begin as soon as possible to draft:

(a) A new State law on environmental protection and all relevant secondary legislation; and
(b) A strategy for environmental protection and sustainable development, in cooperation with the relevant Environment Ministries in the Federation of Bosnia and Herzegovina and Republika Srpska, and with broad participation from all stakeholders.

The strategy should aim at:
* *Strengthening the institutional capacity for designing and implementing environmental policy at all levels;*

- *Developing and institutionalizing communication among sectors and ministries within and among the State, the entities and Brčko District;*
- *Establishing procedures for communication between officials and stakeholders in decision-making for sustainable development; and*
- *Improving the knowledge of the general public about the significance of environmental protection and encouraging the preparation of awareness-raising programmes.*

A review of the institutional framework for environmental protection in Bosnia and Herzegovina shows the weaknesses of the system, including a shortage of staff and funding. Additionally, the number and relative independence of the cantonal ministries in the Federation of Bosnia and Herzegovina may create obstacles to integrated environmental management. A stronger Ministry of Physical Planning and Environment could result in the establishment of uniform regulations, ensuring a consistent standard of environmental licensing throughout the Federation. It would also help standardize inspection procedures and help the Ministry attain the necessary legal competence for its work.

The Ministry of Physical Planning, Civil Engineering and Ecology in Republika Srpska is also understaffed. Its Ecology Sector currently has only seven staff. A stronger Ecology Sector within the ministry or new environment ministry would have several benefits. It would facilitate the integrated management of the main environmental media. Through the clear assignment of authority for licensing and for environmental quality and through better coordination with the other line ministries (agriculture, water, industry, energy and mining) and municipalities, the Ministry could secure standardized environmental licensing, installation inspections and the necessary legal competence.

Recommendation 1.3:
The Federation's Ministry of Physical Planning and Environment and Republika Srpska's Ministry of Physical Planning, Civil Engineering and Ecology should be strengthened, as a matter of priority, so that they are able to:
(a) Prepare all secondary legislation required by the new Laws on Environmental Protection, Air Protection, Water Protection, Waste Management, Nature Protection and the Environmental Fund;

(b) Organize and implement effectively environmental permitting, inspection and control; and
(c) Implement all the tasks incumbent upon them as ministries.

Both Ministries may be strengthened either by increasing the number of permanent staff or by hiring external experts ad hoc.

In the longer term, Bosnia and Herzegovina wishes to accede to the European Union and it, therefore, has to align its legislation with European Community law. The framework environmental laws have been produced under the CARDS Programme for both entities. They transpose to a great extent the most important European Commission's environment-related directives. Although this package of laws was adopted in Republika Srpska in the summer of 2002 and in the Federation of Bosnia and Herzegovina in the autumn of 2003, the legislation cannot be implemented because of a lack of regulations. This situation is all the more problematic because the most important tools for their implementation, such as environmental impact assessment and integrated environmental (IPPC) permits, have only recently been adopted in Bosnia and Herzegovina. It is expected that the secondary legislation will establish procedures, approaches and competences that could contradict the old laws and regulations.

Recommendation 1.4:
The Federation's Ministry of Physical Planning and Environment and Republika Srpska's Ministry of Physical Planning, Civil Engineering and Ecology should develop the necessary secondary legislation for the implementation of the new framework Law on Environmental Protection and other specialized environmental laws as soon as possible. The most urgent issues are:
(a) Establishment of a detailed to environmental impact assessment (EIA) procedure with all the necessary steps: preparation of the list of activities that are subject to EIA, early notification, screening and scoping, public participation at all levels, access to information and decision-making;
(b) Establishment of a detailed SEA procedure for plans and programmes;
(c) Development of a permitting system under the Law on Environmental Protection, including integrated (IPPC) permits; and
(d) Updating of their industrial plant inventories and establishment of new registers of polluters.

Chapter 2

ECONOMIC INSTRUMENTS AND PRIVATIZATION

2.1 Introduction

In the former Socialist Federal Republic of Yugoslavia, Bosnia and Herzegovina was one of the poorer republics. In 1990, its gross domestic product (GDP) was estimated at US$ 10.6 billion, or over US$ 2,400 per capita. On the positive side, it had a relatively diversified economy, a well-developed industrial base, among the best in the region, and a highly educated labour force. Its economy was relatively open (the share of total trade in GDP was over 35%) and market-oriented (with more than half its exports directed to Western markets). At the same time, Bosnia and Herzegovina supplied raw materials to the other republics and imported final products from them. It was also one of the most polluted parts of the former Yugoslavia.

The 1992-1995 war devastated the country and its economy. The recovery started after the Dayton Peace Agreement was signed and brought economic growth averaging 25% a year over the 1996-2001 period, although admittedly starting from a very low base. This average pace is not indicative for the whole period as it was 54.2% in 1996 but only 4.5% in 2001 and 3.7% in 2002 (see table 2.1). The post-war recovery has been fuelled by large amounts of aid – US$ 5.1 billion under the donor assistance programme for 1996-2001. The recovery programme included three main parts: reconstruction and recovery from damage sustained during the war; establishment of a new governance structure for the country with consistent and harmonized policies across its largely autonomous multi-tiered governments; and restarting the transition to a market economy. The structure of the economy changed significantly, from one dominated by industry to one where the service sector prevails (approximately 60% of GDP in 2000-2001). By 2002, GDP reached approximately one half of the pre-war level. Grants continue to constitute a large though decreasing part of the general government budget: from over 20% in 1998 (KM 12.1 million of the total budget revenues of KM 56.7 million) to less than 10% in 2003 (KM 4.2 million of the total budget revenues of KM 50.6 million).

An important feature of the economic development is the disparity between the entities – the Federation of Bosnia and Herzegovina and Republika Srpska. According to World Bank estimates, per capita GDP in 2001 in Republika Srpska was approximately 60% of that in the Federation – US$ 873 and US$ 1,453, respectively. Average monthly net wages that year were KM 305 and KM 433, respectively. Disparities also exist within the entities, particularly in the Federation, which is highly decentralized. For example, estimated GDP per capita in 1999 was US$ 640 in the canton of Bihac and US$ 1,800 in the canton of Sarajevo. Unemployment is high – around 40% – with no significant changes lately. This figure may be an overestimate since it does not account for people engaged in economic activities that are not officially registered. On the other hand, a number of State enterprises functioning at only a fraction of their capacity have many employees on their payroll. Even if these people have not been paid for months and even years, they are not included in the unemployment figures. The process of privatization, which has been going on for several years (so far with limited success) and is now entering the phase of privatization of the largest enterprises, will lead to further changes in the structure of the economy.

Table 2.1: Macroeconomic indicators, 1995-2002

Indicator	1995	1996	1997	1998	1999	2000	2001	2002
Consumer price index (annual average % change)	-14.5	-20.3	8.6	6.8	-0.7	1.4	2.1	1.0
GDP (% change)	..	54.2	36.6	15.4	9.5	5.4	4.5	3.7
Unemployment rate (% of labour force)	..	..	39.0	38.7	39.0	39.4	39.9	42.7

Source: UNECE. Common Statistical Database, 2003.

Various levels of government and the general public are predominantly concerned with the current level of economic development, high unemployment and low standards of living compared both to the pre-war level and to other countries in Central and Eastern Europe. Environmental problems are sometimes viewed as less urgent. A sharp decrease in economic activity, particularly the complete shutdown or operation at low capacity of many polluting industrial enterprises, has led to a certain improvement in the quality of the environment. However, the war also destroyed or shut down facilities designed to prevent or clean pollution, such as municipal waste-water treatment plants. Many State enterprises that continued to operate have not been making the necessary investments in the maintenance of their pollution-prevention equipment or in new, more environmentally friendly technologies. The current decline in pollution is therefore no reason for complacency towards environmental protection.

There are indications that society at large and policy makers have come to understand that developing the economy, solving numerous social problems and protecting the environment must be considered simultaneously and do not have to be mutually exclusive. A recent positive development by the entities is the adoption of the National Environmental Action Plan (NEAP) of Bosnia and Herzegovina in March 2003. NEAP emphasizes both the difficulties and the necessity of balancing environmental protection and job creation. According to NEAP, the development of economic activities that are both labour-intensive and environmentally friendly should have priority in the strategy to further develop the country's economy. Both entities have adopted a set of environmental laws (see Chapter 1 on policy, legal and institutional framework) that, when implemented, could ensure a high quality of environmental protection in Bosnia and Herzegovina. The laws conform to EU Directives and regulations.

The Medium-term Development Strategy of Bosnia and Herzegovina (Poverty Reduction Strategy Paper, 2003-2007), which was adopted in February 2004 by the Council of Ministers, takes into consideration the NEAP findings and recommendations. It sets priorities and specifies measures for managing the environment, particularly in the areas of legislation, air quality and climate change, water, soil and land, forests, waste, land, biological and geological diversity, the cultural and natural heritage, and public health. The Strategy emphasizes the importance of adopting by-

laws and regulations to make the environmental laws operational, and it underlines the necessity of harmonizing environmental protection with sectoral policies in the light of the intersectoral nature of environment issues. It does not have a specific section on economic instruments for the environment.

2.2   Economic instruments for environmental protection

Background, policy objectives and legal framework

There are few environment-related charges and even fewer are effectively enforced. There is little awareness of the existence and use of environment-related economic instruments among government officials, businesses, non-governmental organizations and the general public. There is also a dearth of instruments that have the explicit purpose of limiting environmental pressure or collecting funds for environmental purposes.

Information on the existing instruments, their use and enforcement, and collection rates is not being gathered or studied in any systematic manner and is not readily available. The latest available compilation of economic instruments in Bosnia and Herzegovina was prepared in 1999 by the Regional Environmental Center for Central and Eastern Europe (REC). Some studies of the status of economic instruments for the environment are being conducted at the Hydro-Engineering Institute of Sarajevo, but their results are not in the public domain.

The list of existing instruments includes water abstraction and water pollution charges; municipal user charges for water supply and sewage; municipal waste user charges; excise and customs duties on fuels and cars; annual registration fees for vehicles; taxes on natural resources; air emission charges; wood export charges; fines for exceeding emission limits; and fines for illegal logging. Some of these instruments are relatively well developed, for example charges and fees for water management. Their legal basis is the Federation's Law on Water (Official Gazette F BiH 18/1998) and Republika Srpska's Law on Water (Official Gazette RS 18/1998) and related secondary legislation. Other instruments are not working at all; for example, no charges are being collected from enterprises for the emission of air pollutants. Even those instruments that are in use are not efficient. Charges for public water supply and waste management do not cover maintenance costs. There are no specific indicators to measure collection efficiency, no monitoring and no transparency in the application of existing economic instruments.

With the adoption of new environmental legislation, the legal framework for economic instruments for environmental protection is being put in place. Republika Srpska's Law on Environmental Protection (Official Gazette RS 53/2002) and the Federation's Law on Environmental Protection (Official Gazette F BiH 33/2003) outline economic instruments for environmental protection, including charges, tax incentives for environmentally friendly products, technologies and services, deposit-refund systems, penalties and compensation for environmental damage, and financial guarantees for possible environmental damage. The charges are classified into effluent or emission charges, user charges, product charges and administrative charges. The Laws recognize the "polluter pays" and "user pays" principles by stating that the rates should encourage a reduction in the use of natural resources and in pollution.

The use of economic instruments is also foreseen in other recent environmental laws, specifying fees, penalties and other instruments for the purposes of water protection, air protection, waste management and nature protection. For example, Republika Srpska's Law on Water Protection (Official Gazette RS 53/2002) and the Federation's Law on Water Protection (Official Gazette F BiH 33/2003) state that the Ministry of Physical Planning, Civil Engineering and Ecology and the Ministry of Physical Planning and Environment, respectively, should issue regulations establishing fees for water use and water pollution. The Laws also specify violations for which fines may be imposed.

Even though the environmental laws have officially entered into force, the economic instruments listed in them cannot be implemented until the entities' governments and ministries adopt the necessary secondary legislation (by-laws, regulations and guidelines). This secondary legislation should specify the amount of fees and charges to be paid by polluters and users of natural resources, the details of the environmental fines and the means for

their collection. The development of this secondary legislation is lagging behind and there is no clear time frame for its finalization and implementation. There is also a need to make amendments to other legislation currently in force.

NEAP also makes reference to economic instruments as an important environmental management tool. It provides a brief analysis of the existing economic instruments in water management and waste management, and points out that, as they now stand, they are inadequate in terms of both cost recovery and pollution prevention. NEAP considers the economic instruments identified in the new environmental legislation to be important to improve environmental management.

There has been insufficient discussion in Bosnia and Herzegovina on the practical ways to implement the new legislation and on its social and economic implications. It may be desirable to study the feasibility of the economic instruments foreseen in the new environmental laws. Such a study would allow the fees, charges, taxes and penalties to be set at rates that encourage sound environmental management while taking into account the current state of and prospects for economic development and the affordability for businesses and the population. This would ensure that all stakeholders accept these instruments, make it easier to implement and enforce them and, ultimately, provide for higher collection rates and funds available for environmental financing.

Instruments for water resource management

Currently the most developed instruments in both entities are in water resource management. They include fees for water supply and waste-water disposal services paid by all users (households, businesses and institutions); water abstraction fees paid by *vodovods* (water utilities) – in the Federation only; water pollution fees paid by all companies and institutions, including *vodovods* as compensation for water pollution; and fees for the extraction of material from streams paid by companies excavating gravel and sand. (Water abstraction fees and fees for the extraction of material from streams are further discussed in the section on instruments for natural resource management.)

Table 2.2: Average water and waste-water tariffs

(KM /m^3)

	Water	Waste water	Total
Republika Srpska	0.20	0.09	0.29
Federation of Bosnia and Herzegovina			
	0.40	0.20	0.60
Hungary	0.80	0.80	1.60
Estonia	0.63	0.81	1.44
EU (average)	2.00	1.50	3.50

Source: National Environmental Action Plan. NEAP. March 2003.

The tariffs for water supply and waste-water disposal are set by the (mostly municipal) *vodovods* and approved by the municipalities (in Sarajevo by the canton). Average tariffs for households are given in table 2.2 along with tariffs established in some other European countries (for comparison). The *vodovods* also collect payments. Charges for households in Banja Luka – KM $0.25/m^3$ for water supply and KM $0.10/m^3$ for waste-water disposal – are typical for major cities in Republika Srpska. For businesses and institutions they are significantly higher – KM $1.80/m^3$ and KM $0.70/m^3$, respectively, except for educational, health, cultural, scientific and sport institutions, for which they are KM $0.50/m^3$ and KM $0.20/m^3$. In the Federation of Bosnia and Herzegovina, the combined rate for water supply and waste-water disposal for households is in the range of KM 0.50-$1.00/m^3$, of which approximately 70% is for water supply. Rates for businesses and institutions are 30 to 50% higher. Moreover, the water bills in all municipalities and cantons contain a tax of KM $0.05/m^3$ for water use and water pollution. Even though water rates are set per cubic metre, metering is rare. In the multi-family apartment buildings that have water meters there is usually only one per building. The bill for a particular household is then based on the meter reading for the whole building and the number of people in the household. Therefore, there is no economic incentive for households to save water. In many cases, water meters are not in working order or not installed at all, and the charge in the water bill is based on an estimate.

Water tariffs at their current levels do not cover the full cost of water delivery and sewerage. In addition, many *vodovods* receive less money than they could because of the low collection rates. In Republika Srpska, the average collection rate is estimated to be around 70%; in the Federation of Bosnia and Herzegovina, collection rates vary significantly by municipality from as low as 30% to almost 100% in Breza and Tesanj. The water utilities are generally subsidized by the municipalities and in some cases receive additional subsidies from the entity or the canton (in the Federation). Nevertheless, even with these subsidies their funds are insufficient to meet requirements for normal operation and maintenance. Investments in infrastructure development are low. The poor service also leads to customer dissatisfaction and unwillingness to pay, thus creating a vicious circle. According to officials at the Federation's Ministry of Agriculture, Water Management and Forestry, the high collection rates in Breza and Tesanj are attributed to the public awareness campaign and an improvement in service that became possible thanks to credits obtained by the local *vodovods*.

Water abstraction fees and water pollution fees are collected by public water management companies, two in the Federation (in Sarajevo and Mostar) and one in Republika Srpska (Water Directorate in Bijeljina) (see Chapter 7 on the structure of water resources management). They also receive the taxes on water use and pollution collected by the *vodovods* through the water bills. Water inspectors of the public water management companies control the receipt of payments. These special water compensation charges are distributed as follows: in the Federation, 10% of the revenues are transferred to the entity's budget, 20% to the cantonal budgets and 70% to the respective public water management company; in Republika Srpska, 35% are transferred to the entity's budget and 65% to the Water Directorate.

Box 2.1: Pilot project on the implementation of economic instruments for a sustainable operation of waste-water utilities in the Mediterranean region of Bosnia and Herzegovina

In the framework of the Strategic Action Programme to address pollution from land-based activities for the Mediterranean Sea (SAP MED) launched by the Global Environment Facility, a project component "Development and Implementation of Economic Instruments for a Sustainable Implementation of SAP MED" is being implemented in a number of Mediterranean countries. The Priority Actions Programme Regional Activity Centre of the UNEP Mediterranean Action Plan is in charge of this component. In Bosnia and Herzegovina, a particular focus has been on the use of charges for the collection, treatment and disposal of waste water. For the pilot project, the municipality of Konjic has been chosen. Konjic is located in the upper course of the Neretva river as it flows towards the Adriatic Sea. Waste water from households and industry in Konjic is a significant threat to the Neretva. The key problem identified by the project is the low level of waste-water services and the ineffective maintenance of the infrastructure. If the water utility could be put on a stable financial footing it would be able to make its operation more efficient and decrease river pollution.

The existing waste-water charges are insufficient for cost recovery and rarely collected. The pilot project suggests adapting the current charge system to one based on cost pricing and introducing measures to increase collection rates. The important part of the project is a proper evaluation of the costs of waste-water services incurred by the water utility and developing a waste-water tariff model on this basis. The lack of a metering system, insufficient data, low level of public awareness and the issue of affordability for the population are the main obstacles to introducing a new system of charges. Differentiated rates or subsidies for the poorest sections of the population may be necessary. A public awareness programme, including the establishment of a public relations office at the water utility in Konjic, is important, as are cooperation and acceptance by the municipal authorities. The results of the project are expected in 2004.

Source: Sustainability of SAP MED. Report on the Meeting on Implementation/Evaluation of Pilot Projects, and Proposals for National Action Plans (Split, Croatia, 28-29 March 2003). EI/2003/EM.3/3, Priority Actions Programme Regional Activity Centre.

Another source of financing for water management is the vehicle pollution charge paid by all motor vehicle owners through the annual registration with the police department, even though this type of charge is normally a transport-related instrument (see the section below on instruments for air quality management and instruments related to transport). Incidentally, this charge is a very significant source of revenue for water management. According to Republika Srpska's Ministry of Agriculture, Forestry and Water Management, in the first six months of 2003 revenues from vehicle pollution charges stood at approximately KM 2.5 million, i.e. over two thirds of the total revenues of around KM 3.7 million.

In both entities, water pollution fees for businesses are calculated on the basis of the so-called population equivalent, which takes into account the type of business activity, the quantity of water used and discharged by a company and the chemical and biological indicators of the waste water. In theory, such fees could be an important instrument not only to raise revenues but also to encourage companies to install efficient waste-water treatment equipment. For this to happen, the fees need to be set at levels that would make investments in waste-water treatment financially attractive. In practice, companies find paying the fees at their current levels a less expensive option. The Thermal Power

Plant in Tuzla, one of the largest industrial enterprises in the country, pays KM 2-3 million a year in water pollution fees but currently does not have a waste-water treatment plant and has no plans to invest in water treatment (estimated at KM 20 million or more), according to the company management.

For the Laws on Water Protection in both entities to be implemented, by-laws and regulations have to be developed. For the new charges and fees to become effective instruments in water resource management and water protection, a review of the current economic instruments in water resource management is necessary. The issues that have to be looked at include their efficiency; the reasons for the different collection rates (particularly, to understand clearly what measures made high collection rates possible in certain municipalities); the actual cost of providing water management services; the feasibility of increasing rates for various water fees without hindering economic development or putting an unsustainable burden on the population; and the necessary enforcement measures. Any new economic instrument has to be fully consistent with the "user pays" and "polluter pays" principles. However, when a fee needs to be increased, it may be desirable to do so in increments, taking into account social affordability, with a clear time frame for full cost recovery.

Instruments for waste management

NEAP and the Solid Waste Management Strategy address the current financing of the waste management system and possible ways of improving it. Setting fees (user charges) for waste management services is currently the responsibility of the municipal enterprises that provide the service. The municipalities approve the fee rates. The system is based on charging the population and businesses per square metre of occupied area. The actual fees vary significantly from one municipality to another. In Republika Srpska monthly household charges range from KM $0.01/m^2$ of occupied floor area in Knezevo to KM $0.065/m^2$ in Banja Luka. The situation in the Federation is similar, with waste charges in Sarajevo at KM $0.10/m^2$ (in Sarajevo, unlike in the rest of the entity, the fees are set by the canton).

Rates for businesses are higher and take into account the type of business. In Sarajevo, the range is KM 0.20-$1.50/m^2$ of floor area with the lower figures applicable to offices and the higher rates to meat-processing and meat-selling enterprises, cafes and restaurants. Current rates are too low to recover the cost of waste management services and require subsidies from municipal budgets to cover the shortfall. These rates apply to household waste and other types of municipal waste. Facilities that generate hazardous waste are not obliged to allocate funds for the monitoring and disposal of their waste (see Chapter 6 on management of waste and contaminated sites).

Collection rates are generally low. Exact data are difficult to obtain, but estimates by municipalities and municipal enterprises show that the collection rate for households is close to 50% in Sarajevo and to 45% in Banja Luka. In other municipalities it is even lower, often as low as 10%. Even though the current level of waste charges does not cover the cost of the service, some segments of the population cannot afford even this low rate. In many cases, municipal enterprises issue only one bill covering their various services (water supply, waste-water disposal, heating and waste collection), which may not be itemized. No specific enforcement measures are applied to users who are in arrears. Some of the reasons for not paying up are limited environmental awareness and dissatisfaction with the service.

Republika Srpska's Law on Waste Management (Official Gazette RS 53/2002) and the Federation's Law on Waste Management (Official Gazette F

BiH 33/2003) state that the "polluter pays" principle shall be taken into consideration when implementing their provisions. The producer of waste is responsible for the costs of prevention, recovery and disposal of waste. The Laws also stipulate that waste management services shall be provided for a fee, the conditions and structure of which is to be established in separate regulations. Fines may be imposed for the violation of various provisions of the Laws to be paid to the environmental funds, with their amount and allocation also to be established in separate regulations. No such regulations have so far been prepared in either entity.

Under the new legislation, responsibility for municipal waste management remains with the municipalities. At the same time, it allows the privatization of the municipal enterprises which provide these services, through a tender. In the short term, it is not realistic to expect that user charges to households can be increased to the extent that they will fully cover the costs and that these payments will be collected in full. Therefore, municipalities will have to allocate budget funds to cover the difference. If municipal enterprises are privatized, the new companies may be responsible only for providing the service, while the municipalities will continue to collect the payments. Another option is for the company to collect payments from its customers.

It is critical to get a clear idea of the actual costs of waste management, including operating and capital costs. There are few estimates of such costs. The Solid Waste Management Strategy presents a study on the municipality of Tesanj in the Federation. It estimates that the cost would be approximately KM 32 per ton of municipal waste, with an average of about 0.5 ton of waste generated per capita per year. The average household size is assumed to be 3.4 and the average floor area on which the charges are based is 60 m^2. For households, charging on the basis of occupied area remains a preferred option, according to NEAP. Under these conditions and with a 100% collection rate, the monthly rate should be KM $0.075/m^2$ to cover the estimated cost of waste collection, transport and disposal. Similar studies at other municipalities would be helpful to improve the efficiency of waste management and to have a solid economic basis to make decisions on the service charges.

The Laws also make provisions for collecting waste separately according to type and introducing recycling for certain types of waste. Such changes in the waste management system are certainly desirable from the environmental perspective, but the mechanism for introducing them and particularly the economic aspects are not clear. Waste separation and recycling will need significant capital investment before part of the waste management costs can be recovered through the sale of recycled materials. The only economic incentive for recycling at present is the deposit-refund system for domestically produced glass bottles. Some enterprises recycle, for example, scrap metal that they can use in their own manufacturing process, but data on this are not available.

For industrial and hazardous waste, it is particularly important that the charges should be based on volume or weight, as well as the type of waste, and set at rates that encourage companies to introduce processes that will decrease the amount of waste generated, including changes in the technological process and recycling. NEAP also emphasizes that the cost of the disposal of industrial and hazardous waste should be entirely covered by the industries and businesses generating it.

Instruments for air quality management and instruments related to transport

Air emission charges and emission non-compliance fees were in use in the former Socialist Federal Republic of Yugoslavia and exist in principle in Bosnia and Herzegovina. However, in practice they are not implemented, and industries are not paying anything for air emissions even when the content and amount of air pollution from their activities are known. There is also no requirement for self-reporting of data on air pollution from these companies.

The Federation's Law on Air Protection (Official Gazette F BiH 33/2003) and Republika Srpska's Law on Air Protection (Official Gazette RS 53/2002) state that the "polluter pays" principle should be applied to ensure that the cost of air pollution abatement is borne by the operators of pollution sources. For most activities that may result in air pollution, the Laws specify regulatory, rather than economic instruments, through a system of environmental, urban, construction and user permits. The payment for permits is not mentioned explicitly in the Laws except for a fee for conducting an air study before a permit can be issued. It is not clear whether companies emitting different types or quantities of air pollutants will be charged differently for their permits. The Laws

specify that fines are to be paid for operating without a permit, exceeding emission values specified in the permit and other violations. As with other environmental protection legislation, implementation of the entities' Laws on Air Protection is possible only after adoption of secondary legislation. It is important that the by-laws and regulations contain provisions for differentiating prices for permits depending on the air emissions.

As pollution from mobile sources grows with the increasing number of motor vehicles, the economic instruments related to transport are becoming more important. Currently the following instruments are used: an excise tax on motor fuels and other oil derivatives; a sales tax on vehicles; an import duty on new and used imported vehicles; and an annual registration fee for vehicles.

Taxes on motor fuel do not have an explicit environmental purpose and are used by the entities' central budgets. The rates are KM 0.40/l for leaded petrol, KM 0.35/l for unleaded petrol and KM 0.30/l for diesel fuel. The taxes are paid by the producers and importers of fuel. The price differentiation between leaded and unleaded petrol for the final consumers is relatively small (3-6%). According to the Laws on Air Protection, leaded petrol must be phased out by 2010.

Both the 20% sales tax on vehicles and the 16% import duty on new and used imported vehicles are intended to raise revenue for the entities' budgets. There are limits on the age of imported used vehicles: 7 years for cars and 10 years for trucks and buses.

The annual registration fee for vehicles varies according to the engine size from KM 10 to KM 375. This fee has an environmental component, as mentioned in the section on instruments for water resource management. A portion of its revenues (65% in Republika Srpska) is allocated to the public water management companies. The rest goes to the entities' and the cantons' (in the Federation) budgets and is supposed to be earmarked for road construction and maintenance.

All these instruments are relatively simple to administer and collect, and as such present a stable source of budget revenues. As pollution from motor vehicles has a significant and growing impact on the environment, the Governments of the Federation of Bosnia and Herzegovina and Republika Srpska may consider earmarking a portion of all these instruments for environmental purposes as they already do with the annual registration fee for vehicles.

Instruments for natural resource management

Existing instruments for natural resource management are limited. Information on their legal basis and actual application is not readily available. Among these instruments are water abstraction fees and fees for the extraction of material from streams mentioned in the section on instruments for water management. According to the REC Database of Environmental Taxes and Charges, the water abstraction fee in the Federation is KM $0.1/m^3$ (paid by the *vodovods*). Fees for the extraction of material from streams are applied to companies excavating gravel and sand. In the Federation, the rate is KM $1/m^3$. The total amount of revenues collected is low (KM 12,000-15,000/year), possibly because of under-reporting by companies. In Republika Srpska, the revenues from this fee are higher: KM 200,000 in the first six months of 2003, significantly exceeding the forecast of KM 94,000 for the whole year. The reasons for these differences have not been analysed by the public water management companies responsible for collecting the fees.

Wood export charges are levied in Republika Srpska at the rate of 10% of the export price for raw wood and 3% for cut timber with revenues allocated to the entity's budget. Additionally, in both entities fines for illegal logging in excess of the quantity specified in the licence may be imposed. No information on the revenues from these charges is available. There is strong evidence, according to government officials and academics, that few violations are actually penalized, and illegal logging has become a lucrative business in recent years and presents a serious and growing problem, both environmentally and in terms of lost revenues for the budget (see also Chapter 8 on biodiversity and forest management). No clear information is available on the existence and application of charges for land use in agriculture or revenues from such instruments.

As with the instruments mentioned above, the entities' new environmental legislation outlines the use of economic instruments for natural resources management. Republika Srpska's Law on Nature Protection (Official Gazette RS 50/2002) and the Federation's Law on Nature Protection (Official Gazette F BiH 33/2003) stipulate that polluters and users shall pay fees, charges, taxes or other payments for pollution or for the use of nature or natural resources. The Laws specify which violations of the provisions are subject to a fine. The particulars of the system of charges and fines are to be established by regulations and by-laws adopted by the entities' and the cantons' governments and the ministries responsible for environmental protection.

2.3 Environmental financing and expenditures

The entities allocate few resources from their budgets to environmental activities. After the end of the war, almost all environmental projects were financed by international donors (see Chapter 4 on international cooperation). Recently, some of them have required the entities to co-finance environmental projects. In 2003, the following projects were co-financed by the Government of Republika Srpska: LIFE Third Country Projects "LICENSE – Local Institutional Capacity Development in Environmentally Sensitive Areas" (KM 306,700), "INFRA-RED – Institutional Framework for Regional Environmental Development" (KM 333,200) and "ROSA – Establishment of the Operational Unit of the Steering Committee on Environment" (KM 133,000); and the World Bank Solid Waste Management Project (KM 100,000). For 2004 the Ministry of Physical Planning, Civil Engineering and Ecology has requested approximately KM 1.14 million from Republika Srpska's budget for co-financing LIFE Third Country and other projects.

The Federation allocated KM 96,500 from its budget to co-finance the LIFE Third Country Project "Establishment of the Operational Unit of the Steering Committee on Environment" in 2003. For 2004 its Ministry of Physical Planning and Environment has requested approximately KM 410,000 for the continuation of the LIFE project, the development of the national strategy for the protection of biodiversity and landscape diversity, the development of secondary environmental legislation, the development of an environmental protection strategy, and a programme related to the Una National Park. It is worth noting that in 2003 the Ministry of Physical Planning and Environment's operating budget was more than twice that of 2002 (KM 2.45 million vs. 1.19 million). However, this constitutes only 0.2% of the entity's budget, which is KM 1,217.4 million (Official Gazette F BiH 21/2003).

The entities' other ministries also spend money on environmental protection, as do their municipalities and the Federation's cantons. For example, revenues collected by the entities' public water management companies are used for monitoring water quality, constructing and operating facilities for flood protection, improving existing and constructing new water supply and waste-water systems, riverbed reinforcement, studies and preparing strategic development plans, and implementing projects supported by international donors.

According to officials of the Ministry of Agriculture, Water Management and Forestry, expenditures for these purposes in the Federation total approximately KM 20 million per year. Revenues from particular water-management-related charges are not earmarked for particular activities. Therefore, water pollution fees are not necessarily used specifically for abating water pollution.

According to officials at the Ministry of Physical Planning and Environmental Protection of Sarajevo canton, the canton's budget allocates funds for creating a new sanitary waste disposal site, cleaning up sites contaminated with hazardous waste, exporting medical waste (for which there are no processing facilities in Bosnia and Herzegovina), air quality monitoring, financing two protected areas, and financing projects submitted by NGOs on a competitive basis. Total expenditures are estimated at KM 3 million annually. Some cantons (e.g. Zenica-Doboj and Tuzla) have established environmental funds to be used as a main source for environmental expenditures.

One of the significant drawbacks of the current system of environmental expenditures is the lack of coordination between the entities' Environment Ministries and their other ministries. In the Federation, this is compounded by the lack of clarity in the distribution of responsibilities for environmental protection between the Federation and the cantons. Bosnia and Herzegovina does not have a system for collecting data on environmental expenditure. The Ministry of Physical Planning and Environment of the Federation of Bosnia and Herzegovina and the Ministry of Physical Planning, Civil Engineering and Ecology of Republika Srpska do not have full information or a database on the financing of all environment-related projects in their entities. The Department for Environmental Protection of the Ministry of Foreign Trade and

Economic Relations of Bosnia and Herzegovina does not have this information either.

The entities' Laws on Environmental Protection outline the environmental protection goals and the means of financing them. The goals include fulfilling tasks arising from international obligations, cleaning up environmental damage when the polluter is not known or cannot be held liable, advancing the costs of abating or eliminating environmental damage that requires immediate intervention, and supporting measures to protect the environment, especially developing and operating an information system, control by public administration, education and the dissemination of information, research and public involvement in environmental protection. To this end, the Laws envision establishing environmental funds in the entities and in the Federation's cantons.

The Federation's Law on the Environmental Fund (Official Gazette F BiH 33/2003) and Republika Srpska's Law on the Environmental Fund (Official Gazette RS 51/2002) identify sources of revenue for the funds. These include charges for environmental pollution and the use of natural resources, transfers from the entities' budgets, bank loans and grants from donors. In both entities, the funds are independent bodies. Their statutes and regulations are developed in consultation with the Environment Ministries and approved by the Governments.

In Republika Srpska, the Fund's plans and programmes of work, annual budget and plan of expenditures must be prepared in consultation with the Ministry of Physical Planning, Civil Engineering and Ecology and approved by the Government. Its managing board is appointed by Parliament.

In the Federation, the Ministry of Physical Planning and Environment decides on the methods for determining fees and charges in consultation with the Ministry of Energy, Mining and Industry, and for calculating and paying fees and charges in consultation with the Ministry of Finance. A report on the Environmental Fund's activities has to be submitted to the Ministry every six months. The Ministry also oversees the Fund's management practices and its compliance with relevant laws and regulations. The Ministry nominates the members of the Fund's managing board, who are to be approved by the Government. The managing board also adopts regulations on the Fund's expenditures in consultation with the Ministry. The Law specifies that all the Fund's revenues must be split as follows: 30% for the Federation and 70% for the cantons.

In addition, the entities' Laws on Nature Protection call for the establishment of nature protection funds as part of the environmental funds. As with all new environmental legislation, these laws cannot be operational until appropriate regulations and statutes for the funds are adopted.

The environmental funds may become an important means of financing environmental activities. They may provide better coordination of environmental activities within and between entities as well as be instrumental in setting priorities. Close cooperation with the Environment Ministries is vital for the funds' efficient functioning.

2.4 Privatization and the impacts on environmental protection

The privatization programme in Bosnia and Herzegovina has been developed to assist in the economic and social transition. In both entities privatization is governed by a set of laws. The most important are the Law on the Privatization of Enterprises (Official Gazette F BiH 27/1997) in the Federation of Bosnia and Herzegovina and the Law on the Privatization of State Capital in Enterprises (Official Gazette RS 24/1998, with amendments and additions (Official Gazette RS 62/2002 and 65/2003)) in Republika Srpska. The bodies responsible for privatization are the Agency for Privatization in the Federation of Bosnia and Herzegovina, the Directorate for Privatization in Republika Srpska and Brčko Privatization Office in Brčko District. In the Federation, the cantonal privatization agencies handle the privatization of most enterprises within their jurisdictions with the exception of the largest ones and those that have

branches in more than one canton. The latter are the direct responsibility of the Agency.

The stated goals of privatization include economic recovery, post-war reconstruction and transition to the market economy; social stability; settlement of outstanding claims; increased employment; and liquidation of domestic and foreign debts accumulated by enterprises, banks and the State. They do not mention improving the environmental situation at the privatized enterprises or any other environmental considerations.

Since the beginning of the privatization process, various methods have been used, including voucher sale, direct sale, auctions and tenders. Approximately 1,450 enterprises were identified for privatization in the Federation and 1,100 in Republika Srpska. In the early stages (1997-2000) many companies, particularly small and medium enterprises, were privatized through so-called mass privatisation or voucher sales. While this process allowed their employees and other individuals to become shareholders, it did not bring the necessary investment and new technologies to make them viable. The focus has since shifted to other forms of privatization. In particular, for larger companies (equity exceeding KM 500,000 in the Federation and KM 300,000 in Republika Srpska), the bodies responsible for privatization are organizing tenders to attract strategic foreign investors.

The privatization has had mixed economic and social results at best. Table 2.3 contains selected data on the results at the end of 2002. According to government officials and representatives of non-governmental organizations, public opinion of the privatization process is generally negative. Privatization is perceived to have brought very few benefits so far. In particular, the revenues from privatization are low and unemployment remains high.

Table 2.3: Selected data on the privatization of State property by the end of 2002

	Total number of large enterprises*	Number of privatized large enterprises	Percentage of privatized small enterprises	Revenues from the sale of State property, millions of KM
Federation of Bosnia and Herzegovina	1,064	260	70	326
Republika Srpska	648	271	47	120

Source: Medium-term Development Strategy (Poverty Reduction Strategy Paper) (2003-2007).
Note: * Over 50 employees or over KM 500,000 in capital.

To change that perception the authorities are trying to make the privatization process more transparent and open. Information about upcoming tenders, along with relevant legislation and regulations, is available on the Directorate's and the Agency's web sites. The Directorate and the Agency also publish information about success stories in both entities. Such cases include SHP Celex in Banja Luka, which produces tissue paper. The company was privatized in November 2001 by Ecoinvest, Slovakia, and has since increased production nine-fold. Employment at the factory rose from 288 to 420. The new owner has invested KM 17.5 million in the factory in less than two years.

In many cases, it is not possible to find an investor for companies scheduled for privatization because their equipment and technological process are obsolete, and they are overstaffed and deeply indebted. For a potential investor who wishes to operate in Bosnia and Herzegovina, it is often cheaper to build a new plant than to privatize and refurbish an existing one. This explains why the bodies responsible for privatization are unwilling to attach conditions related to pollution prevention, clean-up and other environmental measures to privatization agreements. Officials believe that such conditions make the privatized company less attractive to potential investors.

In Republika Srpska, privatization agreements contain a general clause on the company's environmental obligations. It states that the newly privatized company must comply with the country's environmental laws. In most cases, the agreements contain clauses absolving the new owners from liability for any prior environmental pollution. As the environment is not seen as a priority in privatization, the Directorate for Privatization does not insist on environmental investments when negotiating with potential investors. There is no coordination between the Directorate and the Ministry of Physical Planning, Civil Engineering and Ecology.

In the Federation, the situation is similar. There is no coordination between the Agency for Privatization and the Ministry of Physical Planning and Environment and, generally, no special environmental clauses. However, according to Agency officials, the international community has recommended the Agency to include environmental protection clauses in the privatization agreements. The Agency also plans to hire an environmental adviser.

Some investors have voluntarily taken environmental measures and curbed pollution. For instance, Kakanj Cement, a large cement manufacturer approximately 50 km from Sarajevo was privatized in 2000 through the sale of 51% of its shares to a German company, HeidelbergCement. HeidelbergCement has invested € 22 million in the plant to modernize it and especially to improve its environmental performance. As a result, the levels of dust emissions declined steadily, and by 2002 they were 96% lower than before privatization. HeidelbergCement has recently acquired another major cement plant in Lukavac and has begun a programme of environmental improvement there.

The privatization process is now moving into a phase when the largest commercial companies in, for instance, energy, water management, forestry, mining, transport and electronic media will be privatized. Because of their importance for the national economy and the impact many of them have on the environment, environmental considerations must be taken into account during this phase.

The Medium-term Development Strategy (Poverty Reduction Strategy Paper) (2003-2007) lists the reasons for the relative ineffectiveness of the privatization, the main obstacles to its success and the priorities for accelerating it. Among these are: strengthening the Agency for Privatization and the Directorate for Privatization; performing pre-privatisation restructuring of firms; introducing measures to resolve the issue of accumulated debts; preparing the privatization of public enterprises and public utilities (telecommunications, mining, forestry, water supply and energy) and parts of the public infrastructure; and campaigning for public support for accelerated privatization. Unfortunately, the Strategy does not mention the environment in connection with the privatization process.

2.5   Conclusions and recommendations

The economic instruments for environmental protection are generally not well developed and their use is limited. Many have been inherited from the former Socialist Federal Republic of Yugoslavia and do not reflect Bosnia and Herzegovina's current economic and social development or the state of its environment. In areas where economic instruments are relatively well developed and used, such as water management, they often remain inefficient because the established tariffs and the rates of collection are too low to cover the cost of services, let alone to make the necessary investment in infrastructure development. In other cases the charges are not collected at all. Often the main purpose of an economic instrument is to raise revenue for the government budget (entities, cantons or municipalities) or for the public utility. Its effect on the environment is not a priority – if considered at all. Few of the charges have an explicit environmental purpose. The purpose of economic instruments and their impact on the environment are poorly understood. Together with the inadequate service and the low incomes of some people, this often results in a low collection rate of user fees.

Recently adopted environmental legislation in the Federation of Bosnia and Herzegovina and in Republika Srpska clearly outlines the objectives of economic instruments for environmental protection. The "polluter pays" and "user pays" principles are an integral part of the legislation. The legislation is almost identical in both entities and so sets a good basis for harmonized policies, including in the area of economic instruments. Unfortunately, the development of secondary legislation (by-laws and regulations) is lagging. Consequently, the provisions of these laws related to economic instruments cannot be implemented until such secondary legislation is drawn up. To make the new economic instruments efficient, several requirements must be met. For instance, the "polluter pays" and "user pays" principles must be implemented; the instruments must be socially acceptable, this means introducing lower rates or subsidies for the poor; and companies must have incentives to apply technologies that significantly reduce pollution and their impact on the environment.

Recommendation 2.1:
(a) The Ministry of Physical Planning and Environment of the Federation of Bosnia and Herzegovina and the Ministry of Physical Planning, Civil Engineering and Ecology of Republika Srpska in cooperation withthe State Ministry of Foreign Trade and Economic Relations, should draw up by-laws and regulations to introduce the economic instruments stipulated in the environmental laws and ensuring the consistency with the State environmental policy.

(b) When developing the secondary legislation, they need to propose adequate levels of charges, fees, taxes and penalties. If it is not feasible to introduce instruments at the desired levels (for example, user fees at the level of full cost recovery for the service provided), the charges may be reduced at first, but should increase incrementally with a clear time frame until they reach the desired levels.

Recommendation 2.2:
The Federation's Ministry of Physical Planning and Environment and Republika Srpska's Ministry of Physical Planning, Civil Engineering and Ecology should establish a regularly updated and readily accessible database of economic instruments for the environment. This would enable all levels of government, businesses and the general public to have a clear understanding of the instruments that exist, their main purpose, the recipients of the revenues (and the amounts) and whether the revenues are used for environmental purposes. The changes in rates, when necessary, and the reasons for such changes would also become transparent. These databases should be made available to the State for policy-making.

Recommendation 2.3:
The Federation's Ministry of Physical Planning and Environment and Republika Srpska's Ministry of Physical Planning, Civil Engineering and Ecology, in cooperation with environmental NGOs, the media and other stakeholders, should organize a public awareness campaign with the aim of increasing collection rates for services related to the use of natural resources as well as for waste management. Such a campaign should inform the public of the importance and the positive impact of economic instruments on the environment.

Until now, the entities have allocated few resources from their budgets to environmental protection. Most environmental projects have been financed by international donors. Republika Srpska's Ministry of Physical Planning, Civil Engineering and Ecology and the Federation's Ministry of Physical Planning and Environment do not have full information on the environmental expenditures of other ministries, municipal and cantonal authorities and enterprises.

The environmental expenditures of various governmental offices are insufficiently coordinated. The adoption of the sets of environmental laws, including the entities' Laws on the Environmental Fund, opens the possibility of better coordination of environmental activities within and between the entities and could be instrumental in identifying priorities for environmental expenditures. Close cooperation with the Environment Ministries is critical for the funds' efficient functioning.

Recommendation 2.4:

(a) The Federation's Ministry of Physical Planning and Environment and Republika Srpska's Ministry of Physical Planning, Civil Engineering and Ecology should draw up by-laws and regulations to make the environmental funds operational.

(b) The Ministries and the environmental funds of the entities and the cantons (in the Federation) should coordinate their activities based on the priorities included in the National Environmental Action Plan for spending on environmental protection and to ensure the most efficient use of environmental expenditures.

The country's privatization process has been going on for more than six years, yet many of its objectives have so far not been realized. There are a number of successful privatization projects, which turned loss-making companies into profitable businesses and even increased employment opportunities, but society's overall attitude towards privatization remains largely negative. For companies privatized through tenders, the privatization agreement either does not include environmental requirements or it has only a general clause requiring the new owner to comply with environmental legislation. As a rule, privatization agreements contain no provisions for past environmental liabilities. Currently, the Agency for Privatization in the Federation of Bosnia and Herzegovina and the Directorate for Privatization in Republika Srpska do not employ environmental specialists.

No coordination exists between the privatization bodies and the respective Environment Ministries.

On the positive side, some newly privatized companies have voluntarily taken effective pollution preventing measures. The case studies of such companies may be instrumental in developing policies to encourage new owners to invest in pollution prevention and resource-saving technologies. The largest energy, water, forestry, mining and telecommunications enterprises are about to be put up for privatization. Because of their importance for the national economy and the impact many of them have on the environment, environmental considerations must be taken into account during this phase of the privatization process.

Recommendation 2.5:

(a) The Federation's Agency for Privatization and Republika Srpska's Directorate for Privatization should strengthen their cooperation respectively with the Federation's Ministry of Physical Planning and Environment and Republika Srpska's Ministry of Physical Planning, Civil Engineering. In particular, they should involve them in the decision-making in the privatization process to promote environmental investments by the new owners by:

- *Developing and introducing clauses on past environmental liabilities into the privatization agreements;*
- *Requiring enterprises and industries put up for privatization to carry out environmental audits; and*
- *Including compliance plans, prepared by the new owner, in the privatization agreement. These plans should specify the measures that enterprises and industries have to take to comply with environmental standards and regulations.*

(b) The Agency and the Directorate should have one or more environmental specialists on their staff.

Chapter 3

INFORMATION, PUBLIC PARTICIPATION AND EDUCATION

3.1   Introduction

The early years after the war may be generally characterized by inertia and unawareness on the part of the population and the authorities of the importance of applying environmental policy and regulations. Most people were not sufficiently aware and informed about the significance of adverse environmental impacts on their health, the environment and the country's natural resource base. Fortunately, over the past few years, environmental issues have been receiving more and more attention from various levels of government. However, the increase of environmental awareness and competence of the authorities has not yet resulted in improved environmental awareness among the general public and better environmental behaviour by individuals.

The various facets of public support (regular payment of municipal fees, appropriate waste disposal, demands for environmental information, scrutiny of public or private bodies) do not sufficiently contribute to environmental improvements. Too often environmental protection is still felt as impeding economic and social development. The public is not used to questioning or contributing to policy development. Civil society is insufficiently informed of opportunities and areas where it can make a difference.

The engagement of the public, cooperation and pressure of civil society on institutions can improve the situation. Much depends on the availability of objective assessments of the state of the environment. This is a great challenge that Bosnia and Herzegovina is facing today.

3.2   Environmental monitoring

Measurements in Bosnia and Herzegovina are generally compared with countrywide environmental standards, if available. Bosnia and Herzegovina has adopted more than 100 environmental standards on the basis of the latest

International Organization for Standardization (ISO) and EU principles. Eight of the adopted standards concern environmental management, some twenty concern air and indoor air, and some seventy concern water quality.

A recent report prepared by the Hydroengineering Institute, Sarajevo, on behalf of the World Bank within the scope of the "Urgent Strengthening of Environmental Institutions in Bosnia and Herzegovina" project provides a detailed assessment of environmental monitoring in the country. The description of the monitoring activities below is based on this report and on additional information collected during the Environmental Performance Review mission.

Water

The water-quality monitoring network is insufficiently developed and covers only part of the country. The quality of surface waters is systematically examined in 58 profiles. The monitoring equipment was destroyed during the war and the re-establishment of water-quality measuring stations is slow and gradual. The system is not yet fully restored and upgraded to modern standards because of financial constraints.

Federation of Bosnia and Herzegovina

The Federation's Meteorological Institute monitors water levels daily and water flow periodically at five gauge stations (rivers Bosna, Jala, Miljacka, Sana and Una). It monitors water levels daily in 13 profiles (rivers Bijela, Bioštica, Bosna, Krivaja, Lašva, Spreca, Stupcanica, Željeznica and Zujevina) and regularly in 9 profiles (rivers Bosna, Crna, Miljacka, Misoca, Sana and Una). It also periodically (seasonally) takes samples and analyzes the chemical water quality in two spots (rivers Crna and Misoca). Twenty-four parameters are measured, including ammonia, sulphate, sulphide, phosphate, calcium, magnesium, nitrate, nitrite, dissolved oxygen and acidity.

Six laboratories have been authorized to check the discharge of pollutants into water. A central water-testing laboratory to meet the needs of the inspectorates and to supervise the operation of the authorized laboratories is being established.

The Public Enterprise for the Watershed Area of the Adriatic Sea Basin, Mostar, and the Public Water Management Enterprise for the Watershed Area of the River Sava Basin, Sarajevo, monitor these water resources at a few locations. The Public Electricity Supply Company Elektroprivreda BiH, Sarajevo, collects and processes hydrologic and meteorological data from 19 automatic gauge stations on the upper and middle course of the river Neretva.

Water utilities monitor physical and chemical water quality at source. The Federation's Institute for Public Health, Sarajevo, carries chemical and bacteriological analyses of drinking water from water utilities. The cantons' institutes for public health occasionally monitor the quality of drinking water in their jurisdictions.

Republika Srpska

Republika Srpska's Hydrometeorological Institute, Banja Luka, operates a network of hydrological stations for surface waters which monitor the state and changes in the water level, flow and temperature and the occurrence of ice. Physical, chemical, saprobiological, bacteriological and hydrological parameters are monitored. Furthermore, the Institute measures beta-radioactivity of groundwater and sea water.

The Institute for Water in Bijeljina undertakes physico-chemical, microbiological and saprobiological analyses of water in all important water streams (rivers Bosna, Cehotina, Crna Rijeka, Drina, Lim, Sana, Sava, Spreca, Trebišnjica, Ugar, Una, Ukrina, Usora, Vrbanja and Vrbas) in 23 profiles and in the Bocac water reservoir including all its tributaries. Physical, chemical and microbiological analyses of groundwater are currently done in the Semberia area only.

The main water management companies located in Gradiška (river Sava), Srpsko Sarajevo (river Gornja Bosna), Bijeljina (Semberija), Zvornik (river Drina), Trebinje (River Trebišnjica), Šamac (mouth of river Bosna), Loncari (middle stream of the river Sava) monitor the use of water and waste-water discharges.

The Institute for Health Protection monitors drinking water quality and waste-water conditions. Most of the water supply enterprises have their own laboratories to control the main physical and chemical parameters of water samples taken from water distribution networks. Other water utilities contract the Institute for Health Protection to test water quality.

Air

Bosnia and Herzegovina and its entities have neither a data collection mechanism for emissions nor a coordinated monitoring network. A variety of air monitoring activities are conducted by various institutions. The equipment used varies and there is no quality assurance and quality control or agreed protocols.

Federation of Bosnia and Herzegovina

The Meteorological Institute monitors air quality (SO_2, CO, NO, NO_2 and NO_x) daily at an automatic station in Sarajevo. Two other monitoring stations in Sarajevo and stations in Tuzla and Mostar measure SO_2 and black smoke daily. With European Environment Agency (EEA) support (funded mostly through the PHARE programme), the Institute obtained monitoring equipment for its automatic station in Sarajevo and introduced the CORINAIR methodology. Data from the automatic station is uploaded daily on the European Environment Information and Observation Network (EIONET) web server of the Ministry of Physical Planning and Environment and transmitted to the EIONET AirBase Air Quality. Data are available to the general public and are published from time to time in the media. The Institute produces air emission data for the State as a whole by calculation and modelling methods.

The Institute for Public Health, Mostar, sporadically monitors air pollution at a few locations in the canton of Herzegovina-Neretva. It submits monthly reports and bulletins to the relevant public authorities and the mass media.

The Institute for Public Health of the canton of Sarajevo measures concentrations of SO_2 and soot at five spots (Vijecnica, Titova street, Otoka, Ilidža and Vogošca). Samples are taken manually. Moreover, the Institute measures air emissions from some burners in the canton and controls the analyses of two companies, Grizelj and Dvokut, which measure the air emissions of most burners in the canton. It regularly submits data to the canton's

Ministry for Regional Planning and the Environment in Sarajevo.

Some air polluters (Pharmaceutical Company Bosnalijek Sarajevo, thermo-power plants of Kakanj and Tuzla, and the Kakanj Cement Factory) measure some of their emissions into the atmosphere.

Republika Srpska

Apart from meteorological observations, the Hydrometeorological Institute is in charge of measuring air quality and radioactivity in the air and in rainfall. Its automatic monitoring station in Banja Luka measures SO_2, CO, NO, NO_2, and NO_x. It cooperates closely with the Federation's Meteorological Institute.

The Institute for Protection, Ecology and Information Science measures black smoke and SO_2 at seven sampling spots in the area of Banja Luka. It also measures black smoke, SO_2 and NO_x at one sampling spot in Gradiska.

Overall, air quality is monitored occasionally in some 20% of municipalities. Among the polluters, only the Thermo-power Plant Ugljevik operates its own monitoring station.

Biodiversity and forestry

One significant achievement was the publication in 1997 of the national Red List of Plants. It covers all vascular plant groups and comprises 678 threatened species.

Federation of Bosnia and Herzegovina

At present, there is no organized monitoring of forests. Periodically, the Forestry Department of Sarajevo University monitors forest health. Its data are stored in a database and transmitted to the Federation's Institute for Statistics.

The Ministry of Physical Planning and Environment prepared terms of reference for COoRdination of INformation on the Environment (CORINE) Biotopes – Bosnia and Herzegovina. The purpose is to select sites of European importance for nature conservation and to describe the habitats and species according to the CORINE methodology to build up a standardized CORINE Biotopes database and the spatial delineation of sites. This project has not yet been realized because of a lack of financial support.

Republika Srpska

The Public Forestry Enterprise Srpske Šume assesses forests for taxation purposes, collects data on the types of forests (quantity of wood, surface and logging), processes and maps these data and makes them available for forest husbandry. The Institute for the Protection of the Cultural, Historical and Natural Heritage collects data on the main cultural, historical and natural heritage. The data can be made available in paper or electronic form upon payment.

Soil

Federation of Bosnia and Herzegovina

Within the "CORINE Land Cover project", the Geodetic Institute in Sarajevo, in cooperation with EEA, carried out nationwide satellite surveying and mapping. The maps contain 44 different layers that can be used to recognize land cover types.

The Institute of Agropedology in Sarajevo is the only institution in Bosnia and Herzegovina that is working on soil analyses. Its activities include: mapping of land by land use, mapping of soil by its use value, and reviewing soil fertility, land-use changes, impact of solid waste dumpsites on soil, soil remediation and amelioration. The Institute studied the land and soil potential in the country to lay down the basis for a soil information system and mapping soil contamination. It has never continuously monitored soil, however. Neither does it publish any regular reports.

Republika Srpska

The Agricultural Institute collects data on total agricultural land, damage to land surface and areas of land under cultivation. The Institute maps these data and stores them in digital form. The data are available against payment.

Waste

Neither the State nor the entities have an institution to collect data on waste generation, transport, treatment or disposal. Information is available only from some landfills that control and weigh incoming trucks. In the preparation of the Solid Waste Management Strategy for Bosnia and Herzegovina, inventories of all legal and illegal municipal waste dumps, including their potential environmental impacts, were made in the regions of Livno, Mostar and Tuzla.

3.3   Environmental information management

The process of strengthening environmental information management in Bosnia and Herzegovina started in the late 1990s, when the country became a collaborating non-member country of EEA/EIONET and the Inter-entity Steering Committee for the Environment (with coordination functions for environmental monitoring and information) was established. As EIONET required communication at the State level, the Steering Committee designated a member from the Federation's Ministry of Physical Planning and Environment as national focal point. EEA, with EC/PHARE funds, provided the Ministry with a modern telecommunications system and training to set up the national EIONET site.

The designation was not officially confirmed and the national focal point could not, therefore, operate as required. Furthermore, the focal point lacked a proper support structure and back-up capacity for carrying out the activities – staff, procedures, tools and training – that were key elements of institutionalizing the work in Bosnia and Herzegovina. No working arrangements were made between the focal point and expert institutions in the country.

Bosnia and Herzegovina does not participate in the UNECE Working Group on Environmental Monitoring and Assessment, which assists countries in transition to strengthen their monitoring and assessment capacities.

The establishment in 2002 of an operational unit under the Steering Committee was an important practical step towards strengthening and better coordinating environmental information management in Bosnia and Herzegovina. The European Community (EC) and the Netherlands Ministry of Foreign Affairs provided financial support to the unit and its activities. The latter include, inter alia, the following:
- Assessment of the current situation with environmental information in both entities;
- Identification of the main professional institutions in both entities that would regularly collect and forward environmental information to EEA;
- Development of channels, rules and procedures of communication and exchange of information between different participants in the process;
- Development of databases and their uploading on the Internet; and

- Selection and presentation of indicators for selected areas (air, water, nature, and waste).

The operational unit was equipped with computers and software for data storage, exchange and uploading on the Internet. A local area network was installed at the Ministry of Physical Planning, Civil Engineering and Ecology of Republika Srpska, along with a web site (http://www.mpugie.rs.ba). The Federation's Ministry of Physical Planning and Environment also set up a web site (http://www.fmpuio.gov.ba). All information related to the activities of the operational unit is uploaded on these web sites regularly. In addition, the Steering Committee's web site (http://www.koo.ba) was established. Staff members of the two above-mentioned ministries were trained in web page design and maintenance, and in data management. The operational unit has circulated a questionnaire to review the current availability of environmental information in Bosnia and Herzegovina and any gaps that need to be filled.

Discussions on an environment agency

A recent project of the World Bank and the Mediterranean Environmental Technical Assistance Programme to strengthen environmental institutions in Bosnia and Herzegovina resulted in a series of proposals for reorganizing the environmental institutions, including their information systems. The establishment of a State environmental protection agency was at the core of the proposals. As a result and in view of the new Laws on Environmental Protection, which envisage the establishment of an inter-entity environmental body that would be much stronger than the current Steering Committee, discussions started regarding future environmental policy at the State level and the possible role of an environmental protection agency.

Work is under way to study the feasibility of a State environmental protection agency. For this purpose, the State could draft a general (umbrella) environmental law and assess the capacity of the entities' ministries and the State ministries so as to propose the most efficient way of establishing an environment agency, the division of work and responsibilities between the agency and other governmental institutions and the methods of cooperation at various levels.

Judging from the discussions held so far, there seems to be a general agreement that the agency's key responsibilities should include, at least, the coordination of environmental monitoring, the development of environmental databases, the preparation of state-of-the-environment reports, cooperation with the European Environment Agency and reporting to governing bodies of applicable international environmental conventions.

3.4 Environmental reporting and statistics

Environmental assessments

An informal report on the state of the environment in Bosnia and Herzegovina was prepared and published in 2002 by an environmental NGO. It was based on internationally available data. No data from domestic sources were used.

A comprehensive report on the environmental situation in Brčko District was prepared by the Centre on Ecology and Natural Resources of Sarajevo University in 2002 under contract with Counterpart International, an NGO from the United States. The report was submitted to the district's administration, but was not widely circulated.

The NEAP contains a broad assessment of the country's environmental situation and mentions the main causes of adverse environmental impacts. It is not a state-of-the-environment report in its conventional sense.

With the support and coordination of the United Nations Development Programme (UNDP) and the Global Environment Facility (GEF), Bosnia and Herzegovina submitted its national report on sustainable development to the World Summit on Sustainable Development in Johannesburg, South Africa, in 2002. It presented, in particular, an overview of its environmental situation, pointed to the main sources of environmental degradation and indicated ways to improve the situation.

The recent Laws on Environmental Protection in the two entities oblige regulatory bodies and public authorities to make environmental information widely available. They explicitly stipulate that the Environment Ministries shall disseminate actively environmental information in a continuous, transparent and effective way. They shall use publications in printed and electronic form which is easily accessible to the public. The Ministries are further obliged to analyse and evaluate the state of the environment and its protection, and the experience in protecting, using and developing the environment. The laws stop short, however, from

explicitly obliging the Ministries to publish a regular state-of-the-environment report.

Some public environmental institutions publish studies, brochures, newsletters and leaflets. For instance, the operational unit of the Inter-entity Steering Committee for the Environment publishes and widely disseminates its newsletter.

Reporting to the international community

Bosnia and Herzegovina regularly provides environmental data to EEA, but the data are incomplete. In 2002, it reported only 29% of the EIONET priority data, against 39% the previous year. The decrease may be explained by institutional problems (see *Environmental information management* above). In 2002, air-quality and river water-quality data delivery improved. However, water-quality data were reported from only 36 stations (71%) identified for EUROWATERNET. Furthermore, only very short time series (2 years) data were given for total ammonium, nitrate and total phosphorus. As in the past, no groundwater data were provided in 2002; only general descriptions for two groundwater bodies were made available. No marine data were reported in 2002, contrary to the two previous years. As in the past, no data were reported on lake water quality, emissions of acidifying air pollutants, greenhouse-gas emissions and ozone-depleting substances.

Data on the state of the environment were collected and included in the two successive environmental assessment reports by EEA for the Ministerial Conferences "Environment for Europe" (*Dobris +3* of 1998 and *Kiev Assessment* of 2003).

Bosnia and Herzegovina does not provide monitoring data related to a number of international environmental conventions to which it is a Party. Examples are the Convention on Long-range Transboundary Air Pollution and the Basel Convention on the Control of Transboundary Movements of Hazardous Wastes and Their Disposal. It has not yet identified its biodiversity component in accordance with annex I to the Convention on Biological Diversity.

Some progress has been made, however. In compliance with the Vienna Convention for the Protection of the Ozone Layer and its Montreal Protocol, a draft national report was prepared recently with an estimation of the total amount of ozone-depleting substances in use and with a list of installations that are major generators of ozone-depleting substances. Supported by GEF/UNDP, Bosnia and Herzegovina is preparing its first national communication in accordance with the United Nations Framework Convention on Climate Change.

Environmental statistics

Although the implementation of classifications according to international and notably European Union standards is progressing well, the statistical capacity in Bosnia and Herzegovina is generally considered to be poor by European standards. There are no proper registers of enterprises, population and territorial units. National accounts do not meet basic requirements. There are no comprehensive agricultural surveys, and too many data rely on experts' estimates. Environmental statistics are not yet a visible part of the national statistical system. The only data of relevance to the environment that are collected by the national Agency for Statistics and the entities' two Institutes of Statistics are meteorological, forestry and water management data.

3.5   Environmental awareness

Bosnia and Herzegovina's mass media take an interest in environmental issues. For instance, there is a periodical magazine *Eko Svijet* (Eco World). The television of Bosnia and Herzegovina has been broadcasting for more than 15 years a TV show "Living with Nature". The radio of Republika Srpska has a similar weekly show. The Federation's radio, too, has for several years been broadcasting a weekly half-hour show on the environment and sustainable development. Some NGOs and individuals produce environmental publications in local languages.

A survey conducted recently by the local office of the Regional Environmental Center for Central and Eastern Europe (REC) under the Regional Environmental Reconstruction Programme (REReP) project "Capacity Building for EU Approximation in South Eastern Europe" revealed that TV spots and programmes, brochures, newspapers and the Internet were recognized by representatives of the national authorities and environmental NGOs as the most efficient tools for information dissemination. More than half the respondents agreed, however, that these tools were not used to their full effect in Bosnia and Herzegovina.

One of the purposes of the recently launched € 1.6 million project on strengthening environmental management institutions under the Community Assistance, Reconstruction, Development and Stabilisation (CARDS) 2002 programme is to assist the Environment Ministries in the two entities in raising public awareness to promote a change in environmental behaviour. A strategy will be prepared for the short (2 years) and the medium term (5 years). The strategy will focus on the development of information campaigns, specific information materials, marketing and advertising, training and education. Assistance will also be provided to the ministries concerned with the implementation of concrete public awareness campaigns.

The Waste Recycling Pilot Project (€ 1.1 million) under the CARDS 2003 programme also has a component on awareness raising and training. Its purpose is to prepare standard awareness-raising blueprints. This could include the preparation of general information leaflets on the advantages of recycling, TV and radio spots, and other material that could be used by municipalities. The project will provide models for easy reproduction.

The entities' new Laws on Environmental Protection envisage the creation of voluntary eco-labelling schemes for products and services, and environmental management systems to raise the awareness of both producers and consumers. They do not stipulate any coordination requirements between the entities on these matters, however. The EPR team has not obtained any information on any practical steps taken in the entities to establish eco-labelling schemes and environmental management systems.

At present environmental awareness activities mostly consist in providing basic information on environmental degradation (usually in relation to municipal waste) and suggesting how citizens can directly contribute to the preservation of their immediate environment. They do not extend to informing people about their rights and the obligations of authorities towards them. Raising awareness about the legal obligations of polluters, the implications of new environmental laws and the rights of citizens to receive information and participate in decision-making on activities, programmes and policies that may affect their environment and health needs to be the next step.

3.6   Environmental education

Curricula and programmes for pre-schoolers include environmental elements. However, due to the overall economic situation in the country, few children attend childcare institutions. The curricula of primary and secondary schools do not teach a subject that deals only with environmental issues. These are partially dealt with within other subjects (such as nature and society, and biology and basic science), which are insufficiently linked and coordinated. This prevents an interdisciplinary approach necessary for understanding environmental issues.

A new subject, democracy and human rights, covering many environmental issues has been introduced during the final years of secondary school. It deals with basic democratic principles and elements of good governance (authority, responsibility, justice, privacy and human rights). It is implemented as part of the Civitas (civic education) programme in Bosnia and Herzegovina supported by the United States Government. 'Project Citizen', a practical part of the programme, is implemented in primary and secondary schools. Pupils are encouraged to choose a problem from their community and investigate existing public policy, develop their own policy for the problem, and develop a plan of action to implement their suggested policy. Through this process, primary and secondary school pupils learn about the role of citizens in a democratic society and practise it. Environmental issues are integrated in the programme as one of six key themes.

At the initiative of Sarajevo University, teachers' training notes for secondary schools on "Exploring Europe's Environment," prepared by EEA and the World Wide Fund for Nature (WWF), were translated into the national languages and 300 copies circulated throughout the country. These notes provide guidance to teachers of different subjects on how to raise schoolchildren's environmental awareness. The University organized a seminar in 2001 for some 100 teachers from six cantons and Sarajevo on these notes.

In higher education, there is no comprehensive curriculum encompassing different aspects of the environment and its protection, and sustainable development. At science and engineering faculties, environmental issues are often unsystematically and insufficiently treated. The Senate of Rectors of the Federation of Bosnia and Herzegovina recommended that a special course on the environment should be included in all curricula. Many universities are following this recommendation. For instance, an environment department was established at the Technology Faculty of Tuzla University in 2001 to teach environmental engineering.

Another proposal is to establish a State education centre in the city of Neum. The municipality of Neum, the Federation's Meteorological Institute, the Hydrometeorological Institute of Republika Srpska, the public water-management companies of both entities and others all back the idea. According to its proponents, the education centre would offer training courses for technical staff, in particular, to operate modern equipment for environmental monitoring and database management, water supply, waste-water treatment, and solid waste collection, recycling and disposal.

The United Nations Educational, Scientific and Cultural Organization (UNESCO) Regional Bureau for Science in Europe (ROSTE) and the University of Bologna have recently developed a proposal for "Environmental Education for Sustainable Development – A Regional Training Project Scheme for the Adriatic-Ionian Basin". The Italian Government has earmarked €600,000 for the three-year project, which should be operational soon. The aim is to strengthen regional scientific cooperation in environmental sciences and education on sustainable development. The beneficiaries are: Albania, Bosnia and Herzegovina, Croatia, and Serbia and Montenegro. Bulgaria, Greece, the Republic of Moldova, Romania, Slovenia, the former Yugoslav Republic of Macedonia and Turkey will also participate. The project foresees the establishment of a regional centre for environmental education at Sarajevo University, which will serve as a focal point for environmental education in the Adriatic-Ionian basin and:

- Train qualified experts in integrated and multidisciplinary environmental know-how by means of specific intensive teaching modules;
- Provide educational programmes for policy makers and administrators to improve their basic knowledge of environmental issues; and
- Offer training modules for schoolteachers, university assistants and young scientists with a focus on learning tools and methods for environmental education programmes.

UNDP is planning to initiate a postgraduate curriculum in environmental management in Bosnia and Herzegovina. No details were provided during the EPR mission, however.

3.7   Role of civil society

There are 127 NGOs with a total membership of 84,676 people in the REC database for Bosnia and Herzegovina. Nearly all these NGOs define themselves as grass-roots organizations or associations of environmental professionals. Most say environmental awareness raising and education are their main activities followed by nature protection and public participation. The majority of NGOs operate locally or regionally. Very few NGOs are involved in advocacy.

There are many examples of concrete action initiated by NGOs. For instance, Kremenik and its 900 members have launched some 60 actions, including clearing river banks, planting trees, promoting walking in nature areas and organizing competitions for young people. The Eco-Rafting Club of Banja Luka actively promotes ecotourism. It has identified all waste dumps along a 15 km stretch of the river Vrbas and collected some 20 tons of waste (including 25 dumped cars) there at its own expense. SECORS, the student ecological association of Banja Luka, promotes the restoration of natural sites and rivers in the area with the support of the city council of Banja Luka. The Centre for Environmentally Sustainable Development works with 10 industries to promote pollution prevention. Ecoteam Sarajevo works with students to promote sustainable waste management and environmentally friendly behaviour.

NGO registration and activities are regulated by the State's and the entities' Laws on Associations and Foundations. They give NGOs a wide range of rights in the scope of their missions. They allow, in particular, NGOs from one entity to operate in the other entity. NGOs enjoy the status of a legal person, which provides them with greater opportunities and makes it easier for them to initiate court proceedings. Associations of citizens enjoy certain tax privileges. Nevertheless, many struggle to be self-sufficient.

Few have paid staff or adequate offices and equipment. The REC local office has been providing institutional and financial support to environmental NGOs in recent years. According to a 2003 publication by REC, foreign support is the

main source of funding of the NGO community: 34% of total funding comes from international organizations and bilateral donors. Support from local institutions (ministries, local administrations) and business is growing, however. Some NGOs are trying to finance themselves by launching their own businesses and collecting membership fees.

The above-mentioned REC study voiced concern over the lack of strategy and capacity development of the country's NGO community. Weak NGO cooperation and networking were considered a basic problem. Attempts have been made recently to have a coordinated NGO approach to environmental issues. Several meetings and seminars have been organized to bring NGOs closer together and closer to the representatives of public authorities and international institutions. Another initiative is the electronic networking of environmental NGOs promoted by the Young Explorers of Banja Luka ("Mladi istrazivaci Banja Luke") through the http://www.ekomrezabih.net portal.

There are some NGO umbrella organizations like NGO Forum Banja Luka, Council of Bosnia and Herzegovina NGOs, Eco-Forum of Bosnia and Herzegovina, and Ecological Association of Bosnia and Herzegovina. For instance, Eco-Forum of Bosnia and Herzegovina was established in 2001 on the basis of an agreement of 38 different ecological societies and associations of citizens for environmental protection. Ecological Association of Bosnia and Herzegovina, registered in 2002, unites 28 NGOs from 44 towns from all over the country to promote environmental awareness. Nearly one third of the country's NGOs cooperate with NGOs from neighbouring countries.

To strengthen the role of NGOs and to raise awareness, the publication "Basic Considerations for Environmental Approximation for the Non-governmental Sector in Bosnia and Herzegovina" was prepared by the local REC office under RERеP project 1.9 "Capacity Building for EU Approximation in South Eastern Europe". Three national meetings were organized in September 2003 to promote the project's results with NGO and ministry officials. Now a similar publication will be prepared for the business sector focusing on the Environmental Management System (EMS) according to ISO 14000 standards.

3.8 Access to information and public participation

Legal basis

The Law on Free Access to Information in Bosnia and Herzegovina was adopted in 2000 (Official Gazette BiH 28/2000). The entities adopted their own laws the following year. These three laws guarantee the right of free access to information and regulate the procedures for accessing information held by bodies in the central State administration as well as their duties to provide information. The laws stipulate that State bodies shall designate information officers. Fulfilment of this obligation is still in an early phase but some information officers have already been appointed and have started their work. For instance, canton Sarajevo published information about its information officer in the daily newsletter. In accordance with the laws, anyone who is dissatisfied with the decision of a public body on his or her request for information has the right to file a complaint in an administrative procedure. The laws provide for the possibility of turning to ombudsmen for information.

The Human Rights Ombudsman was established in Bosnia and Herzegovina in accordance with the Dayton Peace Agreement and its responsibilities are defined in the Law on the Human Rights Ombudsman (Official Gazette of BiH 32/00 and 19/02). In addition, there are ombudsmen in the two entities. They all receive complaints and investigate them, no matter in which part of Bosnia and Herzegovina the issue may have occurred. The Ombudsman of Bosnia and Herzegovina also prepared a guide to good practices by civil servants. The guide states that civil servants should be "helpful, by simplifying procedures, forms and information on entitlements and services, maintaining proper records" and that they should "inform people how they can appeal, cooperating fully in any such appeal and being open to proposals for redress."

The Laws on Physical Planning of the two entities provide for public participation in discussions on development plans.

Their new Laws on Environmental Protection establish that each individual and organization shall have appropriate access to information concerning the environment that is held by public authorities, including information on hazardous materials and activities in their communities, and the opportunity to participate in decision-making processes. They oblige regulatory bodies and public authorities to facilitate and encourage public awareness and participation by making information widely available. They ensure also that effective access to judicial and administrative proceedings, including redress and remedy, shall be provided. The right to access to information will cover, in particular, future registers of installations and of pollution.

The definitions of environmental information, restrictions to its access and other provisions of the entities' laws correspond generally to those established in the UNECE Convention on Access to Information, Public Participation in Decision-making and Access to Justice in Environmental Matters (Aarhus Convention). The same holds for the provisions on public participation and access to justice. The definition of public authority is interpreted in the laws rather narrowly, however, by obliging mainly the Environment Ministries to provide environmental information to the public and to create participation mechanisms for the public.

Current practice

According to a recent survey by the local office of REC, 60% of the country's NGOs considered that State agencies' responses to requests for information required improvement. Slow administrative procedures and unskilled staff were mentioned as major concerns. Only 33% of NGOs indicated that responses were generally provided "in time," and 27% stated that responses "never arrived." Twenty per cent stated they had been denied information. Sixty-six per cent requested better access to regularly updated (weekly, biweekly and monthly) national water, waste, air and biodiversity data. Similar wishes were expressed regarding access to draft environmental laws and policy documents, contact information and decision-making procedures.

Environmental NGOs in Republika Srpska barely participated in the public debate and made no comments during the procedure for adopting the latest environmental laws. The Ministry of Physical Planning, Civil Engineering and Ecology informed a large number of NGOs about the time frame for submitting comments on the draft laws. In the Federation of Bosnia and Herzegovina, NGOs participated more actively: the draft laws were made available on the web sites of the Ministry of Physical Planning and Environment, which also organized workshops for NGOs on the subject.

The NEAP was prepared in a transparent manner with the provision of all information to the public and with direct participation of all stakeholders, including local authorities, institutions, scientists, NGOs and individuals. Apart from the 50 experts who were directly engaged, about 1000 experts in various fields took part indirectly. This was done by means of:

- Four national workshops in which all interested parties took part;
- Field consultations in each of the Federation's ten cantons, each of Republika Srpska's regions, numerous municipalities in each entity and Brčko District; and
- Targeted round tables on specific themes, and lectures (for representatives of businesses, NGOs, scientific institutions and other major groups), as well as media shows and interviews.

The involvement of NGO representatives, and of civil society as a whole, in various bodies (e.g. coordinating committees and working groups) that have significant influence on the formulation of environmental policy has been negligible. NGOs do not participate in the meetings of the Inter-entity Steering Committee for the Environment. The local office of REC is invited and it circulates information about the deliberations among the country's NGO community. Thus far, NGOs and other civil society representatives (education, commerce and labour unions) at the State level are involved only in the National Steering Committee for Environment and Sustainable Development and some of its subcommittees. The Council of Ministers does organize round tables with environmental NGOs. Two meetings have taken place so far.

New initiatives

Bosnia and Herzegovina has not yet acceded to the Aarhus Convention, but the Steering Committee for the Environment has recently initiated the procedure for accession. At the Kiev "Environment for Europe" Conference, the country signed the Protocol on Pollutant Release and Transfer Registers (PRTRs) to the Aarhus Convention. It does not participate, however, in the cooperation on implementation of the Protocol pending its entry into force.

The Law on the Procedure for Concluding and Implementing International Agreements (Official Gazette BiH 29/00) provides NGOs with the opportunity to launch initiatives for the country to conclude international agreements. In February 2003, more than 30 NGOs signed a letter of support for the Steering Committee for the Environment's proposal to accede to the Aarhus Convention. The country's current legislation is a basis to ensure compliance with the Convention's obligations. What remains to be done is to improve the practice of public information and participation.

The local office of REC is coordinating the preparation of action plans for governmental bodies and for the NGO community to ensure that the country accedes to the Aarhus Convention by 2005-2006. Activities include the preparation of implementation guides and manuals in the national languages, training of officials, judges, prosecutors and NGO representatives, launching of a media campaign and the creation of a web page on the Convention in Bosnia and Herzegovina. It organized local training sessions on free access to environmental information for representatives of municipalities and similar sessions for NGO representatives. These events were part of REReP project 2.2 "Support development strategies for implementation of the Aarhus Convention in the South East European region" and sponsored by the Netherlands.

Regional and local authorities with the active participation of civil society have launched a number of initiatives. For instance, Tuzla municipality is preparing a local environmental action plan (LEAP) with active public consultation and participation. One NGO is a member of the steering group. A brochure on the LEAP will be published to canvass citizens' views through the mass media and public discussions. All interested groups, namely industry, NGOs, public health and schools, will be invited to participate. A draft LEAP will then be prepared for a second round of discussion with the public prior to its adoption by the local government.

REReP project 4.3.23 "Promotion of Networks and Exchanges in the Countries of South Eastern Europe," which is implemented in Bosnia and Herzegovina by the local office of REC, helps to promote public participation in environmental decision-making targeting national and local officials, NGOs, journalists and businesses. It allowed, in particular, the establishment of the Neretva Delta Forum as an informal transboundary body composed of representatives of local and regional authorities, NGOs, schools and universities and small businesses. Small grants were awarded to local NGOs and other non-profit organizations and institutions.

A € 1.4 million project, Support to Sustainable Environmental Management – Public Awareness Programme, is being launched under the CARDS 2004 programme. It is expected to:

- Identify opportunities for public participation and information stemming from the Aarhus Convention and its Protocol on PRTRs, and other relevant environmental legally binding instruments; and

- Raise stakeholder interest in environmental activities by informing the public of its right to be informed and involved through nationwide information campaigns, including media campaigns, booklets, training material and training, and by providing grants for concrete small and medium-scale initiatives.

3.9 The decision-making framework

Policies and strategies

The National Environmental Action Plan (NEAP) adopted in 2003 by the governments and assemblies of both entities presents, under the priority area of environmental management, specifies goals and priorities (short- and medium-term) in environmental monitoring, information management and environmental training. The priorities are:

- Establishing a comprehensive monitoring system;
- Establishing a pollutant emission cadastre according to CORINAIR methodology;
- Emission and imission monitoring of large emitters;
- Establishing water, land and forest monitoring;
- Installing a station at Ivan Sedlo for the UNECE Cooperative Programme for Monitoring and Evaluation of the Long-range Transmission of Air Pollutants in Europe (EMEP);
- Establishing monitoring for ionizing radiation sources;
- Projects for the development and upgrading of databases (registries) using geographic information system (GIS) software;
- Establishing an integral spatial information system;

- Establishing a national environmental information system;
- Equipping institutions adequately;
- Establishing a central database, training personnel and improving communication with EEA and its EIONET; and
- Training staff in the collection, processing and archiving of environmental data according to modern methodology.

In pursuance of the NEAP, some concrete activities have been undertaken within both entities and between them with the support of the international community. Efforts have focused on the creation of a national environmental information system, including the establishment of a coordinated database and staff training. Small projects have been initiated to renovate the country's only EMEP station, to establish an air-quality monitoring station in Tuzla canton, to install a monitoring system for air pollution in Republika Srpska, to train officials in GIS information tools and to raise environmental awareness.

The Poverty Reduction Strategy Paper accepted by the Council of Ministers in February 2004 envisages specific measures to strengthen air, water, soil and land, forests, waste and biodiversity monitoring. Some have already been included in NEAP. Others are:

- Improving the hydrometeorological information system and include Bosnia and Herzegovina in the operational system and scientific and technical programmes of the World Meteorological Organization;
- Harmonizing the country's environmental and quality standards with European standards; and
- Drawing up and adopting a red list and a red book of plants, fungi and animals following the criteria set by the World Conservation Union (IUCN).

The Paper does not indicate how these measures should be taken, nor who should pay for them. Neither does it set time frames or benchmarks.

The legal framework

A great number of laws and regulations set requirements and procedures for environmental monitoring, information management, registration and operation of NGOs, access to environmental information, public participation and access to justice on environmental matters. Some of them (like the legislation on hydrometeorological issues, protection against radiation and physical planning) date back to the 1980s and early 1990s. They were adopted in the time of former Yugoslavia and are still in force in Bosnia and Herzegovina as a whole or in its entities. Since independence, many legal and regulatory instruments have been adopted on these subjects in the Federation of Bosnia and Herzegovina and its cantons, and in Republika Srpska.

Important laws for information, public participation and education are the Laws on Physical Planning, Environmental Protection, Air Protection, Water Protection, Waste Management, Nature Protection, Free Access to Information, and Associations and Foundations.

In some cantons of the Federation of Bosnia and Herzegovina (West Herzegovina, Tuzla and Zenica-Doboj), environmental monitoring requirements are prescribed by cantonal legislation.

The institutional framework

At present, various State, entity, inter-entity, cantonal and local authorities are collecting and processing environmental data and information and providing them to the public, as well as promoting public participation in environmental decision-making and raising environmental awareness.

The Ministry of Civil Affairs of Bosnia and Herzegovina is responsible for defining the basic principles for the coordination of the entities' activities and the harmonization of their plans for meteorology and education. The Ministry of Justice is responsible for issues related to citizens' associations and registering the citizens' associations and NGOs operating in the country.

In the entities, five groups of ministries have relevant capacities, resources and experience:

- The Federation's Ministry of Physical Planning and Environment and Republika Srpska's Ministry of Physical Planning, Civil Engineering and Ecology (environmental monitoring and information management, public participation);
- The Federation's Ministry of Agriculture, Water Management and Forestry and Republika Srpska's Ministry of Agriculture, Forestry and Water Management (water quantity, soil and forestry monitoring);

- The Federation's Ministry of Health and Republika Srpska's Ministry of Health and Social Welfare (monitoring of air and water quality and radiation);
- The Federation's Ministry of Education and Science and Republika Srpska's Ministry of Education and Culture (education); and
- The Ministries of Justice in both entities (registration of NGOs).

The entities' new Laws on Environmental Protection entrusted the Federation's Ministry of Physical Planning and Environment and Republika Srpska's Ministry of Physical Planning, Civil Engineering and Ecology with substantially more responsibilities in environmental monitoring, information management, public awareness and participation. However, they did not receive the resources to fulfil them.

The mandate of the Inter-entity Steering Committee for the Environment includes harmonizing and monitoring environmental standards, harmonizing environmental databases and information systems, and collecting and sharing information (between entities and internationally). It coordinates reporting to EEA and promotes the creation of a coordinated environmental information system in accordance with EEA tools and guidelines.

The tasks of the Inter-entity Advisory Commission for the Coordination of Water Management, which is responsible for cooperation between the ministries of both entities in all water-management issues, include harmonizing water-quality monitoring, supervising analytical laboratories, and collecting and sharing information (between entities and internationally). There is no evidence, however, that this Commission has done any of this since its creation in 1998.

International support

A number of internationally funded projects are under way in Bosnia and Herzegovina to strengthen its monitoring capacities. An EU CARDS project (€ 0.8 million) on "Support to the Development of an Institutional Framework for Monitoring and Reporting" is meant to lead to proposals for developing a nationwide system of environmental monitoring and state-of-the-environment reporting. The setting-up of an inter-entity monitoring advisory group is also envisaged. As a follow-up, the CARDS 2003/2004 programme intends to allocate some € 2.5 million for the development of a national environmental monitoring system. Other ongoing internationally funded activities aimed at strengthening the country's monitoring capacities include:

- The CARDS 2003 "Support to Air Monitoring" project (€ 1.0 million). Its purpose is to define and demonstrate economically sustainable means of gathering data (both via statistics and monitoring) in order to describe the air quality and emissions situation in Bosnia and Herzegovina for use in sectoral strategies, and provide reliable data for reporting, resulting in a proposal for a national air monitoring and information system. Project funds will be spent on technical assistance only. Additional funds (€ 0.3 million) have been earmarked under CARDS 2003 for the procurement of supplies;

- The second stage of the Water Institutional Strengthening in Bosnia and Herzegovina supported by the European Union under its CARDS 2002 programme. The purpose is, among other things, to set up a system of surface-water monitoring under the planned river basin authorities in the country; and

- "Support for Improved Waste Management" project under the CARDS 2002 programme.

3.10 Conclusions and recommendations

At present there is no comprehensive environmental monitoring system in Bosnia and Herzegovina, but there are some isolated data collection, maintenance, processing and dissemination. Overall, more than 60 technical (expert) institutions are collecting environmental data with practically no coordination and policy guidance. For some environmental topics, there is not enough monitoring capacity to cover the whole country or even parts of it. Data are frequently collected case by case. There is no monitoring of compliance by economic actors with legal environmental obligations. There are neither registers of polluters nor information systems of environmental inspections.

The institutions in both entities that collect environmental data tend to do so independently, according to their often outdated mandates. Generally, these institutions do not ensure data compatibility or take each other's practices into account when purchasing software and upgrading or developing systems for data collection and

management. There is no systematic use of internationally accepted monitoring methodologies to collect environmental data on particular topics. This is due to the lack of coordination between the monitoring institutions and the absence of commitment to using these methodologies.

The new environmental laws adopted in the two entities provide a much-needed framework to strengthen environmental monitoring in a coordinated manner. The Laws on Air Protection, Water Protection, Waste Management and Nature Protection set specific requirements for collecting, recording, analysing and reporting environmental data. The Laws on Environmental Protection oblige the Federation's Ministry of Physical Planning and Environment and Republika Srpska's Ministry of Physical Planning, Civil Engineering and Ecology to establish and operate systems for monitoring the state and use of the environment in their jurisdictions including the measurement, collection, processing and registration of data. Polluters are obliged to monitor their emissions and the impact of their installations and to provide data to the authorities.

These environmental laws need to be further detailed through regulations. The entities' Environment Ministries should have adopted such regulations within one year of these laws entering into force. This has not been done so far. Neither human nor financial resources were provided to them to cope with their new, expanded responsibilities in environmental monitoring and information.

Recommendation 3.1:
The Ministry of Physical Planning and Environment of the Federation of Bosnia and Herzegovina and the Ministry of Physical Planning, Civil Engineering and Ecology of Republika Srpska should issue, without delay, regulations to specify, in particular:
- *New procedures for setting or revising environmental quality standards harmonized with European standards;*
- *Measurements, monitoring and reporting requirements for operators;*
- *Criteria for the qualification of experts for self-monitoring by polluting enterprises; and*
- *Modalities for the registers of installations and of pollution taking into account the requirements of the UNECE Protocol on PRTRs.*

Recommendation 3.2:
The Inter-entity Steering Committee for the Environment and the Inter-entity Commission for Water with the State Ministry of Foreign Trade and Economic Relations should jointly prepare recommendations leading to the creation of an integrated monitoring system.

These recommendations should be addressed to Ministry of Physical Planning and Environment of the Federation of Bosnia and Herzegovina and the Ministry of Physical Planning, Civil Engineering and Ecology of Republika Srpska, the Ministry of Agriculture, Water Management and Forestry of the Federation of Bosnia and Herzegovina and the Ministry of Agriculture, Forestry and Water Management of Republika Srpska, the Ministry of Health of the Federation of Bosnia and Herzegovina and the Ministry of Health and Social Welfare of Republika Srpska, the Institutes for Statistics of both entities and the Agency for Statistics of Bosnia and Herzegovina, other relevant ministries and the Government of Brčko District. The following steps should be included:

- *To set up an inventory of air emissions including information on transboundary fluxes of harmful substances;*
- *To set up air pollution monitoring in major urban centres;*
- *To strengthen the system for monitoring water quality;*
- *To make an inventory of degraded land and assess the current situation and potential of soil erosion;*
- *To monitor biodiversity and forest health;*
- *To collect systematically data on (a) origins, quantities and types of waste; (b) facilities for handling waste; and (c) waste recycling and final disposal; and*
- *To create a network of authorized laboratories and certification centres.*

Few formal mechanisms exist for the transfer of data and information between institutions dealing with the environment in the two entities. Much exchange is voluntary. The only bodies ensuring some form of homogeneity in data collection and presentation are the Institutes of Statistics of both entities and the Agency for Statistics of Bosnia and Herzegovina. There is no centralized database on the environment at the State level.

There is no environmental reporting either to the State or to the entities. Parliaments and Governments do not receive state-of-the-environment reports to serve as a basis for law- and policy-making. The absence of regular objective scientific assessments of the state of the environment and of trends in the main environmental indicators leads to difficulties in appreciating the impacts and the effectiveness of decisions taken. Information to the general public is provided mostly through some newsletters, irregular brochures and upon request. The authorities do not use international guidelines for the production of environmental reports such as the UNECE Guidelines for the Preparation of Governmental Reports on the State and Protection of the Environment endorsed by the Kiev Ministerial Conference "Environment for Europe".

The newly established web sites of the Federation's Ministry of Physical Planning and Environment and Republika Srpska's Ministry of Physical Planning, Civil Engineering and Ecology provide information on legal and institutional matters mainly. Bosnia and Herzegovina's reporting to the governing bodies of the applicable international environmental conventions and EIONET is poor. The country intends to accede to the Aarhus Convention soon but it risks failing to meet the Convention's explicit requirement to publish regular state-of-the-environment reports.

What is definitely missing is an authority at the State level to take responsibility for data integration and national environmental reporting.

The entities' Laws on Environmental Protection leave important information management functions to the State. According to these laws, an inter-entity environmental body will be in charge, inter alia, of setting and monitoring environmental standards and procedures, coordinating environmental monitoring and information systems, and collecting and sharing information. This should be done through the development of inter-entity environmental programmes and issuing guidelines and expert opinions for the entities' relevant ministries. The laws stipulate that the said body may take decisions that will be mandatory for implementation by governmental bodies and agencies of both entities, as far as such decisions comply with State regulations.

The development of a coherent national environmental information system requires, first of all, a legal and institutional basis at the State level. A legal framework should be established to assign countrywide data collection and reporting responsibilities to institutions at different levels. It should spell out the modalities for sharing information, both horizontally and vertically. An institution (agency) should be made responsible at the State level for providing administrative and expert support to the envisaged inter-entity environmental body. It should, in particular, set up and operate a national environmental information system, publish a national state-of-the-environment report and deliver environmental data and information to the international community on behalf of Bosnia and Herzegovina.

On 16 May 2002, the Council of Ministers adopted a decision instructing the State Ministry of Foreign Trade and Economic Relations to draft an environmental law. No progress has, however, been made so far.

Recommendation 3.3:
When the State Ministry of Foreign Trade and Economic Relations prepares the environmental law for Bosnia and Herzegovina it should cover, among other things, the specific modalities for setting up, financing and operating a national environmental information system. The law should specify the responsibilities of the entities and the State's institutions (including the national agency to be established) regarding:

(a) The collection of environmental data and information, their storage, evaluation and dissemination;
(b) The development, on the basis of international experience, of environmental indicators for data collection in the entities and the State and reporting to them;
(c) The publication of state-of-the-environment reports for consideration by the Parliamentary Assembly and the Council of Ministers of Bosnia and Herzegovina, their circulation among interested institutions at various levels and uploading on the Internet to make them available to the general public;
(d) Transmission of environmental data and reports, on behalf of Bosnia and Herzegovina, to governing bodies of applicable international conventions;
(e) Participation in EIONET, including the designation of a national focal point, national reference centres and expert institutions, and in other international programmes on environmental monitoring and assessment; and
(f) Training of experts in monitoring and information management.

There is no public system of environmental education in Bosnia and Herzegovina. There are some initiatives under way, like the education reform programme supported by the Organization for Security and Co-operation that may lead to improvements. Many NGOs are actively promoting extra-curricular environmental education for children and adults. They cannot contribute to professional training, which is missing in the country. There is a lack of experts on such issues as environmental economics, environmental impact assessment and environmental law, which undermines the effectiveness of environmental policy.

The media generally have little interest in environmental issues. Whether in the press or in the electronic media, information on the environment is limited, while prominence is given to issues that are often opposed to environmental interests. The production of documentaries is reduced to a very small number of programmes that, though popular, deal only to some extent with environmental issues.

The definitions of environmental information, restrictions on its access and provisions for public participation and access to justice of the entities' laws correspond generally to those established in the Aarhus Convention. The laws interpret the definition of public authority rather narrowly, however, by obliging mainly only the Environment Ministries to provide environmental information to the public and to create participation mechanisms for the public.

To establish a wide basis for environmental protection, the entities' new Laws on Environmental Protection require the creation of environmental advisory councils to assist the Environment Ministers and the entities' Governments. The councils should be composed of different stakeholders including environmental associations, organizations and institutions representing professional and economic interests, and scientific circles. The councils should participate in the evaluation of strategic environmental assessments, environmental plans and programmes.

The new laws, furthermore, oblige public education institutions to actively promote environmental education in cooperation with environmental protection associations and professional organizations. The entities' Ministries of Education, in collaboration with their Environment Ministries, will have to prepare annual environmental plans. Professional education on the environment will be the responsibility of the Environment Ministries, which will cooperate with the Ministries of Education. The Environment Ministers should also organize training for environmental NGOs.

Recommendation 3.4:
The Federation's Ministry of Physical Planning and Environment and Republika Srpska's Ministry of Physical Planning, Civil Engineering and Ecology should establish, without any further *delay, environmental advisory councils. The councils' membership and methods of work should be defined in consultation with stakeholders and in accordance with the entities' Laws on Environmental Protection. As a priority, the environmental advisory councils should assist the two above-mentioned Ministries and the Federation's Ministry of Education and Science and Republika Srpska's Ministry of Education and Culture to develop, in close cooperation with media representatives and other stakeholders, environmental communication strategies and education plans.*

Chapter 4

INTERNATIONAL COOPERATION

4.1 Policy background and institutional framework

Since the signing of the Dayton Peace Agreement, there has been considerable ongoing support, in particular from the United States, Japan and the European Union. This will encourage further European integration, as well as closer regional cooperation among the countries of South-Eastern Europe, including within the framework of the Stability Pact.

Because the presence of the international community and its support have been high, it has exerted a particularly strong influence on Bosnia and Herzegovina's efforts to establish an appropriate institutional infrastructure and to initiate activities for environmental management.

As noted in chapter 1, the State Constitution is silent on the environment, leaving responsibility for environmental policy and implementation de facto to the entities and to Brčko District. With respect to international cooperation, however, there are responsibilities at all levels, creating the potential for confusion and a lengthy and slow process of agreement and ratification. For example, the State Constitution makes State institutions responsible for foreign policy, and the State Presidency and Parliamentary Assembly for decisions on the ratification of treaties.

At the same time, the State Constitution gives the entities the right to establish parallel relationships with neighbouring States consistent with the sovereignty and territorial integrity of the country, as well as the right to enter into agreements with States and international organizations with the consent of the entity's Parliamentary Assembly. The Parliamentary Assembly may provide by law that certain types of agreements do not require consent. The Constitutions of the Federation and Republika Srpska are consistent with this approach. In addition, in the case of the Federation, the Constitution also authorizes the legislature to authorize Cantons to conclude agreements with States and international organizations.

International agreements may not be entered into force in the country without the consent of the State Parliamentary Assembly and ratification by the Presidency. This fragmentation of competences is a major obstacle to intensifying international cooperation. It also makes it virtually impossible to identify clear national priorities or strategic objectives for cooperation. Such a situation gives greater power to the donor community to set the agenda for international assistance.

More recently, the Law on the Ministries and Other Administrative Bodies (Official Gazette BiH 5/2003), in article 9, paragraph 2, makes the Ministry of Foreign Trade and Economic Relations "responsible for carrying out tasks and discharging duties which are within the competence of Bosnia and Herzegovina and relate to defining policy, basic principles, coordinating activities and harmonizing plans of the entities' authorities and bodies at the international level in the fields of protection of the environment, development and use of natural resources", thereby strengthening the coordinating role of the State.

The Inter-entity Steering Committee for Environment (see chapter 1 on Policy, legal and institutional framework) provides another mechanism for coordination. One of its more important functions has been to designate a single, State-wide focal point for each international agreement and to organize discussions about international activities between the entities. It is not a policy-making body, however, and the fact that there is no such body at the State level requires further attention.

4.2 Bilateral cooperation

Many European, North American and Asian countries provide bilateral assistance across the board. Support for the environment is much more limited and involves primarily Austria, Germany, Italy, Japan, the Netherlands, Norway, Spain, Sweden, Switzerland, the United Kingdom and the United States, in addition to the European Commission. Most of it is earmarked for institutional capacity-building, environmental monitoring, the legal framework for environmental protection, environmental education and public participation, water management, waste management, energy efficiency, agriculture, forestry, biodiversity, protected areas and eco-tourism. A significant portion is channelled through international and non-governmental organizations, such as the United Nations Development Programme (UNDP) or the Regional Environment Center for Central and Eastern Europe (REC), which facilitates the Regional Environmental Reconstruction Programme (REReP) for South Eastern Europe. Bilateral assistance is also used to support direct financing (including loans and credits) by the World Bank, the European Bank for Reconstruction and Development (EBRD) or the European Investment Bank (EIB), primarily for feasibility studies or the appraisal of investment projects.

At the State level, external assistance for the environment from 1996 to 2002 was US$ 1,581,500, or 6.57% of a total assistance package worth some US$ 24 million. It was provided by the United Kingdom, the European Union, UNDP and the Trust Fund for the Montreal Protocol. For the Federation of Bosnia and Herzegovina, the total amount earmarked for the environment was only US$ 500,000, or 0.014% of a total of US$ 3.65 billion. Comparing the figures for the Federation and Republika Srpska is difficult, because the latter reports "urban planning, housing and the environment" as a single cluster. Nevertheless, the amount given was roughly KM 74.3 million, or 5.17% of a total of KM 1.4 billion. This is a much higher percentage than in the Federation. Yet total assistance given to the Federation is about five times that given to Republika Srpska. In Brčko District, assistance for the environment stood at US$ 149,732, or 0.182%.

4.3   Global and regional cooperation

Bosnia and Herzegovina was admitted as a member of the United Nations on 22 May 1992, when it also joined the United Nations Economic Commission for Europe (UNECE). It then accessed to a number of global and regional conventions. It took an active part in several European institutions, such as the Organization for Security and Co-operation in Europe (OSCE) and the Council of Europe.

Bosnia and Herzegovina cooperates with a number of United Nations programmes and specialized agencies, such as the United Nations Development Programme (UNDP) and the United Nations Environment Programme (UNEP), as well as the United Nations Educational, Scientific and Cultural Organization (UNESCO), the World Meteorological Organization (WMO), the World Health Organization (WHO) and the United Nations Industrial Development Organization (UNIDO).

Bosnia and Herzegovina is a Party to 10 global and regional conventions or agreements on environmental protection and nuclear safety and to 9 related protocols (see annex I). It has started the procedure for ratifying the UNECE Convention on Access to Information, Public Participation in Decision-making and Access to Justice in Environmental Matters (Aarhus Convention) and the UNECE Convention on Environmental Impact Assessment in a Transboundary Context (Espoo Convention).

It has cooperated with UNECE primarily through the "Environment for Europe" process, in which it has begun to participate, through the UNECE Convention on Long-range Transboundary Air Pollution, to which it is a Party, and through the Committee on Environmental Policy. As it becomes a Party to other UNECE conventions, such as the above-mentioned Aarhus and Espoo Conventions, this cooperation is expected to intensify.

The UNDP Country Cooperation Framework for the period 2001 to 2003 focused on capacity-building for an agenda for sustainable development that addressed human development and human security. The environment was one of the four cross-cutting issues of immediate and increasing importance in the country. UNDP ensures that all programme activities are screened for their environmental effects and that opportunities for promoting the environment are not missed. It contributes whenever possible to the development of environmental policy, promotes environmental awareness and integrated environmental issues through area-based, local action programmes and Agenda 21 activities. UNDP is planning to increase its participation in environmental projects over the coming years.

In the framework of its post-conflict activities, the United Nations Environment Programme (UNEP) carried out the first international assessment of the environmental impact of depleted uranium in Bosnia and Herzegovina, in 2002.

Implementation of Agenda 21

Bosnia and Herzegovina participated in the 2002 World Summit on Sustainable Development (Johannesburg, South Africa) and prepared a comprehensive report ("Assessment of the Sustainable Development in Bosnia and Herzegovina") on its implementation of Agenda 21 for this meeting. It also established the National Steering Committee for Environment and Sustainable Development with broad stakeholder participation (see section 4.4 below and chapter 1 on policy, legal and institutional framework).

Its Mid-term Development Strategy, which was adopted by the Council of Ministers in February 2004, is one of the most important documents with regard to sustainable development and international cooperation. It covers many of the environmental issues identified in the National Environmental Action Plan (see Chapter 1) as well as a broad range of sectoral issues, for example water management, industry, energy, forestry, agriculture, transport, education and health.

It is expected that the Strategy will be implemented swiftly to ensure fast growth and avail of the international grants and soft loans needed for public spending reform and investments.

International financial institutions

Following its independence, Bosnia and Herzegovina became a member of various international financial institutions. It joined the World Bank in February 1993, EBRD in June 1996 and the Global Environment Facility (GEF) in October 2001.

Global Environment Facility

Bosnia and Herzegovina's membership in GEF is recent. With its accession to the United Nations Framework Convention on Climate Change in 2000, Bosnia and Herzegovina became eligible for GEF funding, and it is using the opportunity to request funds to help it implement this Convention and those to which it acceded subsequently.

GEF has already approved one project for national capacity self-assessment for global environmental management and two others are in the pipeline. These concern regional ecosystems and forests, biodiversity and international water protection and sustainable use. There are some regional projects from which Bosnia and Herzegovina benefits too, all of which concern integrated river management, including the Danube river basin and the Neretva and Trebišnjica river basin. Bosnia and Herzegovina has prepared proposals for GEF funding of its national biodiversity conservation strategy and action plan, the development of its national implementation plan for the Stockholm Convention on Persistent Organic Pollutants and the preparation of its first national communication to the United Nations Framework Convention on Climate Change.

The Council of Ministers has designated the Ministry of Foreign Trade and Economic Relations as overall national focal point, but issue-specific focal points have also been nominated in the relevant ministries of either the State or the entities, but who are acting on behalf of the State (see fig. 4.1).

World Bank

The first National Environmental Action Plan (NEAP) was completed at the beginning of 2003 with support from the World Bank. NEAP, adopted by the two entities though not by the State, is seen as a key document for Bosnia and Herzegovina to identify and prioritize environmental issues, and it may help international financial institutions in their decisions (see chapter 1 on policy, legal and institutional framework).

The World Bank also actively supports a number of other environment-related projects. One of the most important has been the solid waste management project, which resulted in the development and approval of the Solid Waste Management Strategy, which both entities have adopted (see chapter 6, management of waste and contaminated sites). Other projects include forest development and conservation, small-scale commercial agriculture development, local initiatives, water supply and sanitation, education development and electric power reconstruction. A plan to rationalize the institutional framework for waste-water management is also expected to be drawn up.

Figure 4.1: Coordination and Management of GEF Programmes

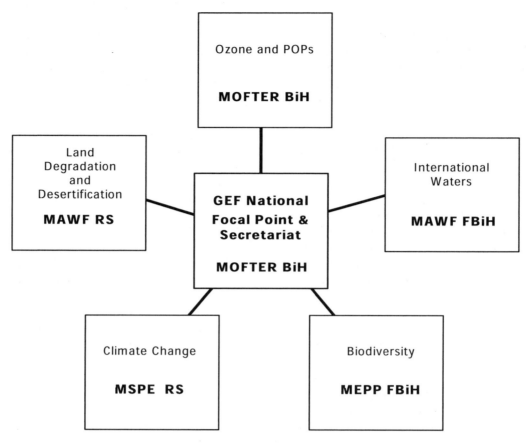

Notes:
MOFTER BiH: Ministry of Foreign Trade and Economic Relations
MAFW RS: Ministry of Agriculture, Forestry and Water Management
MAWF FBiH: Ministry of Agriculture, Water Management and Forestry
MSPE RS: Ministry of Spatial Planning, Civil Engineering and Ecology
MPPE FBiH: Ministry of Physical Planning and Environment

European Bank for Reconstruction and Development

EBRD mainly supports institution building in the enterprise sector, infrastructure development and the financial sector. It requires all projects funded by it to be appraised to ensure that they comply with its environmental policy and procedures, and their environmental impact to be assessed. EBRD has worked on mitigating environmental damage, in particular with industrial clients and the power sector. Together with the European Commission it has also been working on upgrading Bosnia and Herzegovina's environmental legislation.

European Commission

European integration is a foreign policy priority. The completion of the road map for EU integration and rapid progress in the Stabilization and Association Process (SAP) has been declared a top priority by the Government of Bosnia and Herzegovina and was "substantially completed" in September 2002. The next SAP stage will be a feasibility report to assess whether the country is ready to open negotiations on a stabilization and association agreement. If it is to catch up with its neighbours, Bosnia and Herzegovina must accelerate reform and develop truly self-sustaining structures, although it is aware of the amount of work that this will demand. For the environment this would include, for instance, approximation to the EU body of environmental law and policies, resource management and pollution control.

One of the European Commission's main assistance objectives is to support the development of an environmental framework in Bosnia and Herzegovina based on the EU body of law, and to facilitate and encourage cooperation between

Bosnia and Herzegovina and the other countries of the region as part of SAP. In this respect, a current project is focussed on strengthening the capacity of the entities' ministries and agencies responsible for water, waste management and environment, particularly in relation to meeting international obligations, contributing to a more rational and sustainable use of the country's natural resources and improving environmental protection.

At the same time, the European Commission strongly supports the adoption of a State law on the environment that could, inter alia, provide for the establishment of an environmental protection agency. The EU funding programme CARDS would provide up to € 27 million for the environmental programme and projects in Bosnia and Herzegovina over the next 6 years. Most of it will go to institutional strengthening and capacity-building, including the drafting of environmental legislation that is in line with that of the European Union, equipment for an automatic air quality monitoring system, and technical assistance for the establishment of an environmental fund.

The European Commission also supports the development of baseline data and monitoring, multi-municipal waste management, institutional strengthening of water management, public participation and vertical reviews, including of the environment, as a part of public administration reform.

In addition, the European Commission, through its LIFE programme, has provided support for eight projects in Bosnia and Herzegovina, totalling more than € 2 million. The funds were spent on institutional strengthening and capacity-building for environmental management, including the establishment of an operational support unit for the Inter-entity Steering Committee for the Environment. This programme also provided support for strengthening the Office of the Mediterranean Action Plan in Bosnia and Herzegovina, which is the main coordinator for the implementation of the Barcelona Convention for the Protection of the Marine Environment and the Coastal Region on the Mediterranean.

The Regional Environmental Reconstruction Programme (REReP)

Bosnia and Herzegovina takes part in REReP, which is the main environmental component of the Stability Pact. Funding is made available through RERep for regional and subregional activities.

Bosnia and Herzegovina has participated, for instance, in projects related to the ratification and implementation of multilateral environmental agreements (MEAs), capacity-building for environmental impact assessment and strategic environmental assessment, strengthening of environment agencies and inspectorates, developing an environmental information system, hazardous waste management, rehabilitation of urban environmental systems, river basin management and cross-border municipal cooperation.

The Regional Environmental Center

The Regional Environmental Center (REC) established a country office in Sarajevo in 1997 and two field offices in Banja Luka and Mostar. It carries out a number of activities in the country, such as public information and participation campaigns, NGO capacity-building, assistance to municipalities, and support for the institutional strengthening of the entities' environmental authorities and the implementation of MEAs. REC is an important implementation partner for many of the REReP projects and, as noted above, it is a conduit for bilateral projects, too.

4.4 Cooperation in multilateral environmental agreements

Introduction

The State Constitution of Bosnia and Herzegovina stipulates, in its annex II, item 5:

> "Any treaty ratified by the Republic of Bosnia and Herzegovina between January 1, 1992 and the entry into force of this Constitution shall be disclosed to Members of the Presidency within 15 days of their assuming office; any such treaty not disclosed shall be denounced. Within six months after the Parliamentary Assembly is first convened, at the request of any member of the Presidency, the Parliamentary Assembly shall consider whether to denounce any other such treaty."

This is crucial, because it is alleged that this procedure was not always followed for multilateral agreements, including environmental conventions. As a result, Republika Srpska does not recognize their validity (see below).

Bosnia and Herzegovina is a Party to several global, pan-European or regional environmental agreements, which are an important factor for environmental policy development, harmonization and implementation. However, it does not have a strategy to set priorities among the agreements or to establish a timetable for ratifying them. Many of the MEAs to which it is a Party have been inherited from the former Socialist Federal Republic of Yugoslavia and succeeded to by the pre-war Republic of Bosnia and Herzegovina. Little was done in this area immediately after the war, but, in recent years, Bosnia and Herzegovina has sped up the process of ratification or accession, primarily for global conventions. This has helped to make the country eligible for funding, especially from GEF, where being a Party to certain conventions is a prerequisite.

In 2000 Bosnia and Herzegovina adopted the Law on the Process of Concluding and Implementing International Contracts (Agreements) (Official Gazette BiH 29/00). According to this Law, the only body authorized to sign international legal instruments on behalf of Bosnia and Herzegovina is its Presidency, which in turn has the right to authorize the Council of Ministers or other representatives to act on behalf of the State in this respect.

The initiative to sign and ratify international legal instruments, however, may come from any State, entity, cantonal or municipal authority, business association or NGO. Such an initiative is submitted to the Council of Ministers through the competent State ministry, which in the case of the environment is the Ministry of Foreign Trade and Economic Relations. This is followed by a proposal for initiating negotiations, also submitted to the Council of Ministers. The Presidency may adopt a decision to commence negotiations at its own initiative or on the suggestion of the Council of Ministers.

Once an international agreement has been signed, it is submitted to the Ministry of Foreign Affairs, while the Council of Ministers prepares a decision-proposal for ratification and submits it to the Presidency. The Presidency submits a legal instrument to the Parliamentary Assembly to obtain full agreement for ratification. On this basis, the Presidency may sign a decision for ratification. This decision, accompanied by the text of the international agreement is published in the country's Official Gazette without delay, but no later than 90 days after its adoption. Although precise, the procedure is complicated and might be seen as slowing down accession.

To set up an appropriate institutional infrastructure at the State level, the Council of Ministers at its 66th session in May 2002 established the organizational framework and bodies responsible for coordinating and managing the implementation of MEAs (see fig. 4.2).

As shown in figure 4.2, there are eight subcommittees for the coordination and implementation of the most important environmental conventions. They are headed by different State or entity ministries, which serve as focal points on behalf of Bosnia and Herzegovina in the international context. They operate within the framework of the National Steering Committee for Environment and Sustainable Development. The Committee's chairperson and the chairpersons of the subcommittees are members of the Committee's Executive Secretariat, facilitated by the Ministry of Foreign Trade and Economic Relations. Each subcommittee has 10 members: three representatives of the State, three of the Federation, three of Republika Srpska and one of Brčko District, nominated by the respective focal point and appointed by the Council of Ministers. These subcommittees are further authorized to reach common positions on proposals before submission for endorsement.

Global conventions

Convention on Biological Diversity and other biodiversity-related treaties

Bosnia and Herzegovina enjoys a rich biological diversity, with numerous species of flora, fauna and fungi. Yet, the state and management of nature do not meet the requirements of the relevant multilateral agreements owing to weak enforcement.

Bosnia and Herzegovina has initiated the process of ratification of the major global and regional conventions related to the conservation and sustainable use of biological diversity, as well as to the protection of nature and natural heritage. It acceded to the Convention on Biological Diversity in 2002. The national focal point for implementation is the Federation's Ministry of Environment and Physical Planning. As operational focal point, the Ministry is responsible for communication with international bodies, the initiation of activities required by the Convention and coordination with the other relevant authorities and concerned stakeholders.

Figure 4.2: Organizational set up of the coordination and management of the implementation of MEAs

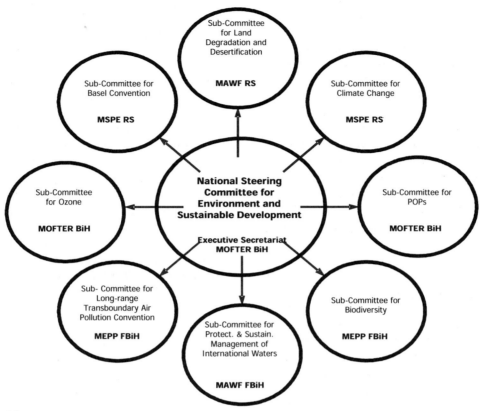

Notes:
MOFTER BiH: Ministry of Foreign Trade and Economic Relations
MAWF RS: Ministry of Agriculture, Forestry and Water Management
MAWF FBiH: Ministry of Agriculture, Water Management and Forestry
MSPE RS: Ministry of Spatial Planning, Civil Engineering and Ecology
MEPP FBiH: Ministry of Physical Planning and Environment

Soon after acceding to the Convention, the State decided to develop a project proposal for GEF to develop a national strategy for biodiversity conservation. In addition, the LIFE project "Setting up an operational unit under the Inter-entity Steering Committee for the Environment" has hired four local nature conservation experts to produce a comprehensive database of the country's natural resources, in accordance with international standards.

Bosnia and Herzegovina has been a Party to the Ramsar Convention on Wetlands of International Importance Especially as Waterfowl Habitat since 1 March 1992, by succession. In accordance with article 2 of the Convention, the new Contracting Party named as its obligatory first wetland of international importance a nature park and important bird reserve called Hutovo Blato near the estuary of the river Neretva.

Republika Srpska, however, does not officially accept the State's succession to the Ramsar Convention. It should be possible to resolve this problem, and it should be done as soon as possible. There are also other areas eligible for the Ramsar list, such as Bardača in Republika Srpska.

The Hutovo Blato wetlands have had the status of nature park since 1995. In 2000 a LIFE-supported project was launched to develop methods for the re-establishment of the original wetlands structure, with special emphasis on migratory fish and bird communities and in line with international regulations and recommendations. The objectives of this project are the restoration of a natural ecosystem structure through conservation and protection, and the elimination of non-native species; the active management of migratory fish species at cross-border level (with Croatia); and the development of a management policy for the wetlands including the above points, plus international regulations and conventions.

Bosnia and Herzegovina recently initiated the procedure for accession to the Convention on International Trade in Endangered Species of Wild Fauna and Flora (CITES) and is expected to become a Party in 2004. This could help to prevent a repetition of a situation that occurred in January 2002, when the media in neighbouring Serbia and Montenegro carried a report on the illegal transport of 120,000 wild birds from the wetland area Bardača (apparently slaughtered). The consignment was intercepted by the authorities at the border between Serbia and Montenegro and Hungary. Accession to CITES will enable Bosnia and Herzegovina to designate a management authority for issuing CITES permits and certificates for import or export and draw up appropriate customs provisions.

<u>United Nations Framework Convention on Climate Change</u>

The United Nations Framework Convention on Climate Change is the first multilateral agreement that Bosnia and Herzegovina ratified as an independent State after the war (Official Gazette BiH 19/2000). It has not yet signed or ratified the Kyoto Protocol, but is considering doing so in the near future

In addition, the new Laws on Air Protection deal with all problems related to emissions of greenhouse gases and provide incentives for users that decrease emissions of CO_2 in a bid to improve energy efficiency, in particular.

It was decided to speed up activities for the development of a nationwide action plan for the implementation of the Convention and the first national communication, which resulted in a project proposal to GEF/UNDP. This is a standard enabling activity project, which will support the country's efforts to draw up the national inventory of greenhouse gas emissions and meet other obligations under the Convention.

Specific suggestions have also been made during a round table on content of the national action plan to be developed under the same project, including a feasibility study on accession to the Kyoto Protocol and other studies related to the impact of climate change on different sectors, and the inclusion of climate change topics in school curricula.

<u>United Nations Convention to Combat Desertification in those Countries Experiencing Drought and/or Desertification, Particularly in Africa</u>

The decision to accede to the Convention to Combat Desertification was published on 26 August 2002 (Official Gazette BiH 12/2002). Bosnia and Herzegovina has no other specific legislation related to soil, since full responsibility lies with the entities. They do have some legislation to address the issue of agricultural land degradation and desertification. This legislation is very precise and restricts non-agricultural use of agriculture land, thus encouraging agricultural production and the sustainable use of land resources. According to the National Steering Committee for Environment and Sustainable Development, the national focal point responsible for this Convention is the Ministry of Agriculture, Forestry and Water Management of Republika Srpska.

After ratification, Bosnia and Herzegovina immediately involved itself in the work of the Convention and participated as observer at the first session of its Committee. However, its communication with the Convention's official bodies is still weak due to its short experience as a Party.

A particular aspect of Bosnia and Herzegovina's interest in the Convention is the fact that a significant area of its territory is still mined, as a result of the war, and this is considered land degradation.

<u>Vienna Convention for the Protection of the Ozone Layer</u>

Bosnia and Herzegovina has been a Party to the Vienna Convention and to the Montreal Protocol since 1992 through succession (Official Gazette SFRJ IA 1/90; Official Gazette R BiH 13/94). It ratified the London, Copenhagen and Montreal Amendments to the Protocol in 2003 (Official Gazette BiH 8/03). The Council of Ministers established a National Ozone Unit in July 2000, and it began its operations activities in January 2001. In the same year, the Bosnia and Herzegovina updated and adopted its Country Programme for the Phaseout of Ozone Depleting Substances. A number of projects have been prepared on the basis of this revised Plan, mostly for the introduction of non-ODS technologies in the industrial sector.

These projects, which have been approved by the Multilateral Fund for the Implementation of the Montreal Protocol for a total of more than US$ 3 million, are currently being implemented.

Basel Convention on the Transboundary Movements of Hazardous Wastes and their Disposal

During the war, Bosnia and Herzegovina was overloaded with different types of hazardous waste, including ammunition and leftover humanitarian aid and medicines, many of which had passed their expiry date. Problems with handling this waste led Bosnia and Herzegovina to accede to the Basel Convention at the end of 2000 (Official Gazette BiH 31/2000). The canton of Sarajevo was among the strongest lobbyists and it immediately concluded agreements to export the hazardous waste that remained from the war. Currently, the same authorities are dealing with the expired medicines.

As with the other environmental issues, the entities have adopted new legislation recently to cover hazardous waste, too. Their Laws on Waste Management deal with the transboundary movements of waste and follow the Convention, stipulating a detailed procedure. Further secondary regulations, however, are still needed.

Bosnia and Herzegovina needs to work out a specific institutional set-up for the implementation of the Convention. In this respect it is important to share and learn from other countries' experience. In particular the Convention's own bodies, on which Bosnia and Herzegovina was not represented in the past, could offer their knowledge and support its efforts to administer this important treaty. Furthermore, awareness and dissemination of information should be strengthened to increase the knowledge of the Convention, in particular of customs officials, who are usually not informed of this kind of legislation but in theory are required to implement it.

Stockholm Convention on Persistent Organic Pollutants

Bosnia and Herzegovina signed the Convention on Persistent Organic Pollutants (POPs) in Stockholm in 2001, when it was first open for signature, but it has not yet ratified it.

In anticipation of ratification, Bosnia and Herzegovina has prepared a proposal for GEF to support the preparation of a national implementation plan and the establishment of an operational unit to facilitate this process.

UNECE regional conventions

Convention on Long-range Transboundary Air Pollution

The former Yugoslavia ratified the Convention on Long-range Transboundary Air Pollution in 1986, and its EMEP Protocol in 1987. As a result, Bosnia and Herzegovina became a Party by succession to both the Convention and the Protocol in 1992. It has not yet ratified any other of the Convention's remaining seven protocols. Most of the implementing legislation stems from former Yugoslav laws and regulations and is outdated. In addition, after the break-up of Yugoslavia and due to internal conflict, Bosnia and Herzegovina was not able to participate in international activities. Its monitoring system also deteriorated and as a result the Convention was not implemented.

Before independence, Bosnia and Herzegovina reported to the Convention's governing body through the former Yugoslav Federal Commission for the implementation of the Convention. Its first independent report on the assessment of SO_2 emissions was issued in 1990, followed by similar reports for 1991-1995.

The new Laws on Air Protection adopted in both entities introduced a modern approach based on EU standards. The NEAP also emphasized the need to re-establish international cooperation and to take a proactive role, and recommended harmonizing the monitoring system with international methodology, so providing a basis for sharing and reporting information. Implementing this Convention will remain a major challenge for the future.

Convention on Access to Information, Public Participation in Decision-making and Access to Justice in Environmental Matters (Aarhus Convention)

The Aarhus Convention is one of the MEAs that are currently going through acceptance procedures. Nevertheless, Bosnia and Herzegovina has taken significant steps to apply the Convention's principles in its national legal system. For instance, the adoption of the Law on Freedom to Information (Official Gazette BiH 28/2000) was a big step forward as this kind of legislation was unknown in the former Yugoslavia. The Law regulates the procedure of access to information used by public officials to ensure its transparency and publicity and to guarantee the right of free access to information. The Law's main part conforms to the provisions of the Aarhus Convention. Similar legislation was adopted in both entities, i.e. the Law on Freedom of Information (Official Gazette RS 5/2001) and the Law on Free Access to Information (Official Gazette FBiH 32/01). In addition, other newly developed and adopted environmental laws by the entities provide for the harmonization of Bosnia and Herzegovina's legislation with the Aarhus Convention.

During the fifth Ministerial Conference "Environment for Europe" (Kiev), in May 2003, Bosnia and Herzegovina signed the Convention's new Protocol on Polluter Release and Transfer Registers.

Convention on Environmental Impact Assessment in a Transboundary Context (Espoo, 1991)

Bosnia and Herzegovina is not a Party to the Espoo Convention and, until recently, there was virtually no requirement for domestic environmental impact assessment (EIA). The entities' new Laws on Environmental Protection now require a formal environmental impact assessment, although the regulatory framework to make this operational remains to be developed (see chapter 1, on policy, legal and institutional framework). Most EIA that has taken place has been done to meet the requirements of international donors.

There is no EIA in an international context. Bosnia and Herzegovina also experiences a negative impact as a result of not being a Party to the Espoo Convention. For example, Croatia initiated the construction of a hazardous waste site very close to the border, without prior notification, since Bosnia and Herzegovina is not a Party to the Convention. Consequently, relevant ministries have recommended State officials to give priority to the ratification of the Espoo Convention.

Convention on the Protection and Use of Transboundary Watercourses and International Lakes (Helsinki, 1992)

Bosnia and Herzegovina has until recently not shown any interest in becoming a Party to the Convention on the Protection and Use of Transboundary Watercourses and International Lakes. The Convention requires its Parties to

undertake comprehensive measures to prevent, control and reduce water pollution, particularly by hazardous substances, and to enter into bilateral or multilateral agreements, or adapt existing ones, with the riparian countries sharing transboundary waters. Bosnia and Herzegovina shares some of its major water bodies with both Croatia, which has ratified the Convention, and Serbia and Montenegro.

Bosnia and Herzegovina is cooperating with its neighbours through the Framework Agreement on the Sava River Basin (see below) and the project proposal with Croatia for the protection of the river Neretva. Acceding to the Convention would greatly benefit the country's overall water management.

Convention on the Transboundary Effects of Industrial Accidents (Helsinki, 1992)

The Convention on the Transboundary Effects of Industrial Accidents requires its Parties to take appropriate preventive, preparedness and response measures to protect human beings and the environment against industrial accidents that are capable of causing transboundary effects. Neither the entities nor the State authorities have thus far shown an interest in acceding to this Convention.

Other regional conventions and agreements: rivers and seas

Bosnia and Herzegovina became a Party to the Convention for the Protection of the Marine Environment and the Coastal Region of the Mediterranean (Barcelona, Spain, 1976) by succession in 1998 (Official Gazette SFRJ IA 12/77; Official Gazette BiH 26/98) and to its four protocols, but not to its 1995 Amendments. Since Bosnia and Herzegovina is a Mediterranean country, this Convention is important. The country has established an office and a national coordinator for the implementation of the Convention, reviewed hot spots and sensitive areas, and prepared its National Action Plan on Pollution Reduction and Integrated Management Application for the Mediterranean Region. It also actively participates in the work of several working groups of the Mediterranean Commission on Sustainable Development.

The Danube river watershed covers 75% of Bosnia and Herzegovina. However, it has not yet signed the Convention on Cooperation for the Protection and Sustainable Use of the Danube River (Sofia,

1994), although there is some indication that it is considering doing so. At the moment, the country participates as an observer in the International Commission for the Protection of the Danube River. Bosnia and Herzegovina has begun the accession process and the ratification of Sofia Convention is expected by the end of 2004.

In addition, the four riparian countries, Bosnia and Herzegovina, Croatia, Slovenia, and Serbia and Montenegro, concluded the Framework Agreement on the Sava River Basin on 3 December 2002, which, inter alia, establishes a framework for joint planning. The Framework Agreement takes into account all aspects of the river basin's sustainable water management, including the use of water resources the protection of the aquatic ecosystem, water quality protection, and protection against the detrimental effects of water.

4.5   Conclusions and recommendations

Since the end of the war in 1995, Bosnia and Herzegovina has made progress in its international environmental cooperation at bilateral, regional, European and global levels. However, there is still important work to be done, in particular in clarifying institutional responsibilities. Some challenges, including many of those that are expressed in the Assessment on Sustainable Development in Bosnia and Herzegovina, the National Environmental Action Plan and the Mid-term Development Strategy, are of transboundary or regional importance and are being considered by the respective ministries as top national priorities. In a continuing process of stabilization and accelerated regional and international integration, Bosnia and Herzegovina will be able to continue to rely on the support of the international community. It can be expected that important cooperation programmes will continue and new ones be created, especially in the context of cooperation with the European Union.

One issue of concern is the lack of a systematic, strategic approach to international cooperation. A strategy and action plan in this area could provide a blueprint for cooperation to assist the country in identifying the bilateral and multilateral agreements most appropriate for it. Such a strategy could also help to prepare Bosnia and Herzegovina to harmonize its legislation with that of the European Union.

Recommendation 4.1:
The State Ministry of Foreign Trade and Economic Relations, working closely with the Federation's Ministries of Physical Planning and Environment and of Agriculture, Water Management and Forestry, Republika Srpska's Ministries of Physical Planning, Civil Engineering and Ecology of Agriculture, Forestry and Water Management and the appropriate authorities in Brčko District, should develop a national strategy and action plan for international environmental cooperation consistent with the Strategy for environmental protection and sustainable development proposed in recommendation 1.2. The strategy should address the role in international cooperation of all relevant actors, including non-governmental.

Bosnia and Herzegovina has ratified or acceded to many of the major multilateral environmental agreements, and the Government is actively participating in numerous international forums. However, an overall assessment of the implementation of these agreements shows that there is still much to be done in practical implementation and enforcement.

One of the most important issues in this regard is institutional strengthening and capacity-building at all administrative levels. It is important to assess the cost of implementation, the most effective institutional arrangement and the importance to the country of the conventions that it has not yet ratified. Treaties affecting shared waterways, transboundary pollution and protection of biodiversity appear to be of particular significance.

Recommendation 4.2:
(a) Bosnia and Herzegovina should speed up its accession to:
- *The Convention on Access to Information, Public Participation in Decision-making and Access to Justice in Environmental Matters;*
- *The Convention on Environmental Impact Assessment in a Transboundary Context;*
- *The Convention on Persistent Organic Pollutants;*
- *The Convention on Trade in Hazardous Chemicals and Pesticides Enters into Force;*
- *The Convention on Cooperation for the Protection and Sustainable Use of the Danube River;*

- *The Convention on International Trade in Endangered Species of Wild Fauna and Flora; and*
- *The Kyoto Protocol to the United Nations Framework Convention on Climate Change.*

(b) Bosnia and Herzegovina should also begin the process of accession to:
- *The Convention on the Conservation of Migratory Species of Wild Animals;*
- *The Convention on the Protection and Use of Transboundary Watercourses and International Lakes; and*
- *The Convention on the Transboundary Effects of Industrial Accidents.*

Bosnia and Herzegovina has been a Party to many conventions for only a short period of time. Implementation is only beginning and has been largely directed towards reporting requirements, for which technical and financial support are available from external sources. Until quite recently, the legislative framework for implementation was also lacking, but this has now changed.

What remains weak is the institutional capacity for implementation, including inspection and other compliance and enforcement machinery. Greater capacity is also needed in municipalities, which have responsibility for implementation too and which, in some cases, receive direct bilateral support.

Recommendation 4.3:
The State Ministry of Foreign Trade and Economic Relations, working together with the national focal points, should assess the requirements for implementation of all the conventions and protocols to which Bosnia and Herzegovina is a Party. The results of this assessment should be reflected in the national strategy for international environmental cooperation, recommended in 4.1.

PART II: MANAGEMENT OF POLLUTION AND OF NATURAL RESOURCES

Chapter 5

AIR QUALITY MANAGEMENT

5.1   Introduction

Before the war overall air quality was poor: large energy and metallurgy plants, built for the needs of the former Yugoslavia, generated much pollution. The overall recession and the decline in activity in particular in the industrial sector, as a result of the war, have significantly relieved pressure on air quality. All inhabitants note that the air is much cleaner now than before the war.

However, the country will face a double challenge to air quality in the coming years. The first will come from the expected improvement in the economic situation, in particular through the progressive restarting and rehabilitation of industrial production. It is therefore necessary to develop adequate air quality management tools so as to prevent harmful effects resulting from air pollution and avoid a return to the pre-war situation.

Moreover, partly because public transport was disrupted during the war, traffic increased rapidly in 2002 and is expected to continue to do so in the coming years. Traffic pressure on air quality will become increasingly intense unless preventive action is taken soon.

5.2   State and determinants

Emissions

Before poring over emission estimates, it is important to note that their accuracy is questionable. Indeed, there is no inventory of industrial plants or register of polluters. Input data were either collected directly from the plants or interpolated from data going back to before the war (such as the vehicle fleet).

Air emissions for the whole country (see table 5.1) have been calculated by the Meteorological Institute of the Federation of Bosnia and Herzegovina. They concern both entities and cover the major pollutants, including greenhouse gases (SO_2, NO_x, NMVOC, CO, CO_2, CH_4 and N_2O).

The values include all emissions from fossil-fuel burning, road transport and agriculture. However, direct emissions from waste and from process industries are not included. They are estimated to represent an additional 5-8%.

As expected, air emissions per capita declined sharply between 1990 (last pre-war data) and the 1999-2001 period:

- From 114.3 kg to 55-60 kg SO_2 per year or a 50% decrease; and
- From 5.4 tons to 3.1-3.3 tons of CO_2 per year or a 40% decrease.

Table 5.1: Air emissions

kilotons/year

	Estimated emissions			Forecast emissions	
	1999	2000	2001	2002	2003
SO_2	244.4	228.9	212.5	200.0	180.0
NO_x	67.1	68.3	67.7	68.0	69.0
CO_2	11,826.6	12,536.0	12,540.4	13,000.0	13,500.0
CO	117.7	115.3	121.6	123.0	125.0
NMVOC	13.6	13.3	14.0	14.0	14.5
CH_4	63.6	60.6	60.6	58.5	57.0
N_2O	1.8	1.9	1.9	2.0	2.0
NH_3	31.7	29.8	29.4	28.1	27.6

Source: Meteorological Institute - Report 11/2003.

Figure 5.1: Air Emissions in 2000

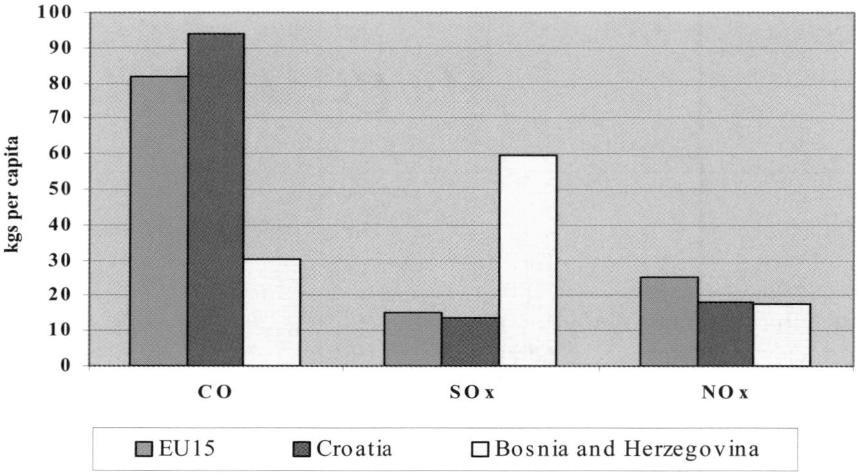

Sources : EMEP webdab.emep.int, 12/2003 and Meteorological Institute report, 11/2003.
Note : EU15 = Austria, Belgium, Denmark, Finland, France, Germany, Greece, Ireland, Italy, Luxembourg, Netherlands, Portugal, Spain, Sweden and United Kingdom.

CO and NO_x emissions per capita appear to be respectively 37% and 71% lower than in the 15 member States of the European Union (fig. 5.1), while SO_x emissions per capita are four times higher. Emissions of SO_x were already high before the war. Anthropogenic emissions of SO_x are due largely to the combustion of sulphur-containing fuels such as coal and oil. Industry and the power sector were and still are, although to a lesser degree, major emitters. However, such comparisons must be seen in the light of the uncertainties linked to the emission estimates for Bosnia and Herzegovina.

The same applies to the division of emissions by sector presented in table 5.2. For example, the figures suggest that the energy sector is responsible for 70% of NO_x emissions while transport contributes only 20%. The opposite conclusion can be drawn for CO, with the transport sector generating 98% of the emissions and the energy sector only 2%.

Sectoral pressures

Energy production

In Bosnia and Herzegovina energy is produced by both hydro and thermal power plants. Only 39% of the country's hydro potential is used. Its geothermal potential is neglected, although some studies are taking place in the area of Banja Luka (see Chapter 11 on Energy and environment).

The country's thermal power plants are major emitters of air pollutants. They are not equipped with adequate abatement devices such as, in particular, deNOx (nitrogen oxide abatement) units. Electrostatic precipitators (ESP) and desulphurization (deSOx) units – if installed – are often deficient.

The power plant of Kakanj has four old and inefficient units of 32 MW, two units of 110 MW and one unit of 230 MW, linked to a 300 m stack. Indicative concentrations in flue gas are around 7,000 mg/m^3 for SO_2 and around 1,200 mg/m^3 for NO_x. These values are well above the European Union (EU) limit for large combustion plants (for solid fuel, 2,000 mg/m^3 and less for SO_2 according to thermal input, 600 mg/m^3 for NO_x). The electrostatic precipitators for particles were rehabilitated in 1999; emission levels fell to 150 mg/m^3, but are still above the EU limit (100 mg/m^3 for thermal input below 500 MW).

Tuzla thermal power plant is slightly more powerful than that of Kakanj, but its emissions are lower partly because the sulphur content of the coal is lower. The figures indicate that the EU SO_2 limit is nevertheless exceeded: the measured values are around 5,000 mg/m^3. With measured values of 480 mg/m^3 for NO_x and 19 mg/m^3 for dust, EU emission limits are not breached.

In the Ugljevik thermal power plant, which burns coal with a high sulphur content, SO_2 emissions are extremely high, reaching 20,000 mg/m^3. The Gacko thermal power plant, which uses coal with a lower sulphur content than that used in Ugljevik, pollutes less but produces more fly ash.

A large number of smaller enterprises have their own power plants. Occasional measurements show that these are inefficient. Poor maintenance and the lack of instruments to monitor combustion efficiency push up fuel consumption and, consequently, increase SO$_2$ emissions. Owing to inefficient combustion, there is also a considerable level of emission of products of incomplete combustion. The situation with district heating boiler plants is similar (many cities have district heating in at least some neighbourhoods). They are not inspected, except in Sarajevo, where the efficiency of combustion is inspected every year.

The main producers of energy such as Energoprivreda are fully aware of the situation. It can be expected that, under pressure from the new Laws on Air Protection (see section 5.4 below) but within the limits of their financial capacities, they will take appropriate measures to reduce air emissions.

Industry

The industrial sector has suffered from recession, which has significantly reduced its operating capacities and hence its pressure on the environment, including air quality. However, it remains a large source of air pollution. Most of the industrial facilities installed before the war are still equipped with obsolete technologies; the general economic context means that maintenance is generally poor and the upgrading process slow. This also affects abatement devices. Another reason for the high air emissions are the poor quality of the fuels burnt as well as the chemical characteristics of the ores used in metallurgy.

The Federation's Meteorological Institute has labelled some of the major industrial emitters "hot spots":

- The Lukavac cement factory is located in the vicinity of the Tuzla thermal power plant. The particle abatement units are designed to prevent particulate emissions exceeding 200 mg/m^3, but they often fail to do so owing to operating errors and inadequate maintenance.

- The Kakanj cement factory was built in the vicinity of the thermal power plant. Problems with dust emissions are said to be related more to the process management than the abatement equipment.

- Zenica Steelworks used to emit very high levels of heavy metals as well as of SO$_2$, mainly caused by the high content of sulphur in the steel ore extracted from Vares mine, near Zenica. The data on levels of lead in the air were kept confidential. An improvement programme is now ongoing but apparently this is carried out without any environmental impact assessment or licensing procedures.

- Owing to the high-sulphur fuel used, the Mostar alumina and aluminium plants emit high levels of SO$_2$.

In this sector, too, the situation is expected to improve progressively under pressure from the new Laws on Air Protection and from international investors demanding environmental impact assessments.

Transport

Both entities have their Ministries of Transport and Communications. Statistics on the transport of passengers and goods in 2001 are presented in table 5.3. For passengers, road transport is clearly dominant over rail in terms of both total number of passengers and passenger kilometres. For goods, rail and road transport have equal importance. The goods transported by rail are mainly ores, cereals and oil.

Statistics for 1997 to 2001 (see table 5.4) do not reveal clear trends, except maybe for the transport of goods, probably linked to the progressive rehabilitation of the network after the war.

Table 5.2: Percentage of air emissions per sector, 2002

per cent

	CO	SOx	NOx
Energy sector	1.8	89.0	70.3
Industry	0.4	9.6	9.4
Transport	97.8	1.4	20.3

Source: Meteorological Institute. Report 11/2003.

Table 5.3: Transport of goods and passengers, 2001

Goods (tons)	Railway		Road	
	in thousands	in millions of kms	in thousands	in millions of kms
Total	5,405	281	1,472	269
Republika Srpska	1,060	119	256	48
Federation of Bosnia and Herzegovina	4,345	162	1,216	221

Passengers	Railway		Road	
	in thousands	in millions of kms	in thousands	in millions of kms
Total	1,298	50	38,453	1,116
Republika Srpska	1,100	41	22,319	646
Federation of Bosnia and Herzegovina	198	9	16,134	470

Sources :

a) Republika Srpska Institute of Statistics. Monthly Statistical Review 4/2002.

b) Federation's Institute of Statistics. 2002 Statistical Yearbook.

The railway network, with some 1,000 km of track, requires upgrading and the standardization of equipment. Considering the geographical characteristics of Bosnia and Herzegovina, in particular its topography, extending the network would require massive investment and cannot be considered as a realistic option in the short term.

The road network, although of poor quality, is far more developed. It is made up of 22,600 km of road, of which 3,800 km are primary roads, 4,800 km regional roads and 14,000 km local roads. Few motorways meet international standards. To a large extent, this network also needs to be rehabilitated.

Between 1990 and 2000, it is estimated that the total number of vehicles for the whole country increased from 575,000 to 800,000-900,000, assuming that both entities have approximately the same number of vehicles (see table 5.5). The number of vehicles more than doubled during the first two or three years following the end of the war. Traffic management is the responsibility of the municipalities and also of the cantonal authorities in the Federation of Bosnia and Herzegovina.

No information was available about the average age of the vehicle fleet. However, from what can be observed in the country, an average of 8 to 10 years is a realistic assumption. Cars that are more than 7 years old and buses or trucks that are more than 10 years old cannot be imported.

Table 5.4: Trend in transport of goods and passengers, 1997-2001

	1997	1998	1999	2000	2001	change 1997 to 2001 (%)
Passengers in thousands						
railway	1,461	1,751	1,481	1,342	1,298	-11.2%
road	35,540	39,290	37,039	37,577	38,453	8.2%
Goods in thousand tons						
railway	1,810	2,870	3,247	4,279	5,405	198.6%
road	1,740	1,895	1,838	1,709	1,472	-15.4%
Passenger kms in millions						
railway	39	58	51	47	50	28.2%
road	1,042	1,306	1,190	1,314	1,116	7.1%
Goods ton kms in millions						
railway	46	84	146	222	281	510.9%
road	323	393	364	334	269	-16.7%

Sources :

Republika Srpska Institute of Statistics. Monthly Statistical Review 4/2002. Federation's Institute of Statistics. 2002 Statistical Yearbook.

Table 5.5: Vehicles in Federation of Bosnia and Herzegovina, 1997 – 2001

	1997	1998	1999	2000	2001	change from 1997 to 2001 (%)
Total	194,930	317,609	416,758	417,784	426,618	118.9%
Passenger cars	172,029	278,293	362,879	366,670	374,224	117.5%
Goods vehicles	18,358	29,481	35,122	35,978	34,192	86.3%
Buses	1,082	2,113	2,837	2,505	2,678	147.5%
Two-wheelers	410	550	1,585	2,061	2,806	584.4%
Other	3,051	7,172	14,335	10,570	12,718	316.8%

Source : Federation's Institute of Statistics. 2002 Statistical Yearbook.

Figures provided by the Federation's Meteorological Institute indicate that 35% of passenger cars are equipped with engines using unleaded fuel, 35% with engines using leaded fuel and 30% with diesel engines. According to the entities' recently adopted Laws on Air Protection, the use of leaded petrol should be phased out before 2010.

In both entities, technical inspection is mandatory once a year for all cars, trucks and buses. Vehicles need to pass for their registrations to be renewed. The Laws on Air Protection specify that motor vehicle emissions must comply with certain limit values, in particular for CO, NO_x and particulates, and this is tested during the annual inspection (State Decision 20/00 in Official Gazette BiH of 25/07/2000 amended by Decision 36/00 in Official Gazette BiH of 31/12/2000); vehicles that fail to meet these emission limit values are barred. Yet, in practice it appears that emissions are not or at least not systematically verified. This inspection is performed under the responsibility of the Ministers of Internal Affairs.

The Federation's Meteorological Institute has already identified traffic as a major source of pollution in Sarajevo and Banja Luka, affecting approximately one fifth of the country's total population. Traffic emissions are expected to increase in the coming years. Main reasons are:
- Incomplete testing and verification during technical inspections;
- Increasing number of cars and average age of the fleet;
- Low quality of fuels;
- Poor maintenance of the vehicles; and
- Poor quality of the road network and traffic management.

5.3 Air quality

The few relevant statistics collected during the environmental performance review (EPR) mission come from the Federation's Meteorological Institute and concern stations located in Sarajevo only. Only fragmentary data were obtained for some other cities and it is not possible to draw any firm conclusions from them.

Figure 5.2 illustrates particles and SO_2 concentrations recorded in one 'old' station operated in Sarajevo between 1990 and 2000. As expected, there is a clear decline over that period.

Table 5.6 presents values recorded in 2002 at the automatic station operated by the Meteorological Institute in Sarajevo. They are difficult to compare with the limit values of EU Directives 1999/30/EC and 2000/69/EC on air quality, since the statistical parameters are not the same. However, the measured concentrations appear rather high for the higher percentiles. Being uphill, this station's concentrations are expected to be higher than in the valley. This could be indicative of possible pollution episodes or peaks mostly in adverse meteorological conditions (temperature inversion) caused mainly by traffic and local combustion units.

Owing to the lack of comprehensive information, the air quality in the country's other cities is largely unknown. Although the overall air quality is probably better now than before the war, it is feared that poor air quality still prevails at the local level and in particular in several cities. The Meteorological Institute has identified at least nine hot spots (Kakanj, Tuzla, Uglevik, Jajce, Mostar, Gacko, Zenica, Sarajevo and Banja Luka), affecting 1.3 million inhabitants, i.e. one third of the total population.

Figure 5.2: Mean concentrations - Sarajevo, Bjelave, 1990 - 2002

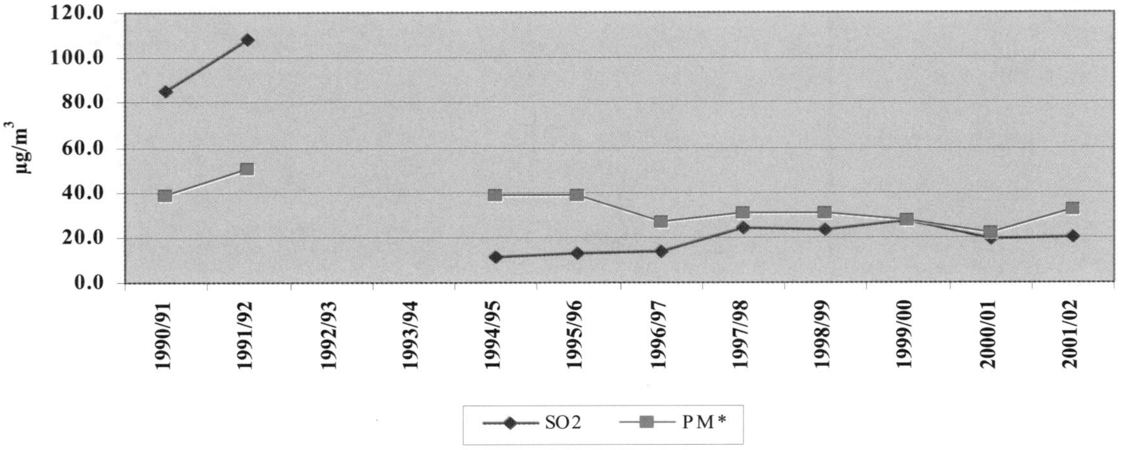

Source : Meteorological Institute, 2003.

Note : *PM =particulate matter

5.4 Policy objectives and management practices

The policy framework

The National Environmental Action Plan (NEAP), adopted by both entities in 2003, aims to identify short- and long-term priority actions and measures providing the basis for a long-term environmental protection strategy. One of its sub-chapters is dedicated to air quality management and focuses mainly on climate change. Although several important measures are listed in this sub-chapter, air quality management is not considered a priority as such, unlike water and waste. However, several priority measures and activities that are recommended could have positive effects on air quality, for instance:

- Establishing a pollutant emission cadastre according to the CORINAIR (COoRdinated INformation AIR) methodology;
- Encouraging environmentally sustainable transport;

- Making fossil fuel use more efficient;
- Reducing SO_2 and NO_x air pollution by applying desulphurization in selected power plants; and
- Preparing a traffic management project for cities.

Another document is the Mid-term Development Strategy (2004-2007) adopted in February 2004 at the State level. It includes a section dedicated to air quality and climate change. Priorities as well as measures in line with those mentioned in the NEAP are identified in general terms. They are mainly focused on reducing the emission of air pollutants by increasing energy efficiency, using renewable energy sources and developing a strategy based on the country's changing climatic conditions.

Beside the limited guidance provided in these documents, no air management policy has yet been developed.

Table 5.6: Air pollutants statistics 2002 - Sarajevo automatic station

$\mu g/m^3$

	SO_2	NO	NO_2	NOx	CO
Average	18	18	27	40	881
Median	6	4	18	22	550
95th percentile	80	87	84	144	2,898
98th percentile	126	169	127	235	4,193
99.9th percentile	285	395	218	456	7,178
Maximum	383	502	277	587	8,192

Source : Meteorological Institute. Report 11/2003.

The legal framework

Both entities recently adopted new laws on air:
- Law on Air Protection of the Federation of Bosnia and Herzegovina (Official Gazette F BiH 33/2003); and
- Law on Air Protection of Republika Srpska (Official Gazette RS 53/2002).

They are the same in both entities and in line with several EU directives. They cover not only emissions of atmospheric pollutants and air quality but also set out a monitoring and reporting framework. Their provisions on air emissions range from the air study necessary for sources that require an environmental impact assessment to inspections of these sources, as well as possible penalties and sanctions for the infringement of emission limits. These limits will be fixed in by-laws.

These Laws foresee specific regulations to be developed for combustion plants and other industrial plants according to their rated thermal input as well as for waste incineration plants. Motor vehicle emissions, volatile organic compound (VOC) emissions and fuel quality (sulphur and lead contents) are also regulated.

A second component of these Laws relates to air quality and follows the principles of EU Directive 96/62/EC on air quality assessment and management. In particular, the Laws call for the development and implementation of action plans in the event that air quality limit values or alert thresholds, to be fixed in by-laws, are exceeded.

The Laws also provide for the development of emission inventories and registers with data measured by large point sources, for regular monitoring and an exchange of information on air quality, and for the preparation of reports describing not only the status but also the trends and measures taken to improve air quality.

As seen above, effective implementation of these Laws requires by-laws: special regulations for specific emitters, provisions and requirements for monitoring, air quality and air emission limit values. Although it was foreseen that these by-laws would be submitted to the competent authorities no later than one year after the entry into force of the Laws, to date none of them has been developed. As a result, air quality management remains in a legal vacuum.

In the Federation of Bosnia and Herzegovina, cantonal air quality policy must be harmonized with the Federation's air quality policy. Cantons have the right to enact their own legislation. In practice, some cantons like Sarajevo, Tuzla and Srednja Bosna have already developed their own law on air quality (see chapter 1 on Policy, legal and institutional framework).

The institutional framework

Air quality management falls within the jurisdiction of the Ministry of Physical Planning and Environment in the Federation of Bosnia and Herzegovina and the Ministry of Physical Planning, Civil Engineering and Ecology in Republika Srpska.

In the Federation, some cantons like Sarajevo, Tuzla and Zenica-Doboj also undertake certain air quality management tasks.

Monitoring

There is currently no plan for measuring air emissions. Emissions are only measured voluntarily by the emitters themselves. The entities but also the cantons (in the Federation) and the municipalities have recently set up inspectorates. Inspections are carried out at the request of or following a complaint from members of the public, but in practice do not result either in penalties or in sanctions.

The statistical data necessary for estimating air emissions rarely exist or are not collected. There is no inventory of industries emitting air pollutants and no register of emissions. In this respect, the new Laws on Air Protection foresee that the emitters, the expert institutions and the Federation's cantonal authorities will communicate all data necessary for estimating emissions or verifying them. These data will be provided to the Ministry of Physical Planning, Civil Engineering and Ecology in Republika Srpska and to the Ministry of Physical Planning and Environment in the Federation of Bosnia and Herzegovina.

Several institutes and bodies in both entities and in Brčko District monitor air quality:

Republika Srpska:
- The Hydro-Meteorological Institute: one automatic station in Banja Luka measuring SO_2, CO, NO, NO_2 and NO_x. This Institute is

the proposed reference centre on air quality for Republika Srpska.

- The Institute for Protection, Ecology and Information Science: seven stations in Banja Luka, three in Gradiska and four in other municipalities. These stations measure particles and SO_2 three times a week.

Federation of Bosnia and Herzegovina:
- The Meteorological Institute: one automatic station measuring SO_2, CO, NO, NO_2, NO_x and one station measuring particulate matter and SO_2 daily. Both stations are in Sarajevo. This Institute is the proposed reference centre on air quality and air emissions for the Federation.

- The Cantonal Public Health Institute of Sarajevo: five stations located in Sarajevo that measure SO_2 and particles daily.

- The Institute for Public Health of Mostar.

- The Department of Environmental Protection in Tuzla with three automatic stations. This Department also operates the two automatic stations (one stationary and one mobile) owned by the thermal power plant of Tuzla. These measure SO_2, CO, NO, NO_2, NO_x, total suspended particles (TSP) and O_3.

- The Cantonal Public Health Institute of Zenica.

Brčko District:
- The Institute of Civil Engineering of Banja Luka: three stations measuring SO_2 and particles daily. These stations belong to Brčko District's Government, but the yearly contracts to operate them are awarded through a tender.

The above list shows that in most cases monitoring takes place only in the cities where the institutes are located.

In addition to these stations run by public institutes, companies and industries also monitor emissions voluntarily, for instance:
- The Kakanj thermal power plant and cement factory (automatic station measuring SO_2, CO, NO, NO_2 and NO_x);
- The Ugljevik thermal power plant; and
- The Tuzla thermal power station (see above).

Although their exact number is not known, there are probably some 40 monitoring stations in the country. Most still use measuring techniques dating back to before the war and monitor only particles and SO_2 on a daily basis. Ozone is measured only in Tuzla. PM10 and metals are not monitored.

Neither the State nor the entities have so far defined a monitoring strategy. Monitoring takes place without any specific objectives such as verifying compliance with limit values, helping policy development, estimating trends or evaluating the population's exposure. Furthermore, there is a lack of coordination and active cooperation between the different institutions. Consequently, the scarce resources available are not used efficiently. For example, the Cantonal Public Health Institute of Sarajevo wishes to renew its network with automatic stations but this initiative is not effectively coordinated with the activities of the Meteorological Institute.

No effective quality assurance or quality control procedures are applied; this affects both the reliability and the representativeness of the few data collected. Communication and dissemination are also unsatisfactory: the few existing reports are of very limited interest, and transmitted only to the bodies that are directly involved in them without any further dissemination.

In the absence of by-laws implementing the Laws on Air Protection, there are no effective limit values. Values adopted in some cantons of the Federation or mentioned in some reports are reference levels of air quality rather than levels determining measures for air quality management.

International cooperation

International conventions

As a successor to the former Yugoslavia, Bosnia and Herzegovina became a Party to the UNECE Convention on Long-range Transboundary Air Pollution in 1992. However, it is a Party to only one of the Convention's eight protocols: the Protocol on Long-term Financing of the Cooperative Programme for Monitoring and Evaluation of the Long-range Transmission of Air Pollutants in Europe (EMEP). It became a Party in 1992 by succession. Despite having monitoring and reporting obligations under the Protocol, it does not report data to EMEP.

Bosnia and Herzegovina also became a Party to the Vienna Convention for the Protection of the Ozone Layer, and its Montreal Protocol by succession in 1992. An Ozone Unit has been established in the

State Ministry of Foreign Trade and Economic Relations. A draft State programme for phasing out ozone-depleting substances has been prepared.

Bosnia and Herzegovina ratified the United Nations Framework Convention on Climate Change on 7 September 2000. The focal point is the Ministry of Physical Planning, Civil Engineering and Ecology of Republika Srpska.

International projects

Several international projects that could help strengthen and develop air quality management are currently under way. The most important are:

- EU Financial Instrument for the Environment (LIFE) project ROSA. This project coordinated by the Regional Environmental Center for Central and Eastern Europe aims at setting up an operational unit under the Inter-entity Steering Committee for the Environment. To that aim, it has established six working groups, one of them dedicated to air quality. These working groups also contribute to the development of secondary legislation.

- EU Community Assistance, Reconstruction, Development and Stabilisation (CARDS) project "Institutional Strengthening in Environmental Management". This project will provide support to the Environment Ministries to develop environmental policies and instruments and to draft secondary legislation.

- EU CARDS project "Development of a National Environmental Monitoring System". The aim of the project is to develop a monitoring system in line with the European Environment Information and Observation Network (EIONET) structure and requirements.

- EU CARDS project "Support to Air Monitoring". The purpose is to define sustainable means of gathering data (both via statistics and monitoring) in order to identify the air quality and emissions situation in Bosnia and Herzegovina and to provide reliable data for reporting on air quality issues.

5.5   Conclusions and recommendations

Although air emissions from industry and the energy sector have likely decreased sharply in recent years, air quality probably remains poor in several cities. The main causes are the lack of abatement devices and obsolete technology at industrial and energy facilities, the use of poor-quality coal as well as the ageing fleet of vehicles and the increasing traffic.

Furthermore, air quality management remains in a legal vacuum until both entities adopt secondary legislation allowing effective and operational implementation of the new Laws on Air Protection.

Recommendation 5.1:
The Ministry of Physical Planning and Environment of the Federation of Bosnia and Herzegovina and the Ministry of Physical Planning, Civil Engineering and Ecology in Republika Srpska should develop the secondary legislation necessary for the practical implementation of their Laws on Air Protection as soon as possible. However, considering the number of by-laws to be developed as well as the scarcity of resources available, the Ministries should prioritize their common needs and the issues to be tackled. A realistic approach taking into consideration the existing and future capacity to ensure effective implementation of the legislation should be adopted in this process.

Air monitoring of both emissions and immissions is a basic component of coherent air quality management. In Bosnia and Herzegovina, several institutes and bodies monitor air quality. Some depend on the Environment Ministries, others on other ministries and yet others are 'independent'. Their activities are not coordinated, resulting in wasted resources. Neither monitoring objectives nor quality assurance/quality control are defined. Data and information on air emissions are scarce and unreliable.

Several international projects currently aim to improve that situation, in particular by developing a monitoring system in line with the EIONET requirements.

Recommendation 5.2:
The State Ministry of Transport and Communications, the Federation's Ministry of Physical Planning and Environment, Republika Srpska's Ministry of Physical Planning, Civil Engineering and Ecology and the environmental authorities of Brčko District should develop a common air monitoring strategy to, inter alia,
(a) Identify the responsibilities of the institutions involved in air monitoring necessary to achieve a cost-effective monitoring approach;
(b) Address the requirements of EIONET and the Convention on Long-range Transboundary Air Pollution; and

(c) Streamline the existing monitoring system. In this regard, the following should be taken into account:

- *Delegating operating responsibilities for running stations;*
- *Transferring and concentrating monitoring activities within a limited geographical zone or region; and*
- *Discontinuing marginal, unrepresentative or inefficient air monitoring.*

Should the proposed Environment Agency be created at the State level, it should take the lead in implementing recommendation 5.2.

Road transport is the most important transport mode for passengers, and traffic is a major source of air pollution in the cities. The number of registered vehicles has significantly increased over the past years and will probably continue to do so in the coming years, aggravating the pressure on air quality.

Beside economic instruments, reducing traffic-related air emissions also requires a number of technical measures at all levels from the municipalities to the entities and the State.

Recommendation 5.3:
In close collaboration with the Environment Ministries and other authorities responsible for the environment, the State Ministry of Transport and Communications, the entities' Ministries of Transport and Communications and the Government of Brčko District should seek to reduce traffic emissions or at least mitigate their impact through a better integration of transport policy and traffic management. This should be achieved by strengthening collaboration between the State Ministry of Transport and Communications, the Ministries of Transport and Communications and the municipal authorities (cantonal authorities in the Federation) responsible for traffic management. Some of the measures to be envisaged are:

- *Effective enforcement of technical inspections (together with the Ministries of Internal Affairs);*

- *Improving road maintenance;*
- *Improving the management of traffic flows;*
- *Improving the quality of fuels in internal combustion engines; and*
- *Promoting and extending public transport.*

Bosnia and Herzegovina is a Party to the Convention on Long-range Transboundary Air Pollution. However, it is a Party to only one of the Convention's eight protocols: the Protocol on the Financing of EMEP. The country does not currently report emission data to EMEP due to the destruction of the EMEP station during the war.

Support from the Convention and its Parties may be forthcoming if the barriers to accession to the other protocols can be identified. Stronger links with the Convention would aid the development of a monitoring strategy, the creation of emission inventories and the development of an air quality strategy in general. While implementation of these protocols may not be a priority for the country, it should be used as a tool for promoting air quality locally, regionally and nationally.

Recommendation 5.4:
(a) The Federation's Ministry of Physical Planning and Environment, Republika Srpska's Ministry of Physical Planning, Civil Engineering and Ecology and the environmental authorities of Brčko District under the coordination and supervision of the State Ministry of Foreign Trade and Economic Relations and in cooperation with the State Ministry of Transport and Communications should develop appropriate and realistic strategies for the ratification and implementation of the protocols to the Convention on Long-range Transboundary Air pollution.

(b) The responsible body should ensure reconstruction of the EMEP station and recommencing Bosnia and Herzegovina emissions data reporting to the EMEP bureau.

Chapter 6

MANAGEMENT OF WASTE AND CONTAMINATED SITES

6.1   Introduction

The management of waste, whether municipal, hazardous or non-hazardous industrial waste, medical waste, obsolete pharmaceuticals or contaminated sites, is one of Bosnia and Herzegovina's environmental priorities. Strategic documents such as the Solid Waste Management Strategy, the National Environmental Action Plan and the Mid-term Development Strategy (2004-2007) provide important guidance for improving this sector in the short, medium and long term. Work has also begun on designing and constructing multi-municipal sanitary landfills to rationalize capital and operating costs.

The development of a legal framework for waste management has begun. Both entities developed and adopted new Laws on Waste Management. Further efforts are now necessary to implement these laws through the development of secondary legislation dealing with specific waste management issues. The framework laws were based on existing EU legislation.

The good start with the development of policy and strategy documents now needs to be complemented with favourable conditions for their implementation, including the drawing-up of concrete regulations, projects, financial support, and the mobilization and training of the population to actively participate in the environmentally sound management of all kinds of waste, including hazardous and chemical waste.

6.2   Waste generation

Municipal waste

Few statistics on municipal waste generation are available because at present there is no regular nationwide reporting system.

Municipal waste contains organic material, durable and non-durable goods, packaging plastics, and textiles. It also contains small quantities of hazardous waste like paint, motor oil, batteries and agrochemicals, from households, shops, small enterprises, workshops, garages, light industry and heavier industry. There is no system for waste separation. Sometimes hazardous waste and medical waste are dumped together with municipal waste.

The demolition of houses during the war and the reconstruction of residential areas in its aftermath have generated large quantities of construction waste. In many cases this waste is disposed of along the riverbanks, constituting a source of contamination and littering rivers. No statistical information on this waste is available. The problem peaked after the war, but is diminishing now. At present construction waste is used to cover illegal landfills on riverbanks.

As economic conditions improve in Bosnia and Herzegovina, consumption patterns are changing and municipal waste is increasing. For example, people buy more packaged food and other goods, and they tend to discard goods more quickly. The share of plastics and packaging in municipal waste is significant. Small plastics bags are a particular problem, as they are being dumped in the rivers and along riverbanks, clogging waterways and generally spoiling riversides.

Municipal and industrial waste estimates for 1999 from the Solid Waste Management Strategy are given in table 6.1. These are the most recent data available. They show that a total of 1,764,893 tons of municipal waste was generated, i.e. 452 kg per capita, which is about average for countries in transition.

Table 6.1: Estimated waste generation in 1999

	Population	Waste generation (tons/year)				Waste per capita (tons/capita/year)		
		Municipal	Industrial	Hazardous waste*	Total	Municipal waste**	Industrial	Total
Federation	2,366,373	1,081,581	495,360	4,953.6	1,576,937	0.457	0.209	0.666
Republika Srpska	1,455,620	650,266	353,081	3,530.8	1,003,349	0.447	0.243	0.689
Brčko District	80,324	33,046	15,191	151.9	48,236	0.411	0.189	0.601
Total	3,902,317	1,764,893	863,632	8,636.3	2,628,522	0.452	0.221	0.674

Source: EU Phare. Solid Waste Management Strategy. Technical Report 1. August 2000.
Notes:
* One per cent of industrial waste is considered to be hazardous.
** The estimated average in countries in transition is 452 kg.

Since the consumption of packaged food and goods has increased in the past five years and will continue to do so, it is expected that more municipal waste will be generated. The amount of industrial waste will depend on the kind of industry and technology that will be developed and applied in the future. Appropriate decisions and measures should be taken to introduce environmentally friendly industrial processes.

Industrial waste, including hazardous waste

Industrial activity in the country has decreased since independence. Industrial enterprises either do not work or work at 10-15% of their designed capacities. Consequently, there is less industrial waste, including hazardous waste.

There are no data on the quantities of non-hazardous and hazardous waste that have been generated or accumulated. Estimates in the Solid Waste Management Strategy are based on the assumption that hazardous waste comprises 1% of industrial waste (see table 6.1). Light industry is estimated to generate an additional 11,000 tons of hazardous waste each year. Estimated quantities of oil waste are between 18,000 and 20,000 tons per year (used oil, lubricants and mixed oil waste, including 1,500 tons of oil contaminated by polychlorinated biphenyls (PCBs)) (see table 6.2). Although there are recovery facilities for oil waste in the country, with a capacity of 10,000 tons/year, they are running at only 10-15% of this capacity because there is no regular collection system for oil waste. Moreover, their oil recovery method is not environmentally friendly, because of obsolete equipment.

Medical waste and obsolete pharmaceuticals

There is no separate collection of medical waste and no treatment. According to the NEAP, an estimated 120 tons of medical (health care) waste is generated per day, of which 15% could be considered as very dangerous and toxic, requiring disinfection or incineration and disposal.

There are some small incinerators for medical waste in Bosnia and Herzegovina, but they do not meet the technical requirements for medical waste incineration. One such incinerator is at the Uborak landfill. The temperature of incineration is very low (400-600° Celsius), and there is no purification system for its exhaust gases. Toxic substances like dioxins and furans are released into the atmosphere in the vicinity of hospitals. To prevent the adverse effects of such incineration on the population and the environment, separate collection systems for medical waste need to be introduced and modern high-temperature incinerators with exhaust gas treatment built.

Significantly compounding the problem with medical waste is the large number of obsolete pharmaceuticals that accumulated during and after the war. There are about 1000 tons of these pharmaceuticals in the country, of which 650 tons are in the Federation of Bosnia and Herzegovina and 350 in Republika Srpska. They are stored at over 90 sites (hospitals, warehouses and pharmacies). Some of these pharmaceuticals have been encapsulated with cement. About 1600 drums were encapsulated according to WHO guidelines; however, only 220 drums were disposed of in a sanitary landfill in Mostar. The rest still pose a health risk. Small quantities of these pharmaceuticals were transported for treatment to other countries under the Basel Convention. The remainder is stored.

Table 6.2: Non-industrial, non-medical hazardous waste

tons/year

Type of hazardous waste	Estimated quantity
Used oil, lubricants and mixed oil waste	18,000 - 20,000
Batteries and accumulators, electrolytes	3,160
Discarded cars (1% of hazardous waste)	5,000 - 6,000
Electrical and electronic equipment	1,500
Paint, thinners and varnishes	200
Packaging materials (1% of hazardous waste)	1,280
Construction waste	1,500
Pesticide waste	64
Photo waste	480
Total, except industrial hazardous waste	31,184 - 34,184

Source: Project on Environmental Protection Assessment of Industrial, Medical and Other Hazardous Waste in Bosnia and Herzegovina, Bosna-S Oil Services Company, book 3, 2002.

6.3 Waste disposal, storage and use

Municipal waste

Bosnia and Herzegovina does not have a system to separate waste. The only separation that takes place is informal, carried out by a few entrepreneurs and individuals who separate small quantities of papers and metals from municipal waste. There is also no recycling or treatment. There is some potential for recycling and reuse, because much of the waste constitutes sources of secondary raw material such as paper, glass, metal and plastic. Organic waste could be composted and used as fertilizer. The main problem with the separation of municipal waste is the unavailability of equipment for processing the separated components (paper, glass, metal, aluminium, organic waste).

There are 25 registered municipal landfills in Republika Srpska and 50 in the Federation. There is no complete inventory of illegal sites, but unofficial sources suggest that they number around 10,000. Illegal landfills are those that are not authorized by municipalities or cantonal governments. According to the NEAP, landfills in Uborak at Mostar, Krivodol, a small landfill in Tesanj and a large landfill in Smiljevici at Sarajevo in the Federation and Bosanka Krupa in Republika Srpska could be defined as sanitary or manageable landfills. The total area of landfills in the country is estimated as 1200 ha.

The landfill in Sarajevo is situated about 3 km from the city and occupies 130,000 m². About 400-600 tons of waste is dumped there each day. It could continue to operate for the next 30 years at least. The site is well organized: it has a gas collection system; methane is collected and used for energy production. There is also an air monitoring system

and a meteorological station. Drainage water is not treated, but there are plans to do so together with sewage. The site is fenced off and has a video control system. It does not, however, include a system for hazardous waste separation, and some equipment and machinery require repair or replacement. There is no inspection service at the site, although it is under consideration. A new pilot project is under development to separate recyclable waste such as paper, plastic and aluminium.

The landfill in Banja Luka has been used for more than 20 years. Eight municipalities (about 500,000 people) dump about 450 tons of waste per day there. The landfill is situated at Ramichi, about 20 km from the city and occupies 36 ha. Two companies serve these eight municipalities: one enterprise called Chistota and a public company named DEP-OT. All eight municipalities have municipal enterprises coordinated by DEP-OT to collect, transport and dispose of municipal waste at this landfill. At present, the municipal enterprises are able to cover only 60% of the population in the main municipalities and an even smaller percentage in suburban areas. There is almost no collection in the rural areas; there are therefore a number of illegal sites along the roads, in abandoned mines and rivers. The Ramichi landfill does not meet international sanitary standards and norms, but there are plans to rehabilitate it through a World Bank project. There is also a plan to eliminate all illegal landfills in DEP-OT's area of operation, which occupy about 100 ha, and to separate municipal waste and have DEP-OT process it.

The Solid Waste Management Strategy calls for an approach to municipal waste disposal that relies on a multi-municipality district. The practical details of this approach, e.g. location of landfills, are still being worked out, but it involves organizing waste disposal for several municipalities around a single site. The population served per landfill should be at least 200,000; the minimum waste disposal should be 200 tons per day; and the transport distance should be no more than 100 km. The country would be divided into 14 or 16 waste allocation districts (depending on the final decision), taking into account overall economic, geographic and local conditions.   In the longer term, the Strategy foresees the construction of five main regional landfills. According to the NEAP, locations for the initial phase are Banja Luka, Tuzla, Mostar, Bijeljina, Bihac, Livno, Sarajevo and Zenica. The Strategy also foresees the rehabilitation of existing sites.

Industrial waste, including hazardous waste and chemicals

As noted above, there are no facilities for treating obsolete pharmaceuticals accumulated during the war, and their storage conditions are generally unsatisfactory.

Industrial waste is either disposed together with municipal waste or stored at the industrial facilities where it is produced. Each industrial plant has its own disposal site. According to the Laws on Waste Management, the operators of installations that require an environmental permit should draw up a company waste management plan, which sets out, inter alia, the storage conditions of waste on the site. These new Laws have not yet been applied, because there are no regulations, norms and standards.

There is considerable wood waste in the country because there are many small wood-processing companies (sawmills). This waste is not being used, but small bricks made of wood waste could be used as a source of energy.

According to the NEAP, about 6000 ha are used for the disposal of mining waste, and about 600 ha for slag and ash from thermal power plants. Red mud from aluminium plants (Mostar and Zvornik) is dumped on 300 ha and not used or recycled.

There is virtually no recycling of industrial waste and no separation and treatment facilities for industrial non-hazardous and hazardous waste. In many cases industrial waste, including hazardous and medical waste, is dumped together with municipal waste at unmanaged and non-sanitary

landfills. An exception is ash generated at the Tuzla power plant, some of which is used in the cement industry.

Electrofilter ash from thermoelectric plants, red mud from aluminium plants, steel slag and mining waste are also sources of secondary raw material and could be used in other industries. This would help to solve two problems by disposing of waste without damaging the environment and manufacturing valuable industrial products, like cement and steel from red mud. Mining waste (overburden) could be used to rehabilitate municipal landfills, repair roads and restore contaminated land for construction. Filtration, extraction and distillation for recovery of spent oil and solvent could be used to produce low-grade solvent and oil.

6.4   Environmental impact

Municipal waste

Many official municipal waste sites are situated about 5 km from residential areas, and about half of the sites are within 10-15 km. Few sites are situated more than 25 km away. Disposal of municipal waste at these sites, which do not meet sanitary norms and standards, has adverse environmental effects, resulting in soil degradation and contamination as well as air contamination by organic substances, toxic dust and methane released from the decomposition of waste. In many cases municipal waste is burned at the sites, and the fumes contaminate the air around the sites, including, sometimes, residential areas. Groundwater is contaminated by heavy metals and organic hazardous substances that are formed during decomposition, and surface water is contaminated by rain water leaching organic hazardous substances, which move to open watercourses.

There is also pollution and contamination of rivers by municipal and construction waste. The landfills are not fenced off, and people and animals have access to contaminated sites, which may result in the spread of infectious diseases.

Contaminated sites

Bosnia and Herzegovina has two types of contaminated sites: sites where industrial toxic waste is stored and sites littered with landmines.

Industrial contaminated sites

There are 15 contaminated industrial "hot spots". These include thermal power plants, and chemical, paper and metallurgical industries. Depending on the industry, the sites are contaminated by heavy metals, different toxic chemicals or asbestos. These sites are listed in table 6.3.

As table 6.3 shows, the main industrial waste storage sites include waste containing heavy metals, ash, metallurgical slag, and waste from soda ash production (white sea). An inventory of contaminated industrial waste sites has been started but is not yet complete. An inventory of all such sites is needed to start their rehabilitation or introduce the technologies for their recycling and reuse.

There is no information on the degree of soil, groundwater and air contamination at industrial sites or in their vicinity, including residential areas of nearby towns. There are no environmental impact assessments (EIA) of these sites or environmental audits of industrial facilities, including industrial storage facilities. A system to monitor soil, groundwater and air needs to be introduced to identify the threats caused by these industries to the population and the environment. Monitoring data are needed to conduct an EIA (or environmental audit, as EIA is only for new facilities) of these sites.

Landmines

Landmines are a significant source of hazardous waste. Bosnia and Herzegovina is the country with the most landmines in Europe. By September 2000, 16 km^2 of land (30,000 landmines and 6,000 items of unexploded ordnance (UXO)) had been cleaned up. However, according to the Bosnia and Herzegovina Mine Action Centre, in 2001, 18,145 minefields remained, 74% of which are located within the Federation, including 2 million items of UXO (see chapter 12, health and environment).

6.5   Policy, legal and institutional framework

The policy framework

The Solid Waste Management Strategy was revised and adopted in 2000-2001 by both entities but not yet by the Assembly of Brcko District. It proposes

concrete measures and recommendations to improve the country's overall waste management and includes, as discussed in section 6.3, the establishment of multi-municipal districts for municipal waste collection, transport and disposal; the construction of regional sanitary landfills; the closure or rehabilitation of uncontrolled disposal sites; and the reprocessing of waste into energy and compost as a long-term priority. The Strategy is divided into three implementation phases: 2001-2005; 2005-2010; and 2010-2015. The first phase is in progress, with support from both the World Bank and the European Commission's Community Assistance, Reconstruction, Development and Stabilisation (CARDS) Programme.

The Strategy is comprehensive. It addresses not only a number of technical issues, but also legal, institutional and organizations issues, and education, professional training and public awareness. It is based on existing European Union legislation, in particular, the EU European Waste Catalogue, the EU Hazardous Waste Directive, 91/689/EEC, and EU Directive 1999/31/EC.

Waste is one of eight priorities identified in the NEAP, which proposes a large number of activities, many of them similar to those in the Solid Waste Management Strategy. The three top priorities are: (1) the adoption of strategies and plans for waste management; (2) the elimination of illegal dumps and the rehabilitation of degraded locations; and (3) the rehabilitation of existing landfills. Attention is also given, among other things, to the return of secondary raw material, its recycling or reuse; increasing energy generation from waste; and establishing a waste market.

The Mid-term Development Strategy, adopted in 2004, refers to the Solid Waste Management Strategy and endorses the concept of inter-municipal organizations for waste management and disposal at regional sanitary dumps. It notes that the Strategy includes 21 priority measures, but it also emphasizes that the problem of waste needs to be extended to mining, power and industry and not treated only, or primarily, as an urban matter. The Mid-term Development Strategy calls for framework laws on recycling and processing secondary raw material as well as on the exploitation of mineral ores. It further proposes that waste exchanges should be set up and encouraged by legal and economic instruments.

Table 6.3: Industrial facilities with hazardous waste storage

Highly toxic waste:	
Category of waste stored	**Location**
Waste from zinc and lead production	- Srebrenica (Lead and Zinc Mines) - Vares (Iron Forge-Vares)
Red mud (aluminium industry)	- Zvornik (TG Birac; Al oxide plan) - Mostar (Aluminij-Mostar)
Asbestos mud	- Bos. Petrovo Selo (Separation Ilici)
Toxic Waste:	
Category of waste stored	**Location**
Thermal power plans (ash and slag)	- Kakanj, Tuzla, Ugljevik, Gacho
Waste from paper production plants	- Maglaj (Natron), Bania Luca (Incel)
Ferrosillicate electrolysis waste	- Jajce (Electrobosna)
Soda ash waste	- Lucavach (Soda Ash Plant)
Leather tanning waste	- Visoko (KTK, Leather factory)
Low toxic waste:	
Category of waste stored	**Location**
Slag from steel industry	- Zenica (Steel plant,Raca steel slag)

Source: Project on Environmental Protection Assessment of Industrial, Medical and Other Hazardous Waste in Bosnia and Herzegovina, Bosna-S Oil Services Company, book 3, 2002.

The legislative framework

The main legislation consists of the Law on Waste Management of the Federation of Bosnia and Herzegovina (Official Gazette F BiH 33/2003) and the Law on Waste Management of Republika Sprska (Official Gazette RS 51/2002). Their operative texts are almost identical but are adapted to each entity's structure. They are also harmonized with EU Decision 94/904/EEC and EU Directive 91/689/EEC. The Laws cover the management of all kinds of waste except radioactive waste. Among other things, they specify: the competent bodies for waste and the definition of waste; the responsibilities of manufacturers; the requirements for permitting, inspection and sanctions; municipal waste management, collection, transport, treatment, use and disposal of waste; landfill requirements; general requirements for hazardous waste and its incineration; and the conditions for the transboundary movement of hazardous waste inside and outside the entities.

The Laws are relatively new and still lack the regulations, norms and standards for implementation, especially for the management of hazardous waste and medical waste, which are a serious threat to the population and the environment.

Bosnia and Herzegovina acceded to the Basel Convention at the end of 2000 (Official Gazette BiH 31/2000). The Federation's Ministry of Physical Planning and Environment and Republika Srpska's Ministry of Physical Planning, Civil Engineering and Ecology issue permits for transboundary waste. For the movement of waste within the country, only notification between these two Ministries is needed. There is no treatment facility for hazardous waste. The entities' Ministries participate in the information exchange under the Basel Convention. Bosnia and Herzegovina uses a classification system for hazardous waste according to the Basel Convention, and it began collecting data for reporting under the Basel Convention in 2002.

The institutional framework

Within Republika Sprska, the Ministry of Physical Planning, Civil Engineering and Ecology is responsible for developing and implementing waste legislation and waste management policy. Within the Federation, responsibilities are shared between the Ministry of Physical Planning and Environment and the cantons' environment ministries.

Municipalities (municipal services departments), through municipal enterprises, are responsible for the collection, transport and disposal of municipal waste. Only in Sarajevo is the cantonal administration responsible for these services. Some municipal enterprises are private companies that have concluded a contract with the municipalities.

The situation is different for industrial waste management (policy, regulation and planning facilities for waste treatment). In this case, responsibility lies with the Federation's Ministry of Energy, Mining and Industry and Republika Srpska's Ministry of Economy, Energy and Development. Industry itself is responsible for the separation, treatment and disposal of its waste.

The Federation's Ministry of Health and the Ministry of Physical Planning and Environment and Republika Srpska's Ministry of Health and Social Welfare and the Ministry of Physical Planning, Civil Engineering and Ecology are responsible for the collection, separation, treatment and disposal of medical waste and obsolete pharmaceuticals. New instructions concerning responsibilities for medical waste management and obsolete pharmaceuticals will be issued under the new Laws on Waste Management.

6.6 Conclusions and recommendations

Waste management is one of the environmental protection priorities in Bosnia and Herzegovina, as evidenced in the NEAP, the Mid-term Development Strategy and the Solid Waste Management Strategy and the entities' new Laws on Waste Management.

The focus now should be on implementing the Strategy and the legislation. It is necessary to develop and implement an overall environmentally sound waste management system to reduce the negative environmental impact of municipal waste disposal. Some of the measures to improve the system are: separating municipal waste (paper, plastic and hazardous waste) and, to the extent possible, recycling municipal waste, such as paper, glass, aluminium and organic waste, and industrial waste; separating and incinerating medical waste; ensuring the environmentally sound disposal of radioactive waste; composting organic waste; ensuring the biological treatment of municipal waste; introducing stricter standards for municipal waste disposal; and introducing economic instruments and improving existing financial mechanisms for the overall waste management system. (See also Chapter 2 on economic instruments and privatization.) Energy production from waste should be considered as a longer-term measure. Attention also needs to be given to reducing waste generation at the source and to introducing life-cycle analysis of goods, with particular reference to those that could be recycled (for example, beverage containers, cars, tyres, and batteries).

At present there is no regular reporting system for municipal and industrial waste, although work has begun to introduce such a system under a project financed by the EU. This information is needed to define methods of waste treatment and disposal, allocating the resources and developing concrete measures to improve the overall waste management system.

Recommendation 6.1:
The Federation's Ministry of Physical Planning and Environment and Republika Srpska's Ministry of Physical Planning, Civil Engineering and Ecology, in cooperation with municipalities, should implement the Solid Waste Strategy. To strengthen its implementation, they should:
(a) Raise awareness and organize training in separation, recycling and reuse; and
(b) Undertake feasibility studies for organizing the separate collection of municipal waste and constructing facilities for its recycling and reuse. The studies should also examine economic aspects including the potential market for such recycled or reused goods.

Few landfills meet sanitary requirements. Most landfills, both legal (official) and especially illegal, are neither controlled nor managed. There is no inventory of landfills and no monitoring system for soil, groundwater and air. In many cases illegal landfills are situated along rivers, which has resulted in the contamination of water. At the same time, the construction of new regional sanitary landfills and the rehabilitation of existing landfills have begun.

Recommendation 6.2:
The Federation's Ministry of Physical Planning and Environment and Republika Srpska's Ministry of Physical Planning, Civil Engineering and Ecology, in cooperation with the municipalities and municipal enterprises, should:
(a) Draw up an inventory of legal landfills and elaborate plans to close dumping sites;
(b) Continue the rehabilitation of non-sanitary legal landfills;
(c) Speed up the implementation of the projects for the construction of regional sanitary landfills meeting European Union standards, including the introduction of a monitoring and maintenance system;
(d) Enforce the law against fly-tipping of both municipal and demolition waste along rivers and other unauthorized sites; and

(e) Increase municipal waste services to cover the entire population in the cities and towns and begin to provide such services in rural areas.

The entities' Laws on Waste Management have been developed and adopted, but not yet the relevant regulations, norms and standards based on EU practice and directives. This is especially important for the management of hazardous and medical waste, which is a serious threat to the population and the environment. This implementing legislation needs to be prepared and adopted at the earliest opportunity.

Recommendation 6.3:
(a) The Federation's Ministry of Physical Planning and Environment and Republika Srpska's Ministry of Physical Planning, Civil Engineering and Ecology should take the initiative to set up a single intra- and inter-entity working group on waste with representatives of the following ministries:
  - *Federation: Ministry of Physical Planning and Environment, Ministry of Health and Ministry of Energy, Mining and Industry; and*
  - *Republika Srpska: Ministry of Physical Planning, Civil Engineering and Ecology, Ministry of Health and Social Welfare, and Ministry of Economy, Energy and Development;*
(b) The intra/inter-entity working group on waste should, inter alia:
  - *Agree on the respective responsibilities of the ministries with particular regard to hazardous and medical waste management; and*
  - *Set a timetable for preparing all implementing by-laws for the Laws on Waste Management, including regulations, norms and standards consistent with EU practices. Urgent attention should be given in particular to preparing by-laws dealing with the management of hazardous and medical waste.*

The situation with obsolete pharmaceuticals accumulated during and after the war, hazardous waste and medical waste is very serious. So far there are no separation and treatment facilities for industrial hazardous waste or for medical waste. For medical waste, there are incineration facilities at some hospitals, but they do not meet environmental requirements.

Hazardous waste and medical waste are either dumped together with municipal waste or stored at industrial sites. There is no monitoring system for soil, groundwater and air. No environmental audits of hazardous waste sites or "hot spots" have been conducted.

Some of the obsolete pharmaceuticals have been encapsulated in cement and small quantities have been exported. There is, however, no precise data on how many of the obsolete pharmaceuticals remain, nor where they are stored.

Recommendation 6.4:
The Federation's Ministry of Physical Planning and Environment and Republika Srpska's Ministry of Physical Planning, Civil Engineering and Ecology, in cooperation with relevant ministries, should:
(a) Draw up an inventory of storage facilities for industrial hazardous waste, medical waste and obsolete pharmaceuticals;
(b) Organize the separate collection and environmentally sound incineration of medical waste;
(c) Continue the encapsulation and cementation of obsolete pharmaceuticals;
(d) Conduct environmental audits of industrial "hot spots" and prepare time-bound work plans for their rehabilitation; and
(e) Introduce a system for the separate collection of oil waste and reuse.

At present there is no industrial waste recycling or reuse as secondary raw material. However, such industrial waste as electrofilter ash from thermoelectric plants, red mud from aluminium plants, steel slag and mining waste are valuable sources of secondary raw material that could be used in other industries. Mining waste (overburden), for example, could be used to rehabilitate municipal landfills and repair roads, restore contaminated land for building; spent oil and solvents could be processed to produce low-grade solvents and oil.

Recommendation 6.5:
The Federation's Ministry of Physical Planning and Environment in cooperation with its Ministry of Energy, Mining and Industry and Republika Srpska's Ministry of Physical Planning, Civil Engineering and Ecology in cooperation with its Ministry of Economy, Energy and Development should:

(a) Conduct feasibility studies on the introduction of environmentally sound processes for the use of some categories of waste or its components as secondary raw material; and

(b) Prepare relevant legal acts on recycling and processing secondary raw material.

Chapter 7

WATER MANAGEMENT

7.1 Water resources

Overview

Bosnia and Herzegovina is under the influence of a moderate continental climate in the north and east (the greatest part of the Sava basin) and a maritime climate in the south and west (Adriatic basins). Some parts of the Sava basin, such as Una-Sana canton, have a continental climate with the influence of a maritime regime. The continental climate is characterized by harsh winters and warm summers with the greatest quantity of precipitation during the summer, as opposed to the maritime climate, which is characterized by mild and rainy winters and dry summers. The annual precipitation varies from 800 l/m^2 in the north-east of Bosnia and Herzegovina to 1500 l/m^2 in the south, with an average of 1250 l/m^2.

Bosnia and Herzegovina is therefore rich in water resources compared to the European average of 1000 l/m^2. Damage to the infrastructure during the war combined with insufficient maintenance and an inadequate regulatory framework have, however, brought the water sector into difficulty. The result is that the water resources are exposed to pollution, the quality of drinking water is deteriorating steadily and the flood control infrastructure throughout the country is damaged and deteriorated.

Rivers and lakes

The total outflow from the territory of Bosnia and Herzegovina is 1155 m^3/s, or 57% of total precipitation. Water from the Sava basin, which covers 75.7% of the country, drains to the Black Sea. The main rivers in the Sava basin are the Una-Sana, Vrbas, Bosna, Drina and Sava, with a mean discharge of 722 m^3/s. The first four flow into the river Sava, a tributary of the Danube, which drains into the Black Sea. In the Adriatic Sea catchment area (24.3% of the country), the main rivers are the Neretva, Trebišnjica and Cetina, with a mean discharge of 433 m^3/s. The river Cetina flows entirely through Croatia, but part of its basin is located in Bosnia and Herzegovina.

River lakes and mountain lakes in Bosnia and Herzegovina are important for recreation and tourism, but less so for other water uses. Flooding of karst areas causes periodical lakes in or near the rivers in the Adriatic Sea catchment area, i.e. the Cetina, Neretva and Trebišnjica river basins. The total volume is around 2.5 billion m^3.

There are also 28 artificial reservoirs in Bosnia and Herzegovina with a volume of about 3.6 million m^3, 13 of which are in the Neretva and Trebišnjica river basins and three on the river Drina. The reservoirs are constructed for power generation, but are also important for regulating river flow.

The figures in table 7.1 show that the pressure on water resources varies considerably between the river basins, and that the situation is the most critical in the Bosna river basin, which is home to about 40% of the country's population but has only 14% of its total water run-off.

Groundwater

Bosnia and Herzegovina has relatively abundant groundwater resources, which can be found in three geographically and geologically separate areas. In the north, the groundwater reserves are within alluvial sediments of uneven granulometrical composition along the river Sava and its tributaries. In the centre, groundwater accumulates in the caves and cavities of the limestone massifs and emerges on the surface as lime wells in the Una, Sana, Bosna, Drina, and Neretva river basins. In the south, there are large karst fields within the Adriatic Sea catchment area, and the most abundant groundwater wells are found in the Cetina, Neretva and Trebišnjica river basins.

Table 7.1: Hydrological characteristics of main river basins

River basins	Area (km^2)	Population in 1991	River length (km in Bosnia and Herzegovina)	Average flow (m^3/s)
Total	**51,309**	**4,527,626**	**901**	**1,155**
Black Sea basin	38,899	4,012,266	795	722
Sana (nearby basin)	5,506	635,353	169	63
Una (in Bosnia and Herzegovina)	9,130	620,373	148	240
Vrbas	6,386	514,038	110	132
Bosna	10,457	1,820,080	232	163
Drina (in Bosnia and Herzegovina)	7,420	422,422	136	124
Adriatic Sea	12,410	515,360	106	433
Neretva and Trebisnijca	10,110	436,271	89	402
Cetina (in Bosnia and Herzegovina)	2,300	79,089	18	31

Source: Okvirna vodoprivredna osnova BiH, 1998.

7.2   Water uses and pressures on the resources

The surface water in Bosnia and Herzegovina is, in general, of poor quality and bacteriologically unsafe due to extensive pollution from numerous sources. The main threats to the quality of water are the discharge of municipal or industrial waste water directly into the nearest rivers or springs, the direct disposal of waste in rivers or along riverbanks and run-off from agricultural areas where pesticides and fertilizers are used. The quality of groundwater is in general considered to be good; the data show few examples of groundwater contamination. The lack of reliable data about the quality of surface and groundwater resources is, however, striking, and groundwater contamination might be more widespread.

Drinking-water supply

About half the population has access to public water-supply systems, mainly in urban areas. The rest uses private wells, small village water-supply systems or local systems which are not under national control. Water supply is mainly based on the use of groundwater (89%), 10.2% comes from rivers and 0.8% from natural lakes and artificial reservoirs.

The extracted water is of varying quality, some is drinkable without any kind of treatment but in other cases the quality is totally unacceptable, especially during the dry season. Water treatment is in many cases insufficient, often just chlorination even when the water needs full treatment. Old and leaking pipelines and insufficient pressure could also pollute water before it reaches the consumers. Gross specific consumption in urban areas ranges from 200 to 600 litres/capita/day, of which 100 to 200 litres are supplied to households.

The maintenance of the water pipelines has been neglected for years, and they are now in poor condition. Some are 50-60 years old, and when serious leaks occur the pipes are often so fragile as to be beyond repair. On average about 40% is estimated to leak from the pipelines, but in some bigger cities it is much higher (Sarajevo 50%, Tuzla 60-65%).

In some parts of the country, water shortage is a major problem, especially during the dry season. The situation is the most serious in some rural areas, but water shortages also occur in urban areas. Around Tuzla for instance, people have access to water only a few hours a day during the dry season. In the future water shortages should also be expected in Sarajevo and Banja Luka unless the capacity of the water-supply system is enlarged. In both cities, however, concrete plans have been drawn up to meet the future demand for drinking water.

The shortage of water in some areas is not only due to seasonal factors, but also to insufficient capacity in the water-supply systems. Leaks from pipelines are also adding to this problem. A special problem is caused by migration within the country as a result of the war or by the general movement of people from rural to urban areas. This has led to substantial pressure on the water-supply system in many areas. During the war nearly 2.7 million inhabitants (about 60% of the population) were displaced, 1,170,000 of them internally and 1,250,000 became refugees. This accelerated the already pronounced movement of people from rural to urban areas.

Table 7.2: Drinking water treatment method

Treatment method	Number of municipalities	
	Republika Srpska	Federation of Bosnia and Herzegovina
Disinfection only	42	47
Filtration	3	3
Chemical treatment	7	13
Number of municipalities	52	63

Source: National Environmental Action Plan (NEAP). Thematic document No. 02. Integrated Water Resources Managemet. Bosnia and Herzegovina, April 2002 (figures for RS) and e-mail information from Public Enterprise "Vodno Podrucje Slivova Rijeke Save", January 2004 (figures for Fed. BiH).

Note: Total number of municipalities in the Federation of Bosnia and Herzegovina is 84, in Republika Srpska 65.

Agricultural uses

Irrigation systems are not very well developed. In fact, only 2% of the total arable land of about 1,123,000 ha is irrigated compared to the world average of 15%. The lack of water during the vegetation period is the key factor limiting the development of modern agriculture, in particular in the west toward the Adriatic Sea. Even if the percentage of irrigated land is higher in this region, the irrigation systems have been seriously damaged due to poor maintenance and the war. The potential for irrigation of arable land in this region has been estimated at approximately 155,000 ha, while only 4,630 ha are irrigated today.

Hydro energy

Bosnia and Herzegovina's total hydropower potential is estimated at 6,100 MW, mostly located within the Drina, Neretva and Trebišnjica river basins. Less than 40% of this potential is so far used, so about 40% of the country's energy production today comes from hydropower. Analyses show that increased use of hydropower would not only be justified from an economic point of view, but would also have positive environmental repercussions (lower emissions of greenhouse gases and fewer discharges of waste water) compared to increasing the use of thermal (coal) energy. Building artificial reservoirs for hydropower could also be advantageous with regard to flood protection, and could make new irrigation systems possible.

Protection from floods

A total area of 250,000 ha is threatened by flooding. This is 4% of the total territory or about 60% of the lowlands. Urban areas that are particularly vulnerable are Tuzla, Banja Luka, Celinac, Prnjavor, Derventa, Modrica, Janja, Zvornik and settlements along the river Sava. Before the war, substantial investments were made to protect agricultural land and urban areas from flooding, mainly along the rivers Sava and Neretva and their tributaries. In 1992 there were about 420 km of dikes, 220 km of boundary channels, 80 km of flood regulation channels and 30 pumping stations with a capacity of 120 m^3/s, and about 80,000 ha of land was protected.

Since the outbreak of the war investment in new flood protection facilities has stopped, and the resources for maintaining existing facilities have been negligible. Some of the installations were also used for military purposes and damaged so badly during the war that they no longer function properly. For instance, the structure of some dikes has been damaged as a result of bunkers being built inside the dikes. In addition mines have been laid around some flood protection installations.

Floods cause enormous damage to crops, private property and infrastructure, lead to the erosion of arable land and increase the likelihood of landslides, in particular along the Sava, but also in other parts of Bosnia and Herzegovina. For instance, the flooding in the Tuzla region in June 2001 was estimated to have caused damage worth approximately € 30 million. In other regions, where there are no flood protection systems at all, the consequences of exceptional high water might be even worse.

To prevent, control and mitigate floods, structural flood protection measures are not sufficient. As set out, for example, in the 2000 UNECE Guidelines on sustainable flood prevention and the recent EU best practice document on the same issue, a combination of structural and non-structural flood protection measures, including the conservation or rehabilitation of natural wetlands and retention areas, is needed.

The past ten years have passed without very high streams in Bosnia and Herzegovina. Situations with exceptionally high water levels must, however, be expected in the future. Unless adequate measures are taken urgently, enormous material damage caused by floods must be expected.

Municipal waste water

In the former Socialist Republic of Bosnia and Herzegovina, the construction and maintenance of sewerage systems and treatment facilities for municipal waste water got limited attention and few resources. The result was that not all towns and cities had sewer systems, and even in the cities where they did exist they often served only part of the population. Today about 30% of the population has access to sewerage systems. In urban areas the connection rate for households is 56%, but in villages and rural areas a maximum of 10% of the households are connected. Due to the lack of resources the sewerage systems are on the whole poorly maintained. In many cases they have not even been completed, often only partially designed and constructed. In some locations the capacity is insufficient for receiving storm waters, and the systems overflow during the rainy season, affecting around 65% of the municipal centres.

At the outbreak of the civil war 1992-95, only seven municipal waste-water treatment plants were built and in operation. Except for one plant, the treatment included biological treatment. The treatment plants were located in Sarajevo, Trebinje, Trnovo, Ljubuski, Grude, Celinac and Gradacac. These plants treated waste water from about 484,000 inhabitants of a total population of about 4.4 million. The treatment plant in Sarajevo was considerably bigger than all the others and received waste water from about 454,000 inhabitants (94% of people with access to waste-water treatment plant before the war) compared to 30,000 inhabitants for all the other plants combined. During the war, five of the seven plants were closed due to war damage, stripping of equipment and installations, lack of maintenance or shortage of electricity. After the war all the plants were put into operation again, except the plants in Sarajevo and Trnovo, and a new treatment plant has been built in Srebrenik. The plants in operation today are, however, all very small, and more than 95% of the municipal waste water is discharged directly into water bodies without any kind of treatment.

Industry, manufacturing and mining

Heavy industry was predominant before the war and the main polluter of watercourses. Combined with weak implementation of environmental measures and the use of obsolete, polluting technologies, industry's impact on water quality was devastating. In 1991 the industrial waste-water load was equivalent to a population of 6.8 million people. By comparison the municipal waste-water load was equivalent to a population of 2.7 million. The huge discharges of waste water polluted almost all rivers, especially the rivers Bosna and Vrbas. Most of the industrial waste water was, like municipal waste water, discharged to the nearest watercourse with little or no treatment. For instance, there were 122 plants for the treatment of industrial waste water before the war, but only 40% of them worked properly.

As many industrial plants have shut down and many others have reduced their capacity, the discharge of pollutants to air and water from industry has been substantially reduced and is today approximately 30-35% of its pre-war level. The big reduction in discharges of industrial waste water has led to a significant improvement in water quality. However, the industrial waste-water load is disproportionately high because there are few treatment facilities for industrial waste water in operation, and the negative pressure on water resources is still very high. When industry recovers from the setback caused by the war, river pollution will rapidly get worse unless waste-water treatment facilities are put in place.

Mining and ore processing are an important sector in Bosnia and Herzegovina. The most important mineral deposits are those of coal, lead, zinc, iron and bauxite. For instance, more than 100 coal deposits are registered. The significant reduction in industrial operating capacity has led to a similar reduction in activity within the mining and ore sector. The production rate for mining and ore processing has declined to about 33% of its pre-war level. Coal and other ore and stone production have been reduced to 40% and 23%, respectively.

When rocks containing sulphuric minerals are exposed to water and air, the ongoing oxidation and acidification will accelerate, and trace metals leach out to the environment. The environmental impact of mining activities on water resources arises at almost all stages of the production phase, and does not end with the completion of mining activity. On the contrary, the environmental impact can last for centuries after the closure of the mine through seepage from waste rock piles, tailing dams and seepage water from abandoned pits and quarries. Acid mine water containing heavy metals represents a serious threat to the environment and to human health in Bosnia and Herzegovina. The problem with mine water pollution is, however, not recognized or regulated, and today there is no treatment of seepage water at all.

Waste disposal

Uncontrolled dumping of waste (fly-tipping) directly into or close to watercourses is a widespread problem and a major threat to water quality, especially in the Bosna, Drina and Una river basins. Hazardous waste from mining and industry is usually dumped at landfills close to the plants or at nearby municipal landfills of poor standards, often directly on the ground without any kind of underground sealing or collection and treatment of seepage water. Coal power plants, the wood and paper industry, the chemical industry and mineral oil processing, the textile and leather processing industry and the metal finishing industry are, in addition to the mining sector, the largest producers of hazardous waste in Bosnia and Herzegovina. The result is that significant environmental problems have been identified in several locations, for instance in Samac, Sava river alluvium (where the spring sources for the drinking-water supply are located), Bijeljina, Modrica, Gorazde and Visegrad.

Fly-tipping of household waste is very visible along the rivers, with plastic and other waste floating on the surface of the water or hanging in bushes and trees along the riverbanks. This is, however, mainly an esthetic problem. A more serious effect on the environment is probably that the waste is a significant source of river pollution with hazardous chemicals. Household waste is also adding to the overall pollution with organic matter, but its contribution is assumed to be rather small compared to other sources.

Forestry and soil erosion

Forestry is an important sector in Bosnia and Herzegovina with about 50% of the total land area, or 2.5 million ha, covered by forests. The intensive use of forest resources combined with outdated technology is, however, causing much organic pollution of many rivers. Another serious consequence of deforestation is increased soil erosion. Deforested and eroded areas were further damaged because they lost their ability to retain precipitation, which caused sudden run-off and increased the risk of flooding. This risk will also increase as a result of deposits in reservoirs and riverbeds in plain areas, which reduce their capacity to receive and transport water. Increased soil erosion will also have a negative influence on the quality of water by increasing its turbidity.

7.3 Policies, strategies and legislative framework

The policy framework

The National Environmental Action Plan (NEAP) of March 2003, drawn up by the entities in cooperation with the World Bank, has a brief chapter on integrated water resources management that sets goals and measures for the water sector. Its main goals are to provide sufficient quantities of high-quality water for water supply and other needs; to protect water resources and preserve surface and groundwater quality; and to protect from flooding.

The Mid-term Development Strategy (2004-2007), adopted by the Council of Ministers on 5 February 2004, notes that the sustainable development of water management requires more attention being paid to: the protection against water-related hazards, the planned use of water resources, and water conservation and protection. The emphasis is on integrated river-basin water management. The Mid-term Development Strategy also identifies nine development priorities for water:
- Repairing flood-control facilities along the rivers Sava and Neretva;
- Regulating the river beds and torrential watercourses in the most vulnerable areas;
- Ensuring an adequate supply of clean water to inhabited areas;
- Improving the quality of water supplied to the rural population;
- Creating the right conditions for the restoration of navigation on the river Sava in cooperation with Croatia, Slovenia, and Serbia and Montenegro;
- Repairing and renovating sewerage systems and rehabilitating water treatment plants for urban waste water, as well as building new ones;
- Introducing measures to protect existing and potential sources of drinking water;

- Ensuring a sufficient volume of water to irrigate cultivated land for intensive farming; and
- Increasing the level of exploitation of hydroenergy by building multipurpose water management facilities not only for power generation but also for the development of tourism and recreation, flood control, irrigation and fish farming, among other activities.

A memorandum of understanding between the Council of Ministers of Bosnia and Herzegovina, the Government of the Federation of Bosnia and Herzegovina, the Government of Republika Srpska and the Commission of the European Communities was signed in September 2004. In it, the Parties agree to reorganize the water sector and to use the EU Water Framework Directive for the purpose of establishing a new water policy.

The legislative framework

Pursuant to the Dayton Peace Agreement, water management is the responsibility of the two entities. There is no responsibility at the State level, although this is likely to change in the near future. In the draft memorandum of understanding with the European Communities, referred to above, the Parties agree to develop a new water law and sub-laws, as well as new organizational and institutional frameworks, based on the principles and goals of the EU Water Directive. Until now, however, two separate legal systems have been developed.

Republika Srpska's Law on Water Protection was adopted in 2002 (Official Gazette RS 53/2002). It establishes river basins (Danube and Adriatic Sea), river sub-basins (Una-Sana, Sava, Drina, Bosna, Vrbas and Trebišnjica) and parts of river sub-basins as the territorial basis for water protection, planning and implementation. The Law calls for the development of a minimum ten-year water protection strategy and protection plans for Republika Srpska, to be an integral part of the National Environmental Action Plan unless an inter-entity agreement states differently. The Law further stipulates that "water protection consent" is required before other permits (e.g. environmental, construction) will be issued, and it establishes an inspection system.

The Law on Water Protection of the Federation of Bosnia and Herzegovina (Official Gazette F BiH 33/2003) was adopted in 2003 and is almost identical. It, too, establishes a regime based on river basin district bodies (Danube and Adriatic Sea) and

sub-basins (Una, Sana, Sava, Vrbas, Bosna, Drina, Trebišnjica, Neretva and Cetina). It calls for the adoption of a ten-year water protection strategy for the Federation, which may be part of the National Environmental Protection Programme, and it establishes consent and inspection systems.

Both Laws intend to ensure that water protection in Bosnia and Herzegovina is in line with EU policy, directives, regulations and standards.

The Federation's cantons also have water laws. In addition, the Federation's Ministry of Agriculture, Water Management and Forestry is finalizing a new water act to address water management.

In 1998 both entities also adopted Laws on Water, which address both water management and water protection, but they do not generally meet EU requirements.

International cooperation

The lack of State institutions to handle water issues have made foreign relations difficult. The result is that Bosnia and Herzegovina has not signed any major multilateral environment and water protection treaties since 1992. It is an observer only to important conventions like the Convention on the Protection and Use of Transboundary Watercourses and International Lakes and the Convention on Cooperation for the Protection and Sustainable Use of the Danube River. As it is not a Signatory to these treaties, Bosnia and Herzegovina cannot obtain financial and technical assistance to implement and monitor international procedures or standards.

The Government has, however, undertaken procedures for the ratification of the Convention on Cooperation for the Protection and Sustainable Use of the Danube River, and is expected to become a Party in the near future. Bosnia and Herzegovina became a Party to the Convention for the Protection of the Marine Environment and the Coastal Region of the Mediterranean (Barcelona Convention) by succession in 1998 (Official Gazette SFRJ IA 12/77; Official Gazette BiH 26/98) and to its four protocols, but has not accepted the 1995 Amendments. To increase cooperation on transboundary waters Bosnia and Herzegovina has also ratified the Framework Agreement on the Sava River Basin, which it signed on 3 December 2002 along with Croatia, Serbia and Montenegro, and Slovenia. The Agreement, which covers all surface water and groundwater of the Sava catchment, aims at establishing an international regime of navigation and sustainable water management. It foresees the drafting of specific protocols to further regulate cooperation on such issues as protection against floods; control of excessive groundwater use; erosion; ice hazards; drought and water shortages and accidental water pollution; protection and improvement of water quality and quantity; and protection of aquatic ecosystems. Bosnia and Herzegovina has also established bilateral cooperation on water with Croatia.

The institutional framework

With the adoption of the entities' new Laws on Water Protection, some questions have arisen regarding institutional responsibility.

The Federation's 1998 Law on Waters assigned responsibility for water management primarily to its Ministry of Agriculture, Water Management and Forestry, two public water management corporations, the cantonal ministries of agriculture, water management and forestry, and municipal authorities responsible for water management. However, the Federation's 2003 Law on Water Protection assigned primary authority to its Ministry of Physical Planning and Environment, with considerable devolution of responsibility for water protection to river Authorities.

The situation is similar in Republika Srpska. The 1998 Law designated the Ministry of Agriculture, Forestry and Water Management and the Directorate for Waters as the institutions responsible for water management. The municipalities were responsible for water supply and sewerage systems, while public utilities were the responsibility of the Ministry of Physical Planning, Civil Engineering and Ecology. The 2002 Law on Water Protection assigned responsibility for "certain issues of water protection" to the Ministry "responsible for environmental protection".

According to the 1998 Laws, the entities' Ministries of Agriculture, Forestry and Water Management are responsible for drawing up strategies, policies and regulations for the management and protection of water resources, issuing agreements and permits, setting standards and securing the enforcement of laws and regulations through licensing and inspections. Republika Srpska's Ministry of Physical Planning, Civil Engineering and Ecology and the Federation's Ministry of Physical Planning and Environment are

responsible for water issues in relation to environmental protection, including setting standards, and monitoring and control. The entities' Ministries of Health are responsible for safeguarding the quality of drinking water.

The new Laws on Water Protection imply that the "Environment Ministries" would develop water protection strategies and by-laws. In addition, in the Federation, a river basin district steering committee would be established for each river basin district with one representative from each of the following: the Ministry of Physical Planning and Environment, each participating canton, the agricultural sector, the respective public company, the main water utility of the river basin district and an appropriate non-governmental organization. The river basin district body is to be responsible for inspections.

In Republika Srpska, a "special organization for water management and protection in the river basin" would be set up. All other issues that are important for the organization of the river basin are to be specified in a special law. A steering committee would also be set up, with one representative each from: the Ministry of Physical Planning, Civil Engineering and Ecology, each town or municipality in the river basin, the agricultural sector, the respective public company responsible for water management, the main water utility of the river basin and an NGO.

The new Laws on Water Protection do not make reference to the 1998 Laws, and it is not clear how the institutional responsibilities identified in the new Laws will affect or be affected by those contained in the 1998 Laws. Further specification is needed to implement the new Laws fully.

In the Federation of Bosnia and Herzegovina some competences for licensing and the allocation of water are delegated to the cantons. For instance, the cantons are responsible for providing drinking water to municipalities that do not have adequate resources themselves by ensuring the construction of water-supply systems to the border of these municipalities. The municipalities themselves are responsible for further distribution to the consumers. The cantons are also responsible for ensuring the construction of installations and equipment needed for waste-water treatment to protect drinking water resources.

Under the Federation's Ministry of Agriculture, Water Management and Forestry two public enterprises have been established, one for the watershed of the Sava and one for Adriatic Sea watershed. The enterprises are responsible, for instance, for the management of rivers and the nearby zones and for the protection of water and water sources to ensure that enough good-quality water is available for the water supply. They also monitor water quality and collect fees for water abstraction and discharges. In Republika Srpska the Public Water Management Enterprise has similar responsibilities for the whole entity. It reports to the Ministry of Agriculture, Forestry and Water Management. These public enterprises do not have direct links with the entities' Environment Ministries. This, together with the responsibilities of these public enterprises and the new river Authorities, is another arrangement that requires clarification under the new Laws on Water Protection.

The municipalities in both entities are responsible for building and operating the water-supply and sewerage systems and the treatment facilities for waste water. In Republika Srpska they are also responsible for urban flood protection. This is not the case in the Federation.

Almost all the main rivers in Bosnia and Herzegovina cross the entities' borders, and there is a considerable need for cooperation and coordination of actions and instruments between the two entities. The Inter-entity Commission for Water was therefore established in 1998 with four members from each entity. The Commission is responsible for the cooperation between the relevant ministries in both entities for all water management issues, including harmonization of regulations and water quality. So far it has been a useful body for sharing information and initiating action of mutual interest. However, if the entities' interests are contradictory, it is difficult for the Commission to make the necessary decisions, and in such cases there is little or no progress.

Many of these issues of coordination and responsibility are addressed in the draft memorandum of understanding with the European Communities. In the existing draft, it is agreed that the Council of Ministers would establish an environment agency at the State level, which would, inter alia, "bear responsibilities in the water sector for fulfilling the following main obligations:

- Address all international issues dealing with water;

- All matters of common interest that the entities want to bring at State level;
- Harmonize data collection/dissemination (IS Standardization/training);
- Assessment of technical performance of river authorities and water boards;
- National public awareness campaign; and
- Coordination of the planning and management of all international and inter-entity flood control projects."

As a part of the memorandum of understanding, the Parties also "pledge" that they will establish river authorities in the entities which will enjoy legal and financial autonomy. The river authorities will, among other things, plan all water and water-related environmental projects within their jurisdiction; collect and process data and maintain the water database; license water abstraction, discharge and water regime changes; and control and monitor floods and flood defence.

Bosnia and Herzegovina has already established water agencies for the river basin Bosna and the river basin Vrbas as pilot projects. The intention is to have water authorities for all river sub-basins, including, as defined in the Laws on Waters, the Una-Sana, Sava, Vrbas, Bosna, Drina, Trebišnjica, Neretva and Cetina.

Monitoring

From 1965 to the outbreak of the war, data for both water quality and quantity were collected from 58 monitoring stations all over the country. During the war, all monitoring stations were destroyed, and there were no data available for the period 1992-97. Since the end of the war the monitoring network has been gradually re-established, partly with financial contributions from donors. Still, the number of monitoring stations seems to be far too low, and few automatically measure both water levels and water-quality parameters. At the other monitoring sites, water quality is measured only occasionally, when funding is available.

To meet the need for reliable data and information on water quality, the information needs for decision-making and water management should be analysed thoroughly before a decision is made to increase significantly the number of monitoring stations, the number of analysed parameters and the frequency of sampling. In any case, the laboratories will have to be upgraded because most of them lack proper equipment for analysing water quality.

Water pricing

The price of water supply and waste-water discharges is far too low to cover the full costs, and the sector is either subsidized by the entities, cantons or municipalities, or it suffers from insufficient maintenance that will jeopardize the water-supply and waste-water systems in the long run. Due to the economic crisis and the poor service, there is, however, stiff resistance against increasing the tariffs. Illegal connections and inadequate systems for collecting the tariffs are also adding to this problem. (See chapter 2, on economic instruments and privatization)

Table 2.2 in chapter 2 shows differences between average water and waste-water tariffs for households in the two entities and some European countries.

7.4 Conclusions and recommendations

Bosnia and Herzegovina is endowed with abundant water resources though they are unevenly distributed and most precipitation comes when it is least needed. However, there should be no doubt that water resources provide an important economic potential for the future.

The quality of water resources is endangered by pollution from various sources, e.g. organic pollution and hazardous substances from municipal and industrial waste water, uncontrolled landfills and tips, industry and mining, pesticides and fertilizers, deforestation and soil erosion. The quality of surface water is considerably influenced by all this pollution, while the quality of groundwater with some exceptions is still quite good. There is, however, an urgent need to take action to prevent the large-scale contamination of groundwater.

To enable prosperous exploitation of the water resources, a number of shortcomings in the water sector have to be overcome. They include a weak and non-transparent administration, an incomplete or confusing legal framework and an unclear division of responsibilities between different authorities.

Recommendation 7.1:
(a) The Government of the State of Bosnia and Herzegovina, in cooperation with the Government of the Federation of Bosnia and Herzegovina and the Government of Republika Srpska, should develop and adopt a new State water law based on the EU Directive that would, inter alia, establish autonomous river authorities.
(b) The Government of the Federation of Bosnia and Herzegovina and the Government of Republika Srpska should adopt the new Water law, which will include institutional responsibilities for both water protection and water management.

The water infrastructure was severely damaged during the war, and even before the war the water-supply systems suffered from a lack of investment and maintenance. So although it is estimated that 90% of the water-supply sector has been rehabilitated to its pre-war level, it still does not reach international standards. The quality of drinking water is on the whole mediocre, and for the nearly 50% of the population who do not have access to public water-supply systems the water quality is probably even more questionable.

Recommendation 7.2:
(a) The Government of the State of Bosnia and Herzegovina, in cooperation with the Government of the Federation of Bosnia and Herzegovina and the Government of Republika Srpska, should develop a new water policy pursuant to the memorandum of understanding with the European Communities and taking into account the Millennium Development Goal to halve by 2015 the proportion of people without access to safe drinking water.
(b) The Federation's Ministry of Physical Planning and Environment and Republika Srpska's Ministry of Physical Planning, Civil Engineering and Ecology, in cooperation with their Ministries of Agriculture, Forestry and Water Management, should start now to:
  (i) Ensure that drinking water is safe by properly treating abstracted water;
  (ii) Develop water protection strategies consistent with the new State policy and the Millennium Development Goals;
  (iii) Establish standards and norms for water quality which are consistent with international ones; and
  (iv) Reduce the leaks from the distribution systems by repairing and replacing old and damaged pipelines. The number of households with access to public water-supply systems should be substantially increased.
(c) As soon as they are established, the river authorities should develop plans for river basin management.

Discharges of untreated municipal waste water have a major impact on the quality of surface water in most of Bosnia and Herzegovina, and they are also potential threats to the quality of groundwater, which are the main source of drinking water. However, the most serious impact is on public health and the environment.

Recommendation 7.3:
The entities' Ministries of Agriculture, Forestry and Water Management in cooperation with the entities' Ministries of environment and with the help of the public enterprises for water management, should assist and require the municipalities to reduce the negative impact of waste-water discharges by:

(a) Reducing the leaks from public sewerage systems and by building new sewerage systems to substantially increase the number of household connections;
(b) Building municipal waste-water treatment plants of environmentally high standards and with sufficient treatment capacity in all the big cities; and
(c) Ensuring that sewage sludge from municipal treatment plants and septic tanks is sufficiently treated for use as fertilizer in agriculture or disposal in sanitary landfills.

Waste water from industrial plants containing organic and hazardous substances are, with very few exceptions, discharged into the nearest watercourse with little or no treatment. This is also true for seepage water containing hazardous substances from mining and ore-processing. The negative impact on water quality is considerable, and there is no doubt that these discharges could represent a threat to public health and the environment. Moreover, this situation must be expected to get much worse when industry recovers from the devastating effects of the war, unless proper action is taken.

Recommendation 7.4:
The Federation's Ministry of Physical Planning and Environment and Republika Srpska's Ministry of Physical Planning, Civil Engineering and Ecology, in cooperation with the other ministries

involved, should take appropriate action to reduce the negative environmental impact of waste-water discharges from industry and seepage water from mining and manufacturing by:

(a) Ensuring that water treatment plants are reconstructed and brought on stream again;
(b) Drawing up a survey of the most polluting mining, manufacturing and other industries; and
(c) Instructing mining, manufacturing and other industries to take immediate and appropriate action to stop or reduce the discharges where drinking-water resources are seriously threatened.

Flood protection installations have been poorly maintained, and dikes, channels and pumping stations were damaged or destroyed during the war. Some large areas that are exposed to flooding do not have flood protection installations at all. Since the end of the war Bosnia and Herzegovina has not experienced extremely high water levels, even if a flood in the Tuzla region caused large-scale damage in 2001. However, extremely high water levels must be expected in the future. If there is no proper flood protection in place, they could cause many casualties and much material damage.

Recommendation 7.5:
The proposed environment agency, with the Federation's Ministry of Agriculture, Water Management and Forestry and Republika Srpska's Ministry of Agriculture, Forestry and Water Management, should work in close cooperation with the new river authorities on an urgent basis to reduce the impacts of floods. Steps to be taken include:

(a) Improving and repairing, in cooperation with the regional and local authorities, existing flood protection systems and building new ones in exposed areas that do not have them, and taking non-structural measures for flood protection, in particular the conservation or rehabilitation of natural wetlands and retention areas; and
(b) Drawing up a comprehensive national flood disaster strategy, which includes preparedness, mitigation, recovery and reconstruction.

Chapter 8

BIODIVERSITY AND FOREST MANAGEMENT

8.1   Current state of nature

Landscapes and ecosystems

Bosnia and Herzegovina is located in the west of the Balkan Peninsula. Due to its complex geological history, especially during the glaciation periods, its central position in the Balkan Peninsula, access to the Mediterranean Sea, and the Dinaric mountain range, its biodiversity is extraordinarily rich. The most important physical-geographic features that support this biodiversity are a very diverse and developed relief, different climate types, the variety of soils, a developed hydrographic system, and the long and rich cultural history.

According to the relief the country can be divided into three main parts: the northern flatland along the river Sava (5% of the total land area), the hilly (24%) and mountainous (42%) central part; and the southern karstic region (29%), characterized by different karstic meso and micro relief forms. The average altitude is about 500 m. The mountains lie in a northwest-southeast direction and belong to the Dinaric mountain range. The highest peak is Maglic at 2,387 m above sea level. The mountains are cut by numerous valleys and gorges, which represent important refugia for biodiversity, especially glacial relicts. The Dinaric mountain range divides the country into two major watersheds: the Black Sea (75.7% of the territory) and the Adriatic Sea (24.3%).

The climate in the country varies from moderate continental to continental to Mediterranean. Average annual precipitation is very high – 1250 mm – but its distribution is uneven, both spatially and seasonally (see chapter 7 on water management). The main landscape types are: (i) Mediterranean landscapes (Neum-Klek), (ii) supra-Mediterranean landscapes (lower flow of Neretva, southeast and southwest Herzegovina), (iii) Mediterranean highland landscapes (eastern and western upper Herzegovina), (iv) highland (hill) landscapes (central, eastern and western Bosnia), (v) mountain landscapes, and (vi) Pannonian landscapes (north Bosnia – Posavina). These landscapes include a great diversity of subtypes and kinds. Although many of the landscapes have been degraded through anthropogenic activities, a large portion of the natural ecosystems remain in their pristine natural or semi-natural form.

In addition, major ecosystem types abound with a great diversity of habitats ranging from bare rocks (especially in the karstic region – Mediterranean highland landscapes), to different grasslands, a variety of broadleaf and coniferous forests and wetlands. There is no inventory of all these habitats according to the methodology of European conventions (Bern Convention particularly) or directives (Habitat Directive), although an extensive and precise phytocoenological division exists in the scientific literature. The terms of reference for a COoRdination of INformation on the Environment (CORINE) Biotope project has been prepared, but the project has not yet been carried out. The CORINE project will provide the basis for the transposition of a purely scientific phytocoenological division onto an applied habitat-based division of Bosnia and Herzegovina's biodiversity, and it will enable registration of its habitat types into common European databases.

Species diversity

Bosnia and Herzegovina has rich species diversity, corresponding to the ecosystem and habitat diversity. According to data published in a 2002 study on the influence of forestry on biologically sensitive areas by the Federation's Institute for the Protection of Cultural, Historical and Natural Heritage, there are about 3,700 species of spermatophytes, 60 species of pteridophytes, 250 mosses, 250 lichens and about 520 fungal species. Other sources estimate the number of fungal species at several thousands. There are no reliable data on the number of bacterial and algal species. Vascular flora is plentiful with endemic species. About 30% of the total endemic species in the Balkans can be found in Bosnia and Herzegovina (540 species). Several centres of floral endemism are recognized in the centre, south-east and north-west of the Dinaric Mountains, central Balkan and Adriatic areas.

The fauna inventories are more advanced, but the data are scattered in different scientific papers and not accessible to the broader public. However, it is known that animal diversity is very rich.

The threats to species are many and increasing. Endemic species are especially threatened since they are in few areas, which are under high anthropogenic pressure. Examples of the threats include unbalanced land management (urbanization, transport infrastructure), degradation of wetlands, extensive livestock-breeding, drying of high mountain pit-bogs, buildings and infrastructure above the upper timber zone, pollution of natural freshwater ecosystems, introduction of alien species, and excessive exploitation of natural resources. The lack of a biodiversity strategy makes it virtually impossible to develop action plans or take other measures to protect the threatened species.

One of the actions that are necessary is the production and adoption of red data books and lists of flora, fungi and fauna according to the World Conservation Union (IUCN) methodology. There are various scientific papers that contain information on biodiversity, and these could be a source of information for anyone preparing red data lists. At present, however, there are no such lists. Red books for some animal groups are being prepared. There do not appear to be any real obstacles to preparing, adopting and publishing red data books.

In addition to wild flora and fauna diversity, there are many domesticated plant varieties and animal breeds registered in Bosnia and Herzegovina. These include fruit varieties, grapevines and vegetables, as well as indigenous breeds of cattle, sheep, goats, horses, donkeys and dogs. The most important threat to this rich agrobiodiversity is its decreasing economic value (see chapter 10, on agriculture and environment).

Brčko District's biodiversity is very well documented. There is an extensive study on its habitats, flora, fungi and fauna as part of a broader study, "Evaluation of Natural Values of the Environment in Brčko District". The study was carried out by the Sarajevo Centre for Ecology and Natural Resources at the Faculty of Science (CEPRES) in 2002 with the assistance of experts from the two entities at the request of the District's Government. It is complex and extensive and could be a basis for developing the District's environmental policy.

Little attention has been paid to biodiversity in the Adriatic Sea, partly because Bosnia and Herzegovina has a short coastline and partly because until recently (in the former Yugoslavia) sea investigation and protection was the responsibility of Croatian institutes. None of the available biodiversity documents or even the recent National Environmental Action Plan (NEAP) mentions the Adriatic coast and Sea. Yet, the Adriatic is threatened by industry, traffic related to the harbour and tourism. Due to the poor economic situation and the recent war, solving the problems related to biological diversity has been given a low priority.

Forests

About half the country is covered with forest or is declared forestland (see fig. 8.2). Of the total forest area, 81.3% belongs to the State and 18.7% is private. However, more than half the forest is low forest or shrub land (see fig. 8.3). Most of the low forests are in the lower oak region bearing the highest human impact since they are close to human settlements. About 10% of the country is bare land (or about one fifth of the forestland). Much of the low forest and shrub land is in the karstic and sub-Mediterranean region. It has little production value, but is important from a biodiversity point of view as it shelters a number of endemic species.

Another important characteristic is the presence of large portions of virgin forests or forests in a near-natural state. A very well known example is the Perucica virgin forest (in Sutjeska National Park) and other smaller reserves of about 2,000 hectares. Most of the other forests are naturally reproduced, thus maintaining the original gene fund. There are more than 25 distinct forest communities on the country's Map of Potential Vegetation, excluding refugial and azonal communities on restricted areas.

The forests are facing many threats, related mostly to the war and to post-war activities. The basic threats are minefields (it is assumed that more than 10% of the forest area is still mined), degradation due to the illegal exploitation and uncontrolled change in land use in favour of urbanization and infrastructure. Mines are a big problem since access to many forests is limited and interventions during forest fires and forest disease outbreaks are impossible.

Figure 8.1: Map of forests

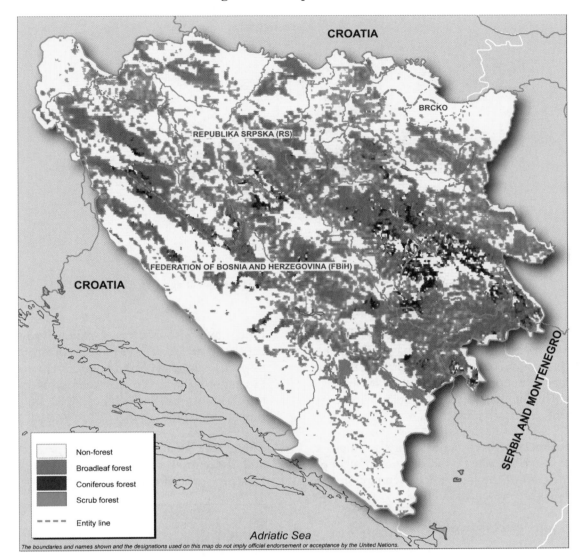

Protected areas

According to the Law on Nature Protection of the Federation of Bosnia and Herzegovina (Official Gazette F BiH 33/2003) and the Law on Nature Protection of Republika Srpska (Official Gazette RS 50/2002), there are four types of protected areas: nature protection areas, national parks, natural monuments and landscape protection areas.

Although many areas were protected in the former Yugoslavia, the total protected area is very small (0.55%). This is among the lowest percentages in Europe, and it is likely one of the reasons that the NEAP identifies the enlargement of protected areas as a priority. The 1981-2000 Physical Plan for

Bosnia and Herzegovina proposed 16 national parks and adopted a target for protected areas of 16% of the territory; however, due to the intervening war, this goal was not achieved.

The current structure of the protected areas' system, which remains based on the old system used by the former Yugoslavia, does not correspond to the categorization in the new Laws on Nature Protection or to the IUCN classification. It is therefore important to revise the system in line with the new Laws. Such a revision should also include different ecosystems in the system, since at present most protected areas are forests. The current types and the number of protected areas and individual species are presented in table 8.1.

Figure 8.2: Forest structure

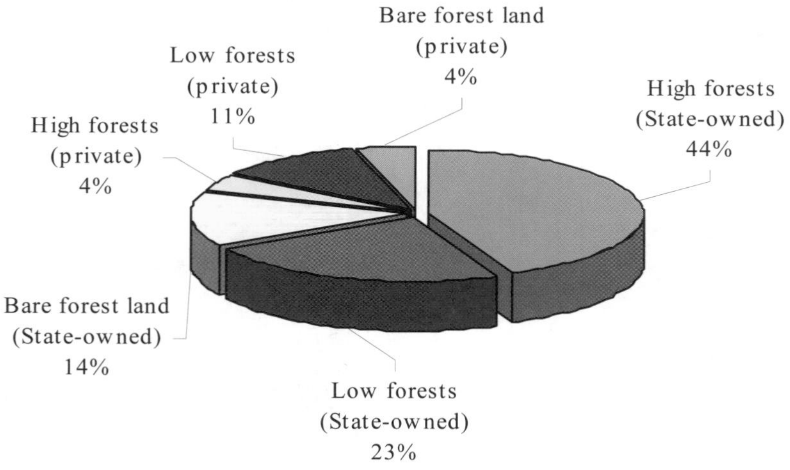

Source: Federation's Ministry of Agriculture, Water Management and Forestry, 2003.

Of the small area that is officially protected, little is really protected. There are no management plans, and the protection regime in the protected areas (except for the national parks and the new Hutovo Blato and Blidinje nature parks) does not meet the requirements of nature protection.

There have recently been major efforts to improve the system and to enlarge the area of protection with the support of the international community. A few examples are presented in box 8.1.

8.2   Pressures on biodiversity

Forestry

According to the new Law on Forests of the Federation (Official Gazette of FBiH 20/02 and 29/03) and Law on Forests of Republika Srpska (Official Gazette of RS 66/03), the entities should develop forest management plans for a period of 10 years and annual management plans. These plans, even the new ones, are based on very old forest inventories (from the 1960s) and are outdated.

The new Laws created an institutional base for the preservation and protection of forests, established guidelines for programming and planning for forest management (e.g. forest cut, reproduction, protection against pests, sanitary cuts, wood and other forest products), set practices for management of special forest regimes (protected forests and forest for special use), and covered issues such as ownership, the cadastre, financing and supervision.

Both Laws also addressed national parks, nature parks and nature reserves in the forests and, in this respect, overlap with the entities' Laws on Nature Protection and create confusion regarding responsibilities. (See section 8.3, on the legal framework, below.)

Table 8.1: Protected objects (protected areas and individual species) according to the 1965 Law on Nature Protection

I	Strict natural reserves	5	
II	Managed natural reserves	3	
III	National parks	2	
IV	Special reserves	14	
	Geological		6
	Botanical*		6
	Ornithological		2
V	Natural landscape reserves	16	
VI	Individual plant species	7	
VII	Individual animal species**	257	[++]
VIII	Monuments of nature	141	
	Geological***		1
	Geomorphological[+]		93
	Paleonthological		2
	Individual stems		39
	Groups of stems		5
	Tree lines		1
IX	Memorial monuments of nature	7	

Source: Law on Nature Protection (Official Gazette SR BiH No. 4/65)

Notes:

* *Picea omorika* (one of six) - in 16 localities

** in five categories - one mammal, one amphibian and the rest are birds

*** sedra (gipsum) in eight localities

[+] Category "Sources" comprises 25 different springs

[++] Not included in the total number

Box 8.1:   Proposals for enlarging the system of protected areas

Igman/ Bjelašnica feasibility study, 2001: The Igman/ Bjelašnica feasibility study is a sub-component of the National Forestry Programme implemented by the World Bank and EU PHARE with financial support from the Governments of Italy and Norway. The study examines the feasibility of declaring a new national park in the Igman/ Bjelašnica area, close to Sarajevo. The area supports at least 32 globally threatened plants and many endemics. Its fauna includes a number of globally threatened bats and rodents, large mammals, a variety of birds, including globally threatened species, and globally threatened reptiles and amphibians. The study concluded that the area should be enlarged and that Igman-Bjelašnica-Treskavica-Visočica should be designated a national park. Development of tourism was foreseen as part of this project.

Study on the influence of forestry on biologically sensitive areas in Bosnia and Herzegovina, 2001: This is another study supported by the same National Forestry Programme. It was carried out by the Institute for the Protection of Cultural, Historical and Natural Heritage in Sarajevo. The main objectives of the study were to define the anthropogenic influence on the forests, to describe the present status of the forestry sector, to stress the country's biodiversity value, and to propose protected areas. The study concludes that the following areas should be proposed for protection as national parks: Igman-Bjelašnica-Visočica, Prenj-Čvrsnica-Čabulja, Vranica, Šator, Zvijezda, Konjuh and Tajan.

Integrated ecosystem management of the Neretva and Trebišnjica river basin: This project is expected to begin in September 2004 with GEF support. One of its main objectives is to improve biodiversity conservation in the Neretva river basin through a comprehensive ecosystem-based approach in managing international waterways. The lower flow of the Neretva contains the largest and the most valuable remnants of the Mediterranean wetlands on the eastern Adriatic coast. The wetlands are a Ramsar site and are included in the Important Bird Areas programme. The upper part of the delta (20,000 ha) in the Federation is a protected area (Hutovo Blato Natural Park).

Forest and mountain biodiversity conservation project: This project is being prepared and will be submitted for possible GEF funding. It should build on the results of the National Forestry Programme and, among other things, enlarge the protected areas' system and create bio-corridors.

Forestry in Bosnia and Herzegovina has suffered from the war and post-war activities. The damage is estimated at about € 2 billion. However, based on information from the Ministries of Agriculture, Water Management and Forests in both entities, the situation is now improving; control over illegal activities is being re-established, illegal cutting has almost stopped, and the illegal timber trade and export, with some exceptions, is being restrained. Nevertheless, problems remain: about one tenth of the area is still inaccessible due to landmines; there is clear-cutting along existing roads; and the forest structure has been damaged from over-ageing, landmines and other problems.

Forest exploitation is low overall, but excessive in certain areas. The estimated volume increment (in the Federation) was 4.12 million m^3 in 2001, but only 2.48 million m^3 were cut (see fig. 8.3). However, given the minefields and the poor access to large areas of mountain forests, this amount seems overestimated. There are only 8 km of forest roads on 1,000 ha in the country, which is far below the European average. Consequently, accessible forests are overused, remote stands are becoming overgrown and the quality of wood is decreasing.

Forestry has also been affected by the total collapse of the pre-war lumber and paper industry. While tree trunks are easily used, there is no market for cellulose wood, veneer trunks and wood for other final products. At the same time, even legal sawmills have much larger capacities for trunk processing than the forest enterprises can supply, and there are many (700-900 in Republika Srpska alone) private "illegal" sawmills that are working very efficiently.

The total standing crop (timber volume) and annual wood volume increment (timber production) are shown in table 8.2. The ratio between the two entities does not differ greatly. Generally, timber production in the forests is relatively low. There are two basic reasons for this. First, forests that can be managed profitably cover only about 13,000 km^2 (less than half the total forestland) and, second, even these have small timber reserves (no more than 216 m^3/ha). The annual timber increment is 5.5 m^3/ha, which is half the potential of the habitat. Based on this growth, about 7 million m^3 annually used to be cut before the war, which should be the basis for the strategic development of the wood-processing industry. There are about 9,000 km^2 (about one third of total forestland) of low and degraded forests (see fig. 8.3).

Figure 8.3: Logging in State-owned forests

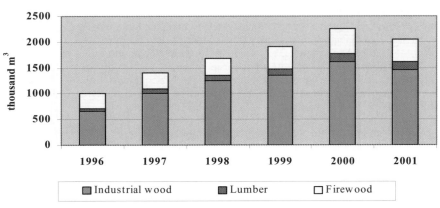

Source: Bosnia and Herzegovina. Federal Office of Statistics. 2002 Statistical Yearbook. Sarajevo, 2002.

The rest is bare land. Most of it (about 4,000 km² or four fifths) is suitable for reforestation. The annual afforestation rate during the past five years has been about 2,500 hectares.

Hunting

Hunting is regulated by the Law on Hunting in Republika Srpska (Official Gazette of RS 4/02). A similar law was drafted in the Federation and is now going through parliamentary procedure. The Federation's current law dates from 1990. The hunting grounds are used by hunting associations, forestry enterprises and other organizations registered for hunting, which have the right to do so in accordance with the law. The hunting grounds are managed according to hunting management plans for a period of at least 10 years. These are based on inventories (or more precisely censuses) drawn up by hunting associations and by experts from the faculties of forestry in Sarajevo and Banja Luka. Application of the Law on Hunting is verified by the State Inspectorate for Forestry, which is part of Republika Srpska's Ministry for Agriculture, Forestry and Water Management, as well as by municipal inspectorates.

Republika Srpska's Law on Hunting grants 10 mammal species and a large number of birds protection (seasonal limitations). The otter and the squirrel, as well as many birds (including vultures), enjoy permanent protection. All game species are listed in the Law. They all fall under a hunting regime defined by the annual plan of the association that manages the particular hunting ground. For protected species there is a special hunting regime with different types of limitations,

and the hunting of permanently protected species is banned.

There is no evidence in official papers or in other documents that hunting poses a serious threat to biodiversity. However, there are no recent inventories of game or official statistics on the number of hunted game. The general view is that game numbers have decreased since the war to a biological minimum. The users of hunting grounds carry out regular counts (censuses) to draw up annual hunting plans, but these data are not published. According to ministry officials in the two entities, the situation is now improving. Poaching has been reduced and game populations are not disturbed on the same scale as during the war.

Other issues

There are no mechanisms to control the use of plant and animal (excluding game) products, and there are no charges. Statistics on the use of wild plants and animals are not available, but it appears to be insignificant. There are no enterprises for processing mushrooms and berries, but there is some indication that the economic performance of the companies in the sector of medicinal and aromatic plants is improving and export volumes are increasing. Measures are being taken to introduce sustainable aspects (bio-certification) in cooperation with foreign experts. In that respect the ratification of the Convention on International Trade in Endangered Species of Wild Fauna and Flora (CITES) would be an important step. Bosnia and Herzegovina is one of the last countries in Europe not to have ratified it.

Table 8.2: Estimated forest resources in the Federation

thousand m^3

Forest type	Coniferous forests	Deciduous forests	Total
Wood volume			
Total	107,385	183,279	290,664
State-owned	105,236	167,413	272,649
Privately owned	2,149	15,866	18,015
Annual volume increment			
Total	3,122	4,817	7,939
State-owned	3,037	4,020	7,057
Privately owned	85	797	882
Annual wood cut			
Total	2,588	4,644	7,232
State-owned	2,503	3,848	6,351
Privately owned	85	796	881

Source: Federation's Ministry of Agriculture, Water Management and Forestry, 2003.

Pollution, although it has decreased as a result of the recession, is still a serious threat to biodiversity. Aquatic ecosystems are under great anthropogenic pressure, not only from industry, but also from mining, municipal waste water and agricultural run-off. The upper flows of pristine rivers are being polluted with waste from illegal sawmills. Air pollution is still a problem in some areas (e.g. Tuzla canton). Erosion has damaged 89% of the land, 10% badly. There are an estimated 20,000 hectares of "technological deserts." Although soil is not monitored, it is expected that it was heavily polluted prior to the war, when pesticide use was uncontrolled and excessive. (See also chapter 10, on agriculture and environment)

Energy, and particularly hydropower, may pose a threat to biodiversity. Most rivers in Bosnia and Herzegovina are dammed, leading to habitat degradation and conversion and watercourse fragmentation. This should be kept in mind when new reservoirs are planned through appropriate EIA. Acceptable mitigation measures should be recommended and respected. The collapse of energy supply during and immediately after the war has resulted in widespread illegal logging for firewood close to settlements. It is estimated that forest density and production will take up to 50 years to recover.

Road and railway transport are not very well developed in the country. There are no major highways, so transport is not a significant threat to biodiversity at present. However, the plans to build a highway as part of the European Transport Corridor 5C could be a serious threat if nature conservation concerns are not taken into consideration. So far there are no positive examples of good EIA practice in Bosnia and Herzegovina.

8.3 The decision-making framework

Policies and strategies

At present there is no strategy for nature in general or for biodiversity protection in either entity, but project proposals are being drafted to request GEF funding to support the drawing-up of a national biodiversity protection strategy and action plan.

The National Environmental Action Plan, adopted by the two entities (but not the national Government) in 2003, identifies a number of biodiversity priorities. Several of these relate to the need for the categorization and development of inventories, for example, of habitats in the Mediterranean coastal belt, of invasive species of plants, animals, fungi and monera, and of native types of plants and breeds of animals. The NEAP calls for an assessment of the current state of endangered plants, animals and fungi, the preparation of red lists, based on IUCN criteria, and the preparation of maps of flora, fauna and fungi. It also foresees the creation of a national gene bank of domestic plants and animals and the propagation of endangered plants and animals in ex situ conditions. The NEAP also stresses the importance of preparing a national strategy and action plan for genetically modified organisms (GMOs) and invasive species, preparing programmes and standards for the sustainable use of biological resources, passing legislation on biodiversity in accordance with EU criteria and ensuring the conditions for signing and ratifying relevant international documents.

The Mid-term Development Strategy (2004-2007) was adopted by the Council of Ministers in 2004 and is much broader than the NEAP. It addresses economic development, social issues, the environment and poverty. It also includes a number of priorities for biological and geological diversity, most of which are the same as those stressed in the NEAP. Some of the priorities identified in the Mid-term Development Strategy but not in the NEAP are:

- Draw up a strategy and national action plan for the balanced management of biological, geological and landscape diversity;
- Conduct ecological categorization of habitats following the CORINE biotope mapping methodology;
- Conduct ecological categorization of swampland following Mediterranean Wetland (MedWet) methodology;
- Design an integrated management programme for the Adriatic coastal zone;
- Set up a system of sustainable management of endemic and refuge centres (the Una and Sana river gorges, the Neretva, Vrbas, Drina, Trebizat valley, Pliva and Tinja);
- Design a programme for the balanced protection of geo-biodiversity (ecosystems in rock clefts, rock creep, rocky ground); and
- Develop a programme to place 15-20% of the territory under appropriate protection.

For forestry, there are no official strategic documents either, but the NEAP proposes a number of measures and activities, including the development of a long-term programme for forest development, mid-term forest management plans, a programme of widespread forest reproduction, the expansion of protected areas, forest certification, improved accessibility of the forests through road building, removal of mines from the forests and monitoring.

The Mid-term Development Strategy devotes considerable attention to developing the forestry sector more sustainably. It prioritizes all of the measures identified in the NEAP and also calls for:

- The adoption of by-laws that are lacking;
- A forestry and wood processing development strategy;
- Programmes to distinguish and extend special-purpose protected areas;
- Revitalization programmes for severely degraded forests, underwood and coverts and bare land;

- Revitalization programmes for karst areas;
- Academic research and education in forestry; and
- Equipment for seed centres and plantations.

The Action Plan for the Mid-term Development Strategy also calls for, inter alia, the privatization of the Public Forestry Corporation in the Federation, the harvesting of non-timber forest products in an organized fashion, forest surveys and the unification of the information technology system.

Most of the priorities and objectives set in these strategic documents can be reached by effectively implementing the new Laws on Forests in both entities. This is especially true for the Law on Forests of the Federation.

Legal framework

Biodiversity protection and the sustainable use of natural resources are governed by the Law on Nature Protection of the Federation of Bosnia and Herzegovina (Official Gazette FBiH 33/2003) and the Law on Nature Protection of Republika Srpska (Official Gazette RS 50/2002). In Republika Srpska, the Law on National Parks (Official Gazette RS 21/1996) also has direct relevance to nature protection. The Federation's cantons are adopting their own laws on nature protection.

Forest management is regulated by the Federation's Law on Forests (Official Gazette of FBiH 20/02 and 29/03) and Republika Srpska's Law on Forests (Official Gazette of RS 66/03). Both are new, and it is expected that they will lead to a better organization and development of forestry.

In Republika Srpska the other sectoral laws directly connected to nature protection and especially the sustainable use of biological resources are:

- The Law on Hunting;
- The Law on Plant Protection (Official Gazette RS 13/97); and
- The Law on Seeds and Seeding Material (Official Gazette RS 13/97).

Except for the Federation's Law on Forests and its Law on Seed and Seeding Material (Official Gazette FBiH 55/01), its respective laws are still being drafted or are in the adoption process. The laws of the former Yugoslavia that are consistent with the Federation's Constitution remain applicable.

As noted in section 8.2, the entities' new Laws on Forests assign institutional authority for national parks, nature parks and nature reserves in the forests. They also prescribe the measures and management that should be undertaken in these areas although they are already regulated in the Laws on Nature Protection. Potentially causing even greater confusion, Republika Srpska's Law on Forests provides for the Law on National Parks to regulate national parks (but not nature reserves and other protected areas). The Federation's Law on Forests includes provisions for biodiversity protection (of plant and game species) in forest management.

This integration of environmental concerns in sectoral laws may be valuable, but, without further regulation and specification, it could also lead to a serious overlap with the Laws on Nature Protection. In the current situation, the entities' Environment Ministries as well as those responsible for forestry have jurisdiction over the management, monitoring, cadastre and other matters concerning national parks and other protected forests.

Permits and licensing

In practice, there are no licensing mechanisms for the use of bio-resources.

International agreements

Bosnia and Herzegovina has ratified the following treaties on biodiversity protection and conservation:

* The International Plant Protection Convention (Rome, 1951) (Official Gazette R BH 13/94) in 2003;
* The Convention on Biological Diversity (Rio de Janeiro, 1992) by accession in 2002;
* The Convention on Wetlands of International Importance especially as Waterfowl Habitats (Ramsar, 1971) by succession in 1992;
* The United Nations Convention to Combat Desertification in those Countries Experiencing Drought and/or Desertification, Particularly in Africa (Paris, 1994) by accession in 2002; and
* The United Nations Framework Convention on Climate Change (New York, 1992) by accession in 2000.

So far very little has been done to implement their requirements. The development of a national biodiversity strategy and action plan could provide a solid base for the beginning of implementation of the Convention on Biological Diversity. The lack of

implementation of international conventions is largely due to the lack of staff in both entities' Environment Ministries, the country's complex administration and its lack of financial resources.

Institutional framework

The State

The Ministry of Foreign Trade and Economic Relations is responsible for environmental protection, but only to a very limited extent. Current developments suggest that this could be broadened in the near future. Within the Ministry there is a Sector of Natural Resources, Energy and Environmental Protection, which includes a very small Department for Environmental Protection and a Department for Coordination of the Management of Natural Resources. In addition, there is the National Steering Committee for Environment and Sustainable Development (see also chapter 1, policy, legal and institutional framework). The National Steering Committee includes a subcommittee for biodiversity (10 members – 3 State representatives, 3 representatives from each of the entities and 1 from Brčko District) that is responsible for advising the competent ministries, drawing up a "red list", drafting guidelines for the introduction of species in the country, drawing up a nature protection strategy, and coordinating and cooperating on transboundary protected areas (according to the entities' Laws on Nature Protection).

Federation of Bosnia and Herzegovina

The Ministry of Physical Planning and Environment is responsible for protecting biodiversity, including protected areas. Among other things, it is responsible for submitting proposals to the Federation's Parliament for new nature protection areas and national parks and for natural monument and landscape protection areas. The cantonal ministries responsible for environmental protection are also responsible for nature protection.

The Ministry of Agriculture, Water Management and Forestry is responsible for the management of agricultural land and pastures, forests and water ecosystems. It is also responsible for protected areas, especially national parks. It is not clear how responsibility for protected areas is shared with the Ministry of Physical Planning and Environment. Article 40, para. 1 (a), of the Law on Forests provides for the declaration of national parks as forests with a special purpose. On the other hand, the Law on Nature Protection governs matters connected to protected areas (national parks included).

The management of protected areas is usually in the hands of their management bodies or of the relevant municipality or forestry unit.

The Federation has a public enterprise for forestry, *BH šume*, and seven cantonal forest enterprises. In addition, the new Law on Forests set up 45 forest management units.

Republika Srpska

The Ministry of Physical Planning, Civil Engineering and Ecology is responsible for protecting biodiversity. It submits all categories of protected areas to Parliament. Lower-level authorities (municipalities) can only recommend that a certain area should be protected.

The Ministry of Agriculture, Forestry and Water Management is responsible for managing the most important natural resources: agricultural land and pastures, forests and water ecosystems. It is also responsible for protected areas, especially national parks. Again, it is not clear how responsibility for protected areas is shared with the Ministry of Physical Planning, Civil Engineering and Ecology.

Forestry is integrated within the single public enterprise, *Srpske šume*. On the basis of the new Law on Forests, 42 forest management units were established. These enterprises are responsible for hunting activities and for other uses of forests and forest products, as well as for the management of some protected forests.

Brčko District

Responsibility for environmental management lies with the Department of Utilities, which includes a logistics unit with responsibilities for environmental protection. The Department of Agriculture and Forestry is responsible for forest management.

Throughout Bosnia and Herzegovina, in addition to the potential institutional conflict between the Environment Ministries and those responsible for forestry, another significant obstacle is the lack of staff in the Environment Ministries. Staffing is insufficient to implement national laws and international conventions. There is less of a problem in the scientific institutes, and it might be useful for the Ministries to explore the possibility of receiving temporary staff seconded from these institutes.

Financial mechanisms

The Federation's Law on Nature Protection (art. 41) stipulates three main sources of financing for nature conservation – the Federation's budget, collected fines and other sources (e.g. donations, taxes). It also calls for the establishment of a nature protection fund as part of the Environmental Fund, but this has not yet been set up. Republika Srpska's Law on Nature Protection (art. 44) stipulates the budget as a source of financing for nature conservation together with the Environmental Fund. The legal basis for the establishment of the Fund was provided in 2002 (Official Gazette of RS 51/02). Sources other than the entity's budget for the Fund are foreseen, such as licences for the use of natural resources, funding from polluters and donations. The distribution of the funds will be according to the Fund's annual financial plan as approved by the Ministry of Physical Planning, Civil Engineering and Ecology. Conservation of the protected areas is one of the Fund's main aims. However, there is no substantial domestic funding for nature conservation so far. All funding comes from international donors. The non-existence of permanent financial resources for the protection of biological diversity is a serious problem.

Monitoring

There is no official biodiversity monitoring. Although Bosnia and Herzegovina is a member of the Environmental Information and Observation Network (EIONET) of the European Environment Agency, the responsibilities for data flows are difficult to meet owing to the lack of human and technical resources of the Federation's Ministry of Physical Planning and Environment (The establishment of a centre in Banja Luka is foreseen). The recent report of the EEA Topic Centre on nature conservation shows this.

Concrete measures for establishing and improving the information collection and dissemination system are taken within the framework of the LIFE Third Country project "Establishment of the Operational Unit of the Steering Committee on Environment". Working groups on data collection and reporting for nature, waste, water and air have been established.

Before the war, the Institute for the Protection of the Cultural, Historical and Natural Heritage of Bosnia and Herzegovina used to monitor biodiversity (although not fully). For instance, endemic flora and fauna were observed and monitored. Some of the locations that were monitored were: Hutovo Blato, Bardaca near Srbac, Modrac Lake near the city of Lukavac, Sijekovac near the city of Bosanski Brod. Observations were irregular, two or three times a year. At present the Institute does not carry out any observations and monitoring.

Republika Srpska's Institute for the Protection of the Cultural, Historical and Natural Heritage has enjoyed independent status in the entity since 1994 and no longer operates as a regional institution under the umbrella of the former national Institute in Sarajevo. Its main activities and data concern: the valorization of the cultural, historical and natural heritage, recording protected natural wealth, plans for the protection and presentation of protected natural wealth, short studies on individual objects, photo collection, expert opinions and approvals for natural wealth protection, caves. These data are based on field studies and are available on paper or electronically for a fee.

At present, there is also no organized forest monitoring in the Federation. A team from the Faculty of Forestry – Sarajevo irregularly monitors only forest health locally. There is no information on any monitoring of forestry by other organizations. In Republika Srpska the public forestry enterprise *Srpske šume* is authorized to conduct monitoring. The previous network of stands to monitor forest health is no longer functioning.

8.4   Conclusions and recommendations

Due to its complex geological history, especially during the glaciation periods, Bosnia and Herzegovina's biodiversity is extraordinarily rich, but it is under considerable anthropogenic pressure, which may cause some species to be lost forever. There are no inventories or databases to track these changes, no assessment and no red lists. There are no data on forestry either. There is information in the scientific literature, but it is not systematic or easily accessible. It is therefore impossible to discuss the integration of national data into a European database or the participation in international data exchange networks. (See chapter 3, on information, public participation and education for a recommendation.)

The area under protection is very small, and biodiversity is threatened by many factors. The only protected species are several tree species and some game species. Wetlands are considered to be among the most endangered habitats. Apart from forests, other ecosystems and habitat types are not well represented in the protected areas.

Forestry is also facing significant problems related to the recent war and post-war activities. Large portions of forests have been degraded. Forests are inaccessible mainly owing to the underdeveloped forest road network and the minefields. The timber and paper industries have collapsed.

Although there should be a nature protection fund, there is no solid financial mechanism for biodiversity protection. The constant lack of finances is one of the main reasons for poor biodiversity management and increasing biodiversity loss. The lack of monitoring is also a serious problem.

The legal framework for nature protection and forest protection has recently been established. Now it is important to proceed with the drafting of the necessary by-laws, which are the basis for effective implementation of the laws. The absence of overall national strategies for biodiversity and for forestry development is an obstacle to long-lasting biodiversity conservation and the sustainable use of bio-resources as well as sustainable forest management. There are many strategic documents in different fields of biodiversity and forestry that could be used as the basis for developing these strategies.

Recommendation 8.1:
The Ministry of Physical Planning and Environment of the Federation of Bosnia and Herzegovina, the Ministry of Physical Planning, Civil Engineering and Ecology of Republika Srpska and the Logistics Unit of Brčko District should accelerate the drafting and adoption of a national biodiversity strategy and action plan. The national strategy should be in line with the Pan-European Biological and Landscape Diversity Strategy. It should be drawn up in close cooperation between the two entities and Brčko District.

At present, the new Laws on Forests define the action to be taken in forestry, including a reorganization of the forestry authorities, and the role of commercial companies. However, there is no overall forestry strategy either nationally or in the entities, and there are no official forestry development programmes. To facilitate the appropriate management of the forests and their sustainable development, it is important that a strategy should be drawn up and an action plan developed.

Recommendation 8.2:
Republika Srpska's Ministry of Agriculture, Forestry and Water Management, the Federation's Ministry of Agriculture, Water Management and Forestry and Brčko District's Department of Agriculture and Forestry, in cooperation with the respective entities' ministries of environment, should:
(a) As soon as possible, develop a national forestry strategy (including forest use and timber industry) applying Strategic Environmental Assessment. The Strategy should ensure the gradual recovery of the forests and sustainable forest management, and include the development of a programme for forest certification as a first step toward sustainable forest use and management.
(b) Draw up action plans on the basis of the strategy.

The two entities have made significant progress by adopting and harmonizing their new Laws on Nature Protection. However, they cannot be implemented without by-laws. This requires, among other things, that the entities and Brčko District should prepare and adopt red lists and a red data book. Similar progress has been made by the entities through their new Laws on Forests, but these, too, need by-laws to facilitate their implementation. In the development of all these by-laws, it is essential to clearly define institutional responsibility for protected area management.

Recommendation 8.3:
(a) The Federation's Ministry of Physical Planning and Environment and Republika Srpska's Ministry of Physical Planning, Civil Engineering and Ecology should:
• Finalize and adopt red data books for plant and animal species according to the IUCN classification; and

• Accelerate the development of the by-laws for the respective Laws on Nature Protection.
(b) Republika Srpska's Ministry of Agriculture, Forestry and Water Management and the Federation's Ministry of Agriculture, Water Management and Forestry should similarly accelerate the development of by-laws for the respective new Laws on Forests.
(c) In developing these two sets of by-laws, it is essential for the Federation's Ministry of Physical Planning and Environment and Ministry of Agriculture, Water Management and Forestry and Republika Srpska's Ministry of Physical Planning, Civil Engineering and Ecology and Ministry of Agriculture, Forestry and Water Management to work together in order to define clearly the institutional responsibilities for nature reserves, protected areas and national parks.

The total protected area in Bosnia and Herzegovina is very small. The 1981-2000 Physical Plan had proposed a significant increase – from 0.55% of the territory to 16% – however, the war intervened and it has been difficult to make any progress. The Mid-term Development Strategy (2004-2007) proposes a programme that would place 15-20% of the territory under appropriate protection. The country is now stable, and it is increasingly important for Bosnia and Herzegovina to take action to protect its rich biodiversity before it is lost.

Recommendation 8.4:
The Federation's Ministry of Physical Planning and Environment and Republika Srpska's Ministry of Physical Planning, Civil Engineering and Ecology should:
• Substantially enlarge the system of protected areas;
• Apply the IUCN classification system for protected areas; and
• In developing these activities, apply to Natura 2000 network.

PART III: ECONOMIC AND SECTORAL INTEGRATION

Chapter 9

TOURISM AND ENVIRONMENT

9.1   Present situation

Bosnia and Herzegovina's tourist sector is in a similar situation as that of the other new States of the former Yugoslavia that do not have a significant coastline. The tourism industry in the pre-conflict era was mainly developed along the Adriatic Sea. Bosnia and Herzegovina was therefore only a destination for transit tourism: people spent a few days in Sarajevo, Mostar and other attractive places on their way to the coast.

Tourism development was strengthened by the hosting of the Winter Olympics in Sarajevo in 1984, at which time tourism infrastructure was developed in the mountains of Jahorina and Bjelasnica. Historic monuments, dating from the Medieval period, Ottoman Empire, and the Second World War, the religious pilgrimage of Medjugorje, and the Mediterranean tourism in the city of Neum have been the main attractions for tourists for many years.

It is very difficult to describe the present situation given the poor quality of the statistics. The Ministry of Trade and Tourism in Republika Srpska and the Tourism Department of the Ministry of Trade in the Federation report that no reliable information is available on the number of tourists in the country due to scarce enforcement of reporting regulations.

No precise information is available on the number of hotels and their categorization either. There is no estimate of the percentage of the national GDP that is accounted for by the tourism industry.

Table 9.1 summarizes the available data regarding tourist numbers in the past six years.

The lack of reliable statistical data on the tourist sector, the recent war, the limited road and rail network for fast transit, all constitute important obstacles to the further development of the tourist industry.

9.2   Ecotourism

Ecotourism or sustainable tourism is a term used to define tourism activities that respect the surrounding natural resources. Particular attention is also given to the socio-economic context of the local community in an effort to create sustainable activities that enable the local community to sustain itself without damaging or destroying its natural resources.

In rural communities the focus is on the creation of economic activities that enable inhabitants to remain on the territory rather than migrate to urban environments in search of work. This is done through the valorization of the local cultural and natural heritage.

Typical ecotourism activities have a low environmental impact and may include rural tourism, spas, trekking, bicycling, rafting and kayaking.

Table 9.1: Tourists and overnights, 1997-2002

Year	Federation of Bosnia and Herzegovina		Republika Srpska	
	Tourists	Nights	Tourists	Nights
1997	160,000	415,000	108,009	362,243
1998	189,000	453,000	148,175	437,736
1999	199,300	474,327	168,375	473,705
2000	221,418	511,048	169,720	440,760
2001	184,193	415,584	146,133	359,890
2002	214,640	505,772	151,838	384,187

Source: State Agency for Tourism, 2003.

Prospects for sustainable tourism development

The territory of Bosnia and Herzegovina is endowed with a valuable natural and cultural heritage, which, if carefully administered, may become the source of one of the country's most valuable and profitable development sector: tourism.

The main possibilities include:
- Mountain and adventure tourism (rafting, canyoning, trekking, skiing);
- Thermal spas;
- Cultural and rural tourism; and
- Transit tourism.

Mountain and adventure tourism

Enclosing part of the mountains belonging to the Dinaric range, which extends to the Prokletija Mountains bordering with Serbia and Montenegro and Albania, the Sutjeska National Park offers a wide range of ecotourism activities. It is the home of Perucica, Europe's last primeval forest, and of Maglic Mountain, Bosnia and Herzegovina's highest peak, and it is crossed by the Sutjeska river, which has carved deep canyons. It therefore offers a potential for mountain sports ranging from trekking to more adventurous winter mountaineering, rafting and canyoning.

The Kozara National park is a protected national forest situated between the rivers Una, Sava, Sana and Vrbas in the northwest. It is a popular hunting spot with over 18,000 hectares of regulated hunting grounds with a wide range of game. It also offers more relaxing activities such as photo safaris, walking and biking.

Hutovo Blato is a reserve along the southern border with Croatia, not far from the ancient Roman settlements near Čapljina. It is a shelter for hundreds of species of birds and game, and therefore offers activities such as boating, bird-watching and fishing.

Adventure sport activities

The pristine natural sites of Bosnia and Herzegovina offer great potential for adventure tourism. Close to Sarajevo is the Bjelašnica mountain range, which hosted the 1984 Winter Olympics. It stretches from Sarajevo to Konjic and includes traditional Bosnian villages, watermills

and mountain huts along canyons, waterfall, rivers and lakes.

There are many mountain huts operated by the Mountain Association of Bosnia and Herzegovina, which is trying to rebuild and renovate the damaged buildings. Many huts used to be located in the Neretva valley and in the Prenj and Cvrsnica mountain ranges. The Bjelašnica and Igman mountains and the Vlasic and Vranica mountains also have huts to accommodate the hikers that follow the mountain trails.

Paragliding is possible from the Visocica Peak over the Rakitnica canyon, and rafting and kayaking may be done along the Tara, the Una and the Neretva rivers. The highland plateau of Prenj, also known as the Himalaya of Herzegovina, is exceptionally suited for mountain biking.

Cultural and rural tourism

The villages and towns of Bosnia and Herzegovina are testimony to the different cultures that have passed through the country over the centuries. From the unique *stecci* – medieval tombstones dotted all over the country – to Roman mosaics, Ottoman architecture and ancient Catholic and Orthodox decorations, the country is rich in cultural heritage.

Some of the more noteworthy towns are Mostar, Jajce, Bihac, Trebinje, Travnik, and Neum on the Adriatic, the former residence of Ottoman rulers. Also of interest are the capital cities of the two entities, Sarajevo (Federation) and Banja Luka (Republika Srpska). Medugorje, close to Mostar, is well known for its Catholic shrine of the Virgin Mary.

9.3   Ongoing initiatives

National parks

At present, only 0.5% of Bosnia and Herzegovina's total territory is protected under two national parks in Republika Srpska (Kozara and Sutjeska). There are current initiatives for enlarging existing protected areas (National parks Sutjeska and Kozara) based on the IUCN categorization. Particular attention is given to the protection of virgin forests in the zones of Lom, Janj and Perucica near Sutjeska.

The Federation of Bosnia and Herzegovina's Ministry of Physical Planning and Environment is concentrating on the establishment of new national parks in the following areas:

- River Una on the border with Croatia, for which a feasibility study has been requested by the Ministry to be financed by the Government's budget;

- Igman/Bjelasnica mountain: a feasibility study was financed by EU in 2001 and is now awaiting financial support for a physical plan;

- The Prenj-Cvrsnica-Cabulja area for its biodiversity characteristics: a feasibility study was also financed by EU in 2001 and is now awaiting a physical plan; and

- Vranica mountain: a very interesting karst and water area that encloses architectural monuments and the village of Blagaj. The area was also the object of an EU PHARE and World Bank study, which was finished in 2001, and is now awaiting a physical plan by the Government.

However, many problems need to be solved. First of all, there is a need for an efficient regulatory and institutional framework to support development and to protect the natural heritage.

Second, at present, Bosnia and Herzegovina does not have the infrastructure to support such diversified tourism. Providing good-quality rural hotels or guest houses, hiking trails and cycling circuits would help develop sustainable tourism. There are some old hiking trails, but they need to be upgraded and maintained. There are no cycling circuits, and good-quality rural hotels and guest houses are very scarce.

In addition, there must be efficient and adequate planning for waste management and other support services to guarantee the proper protection of the surrounding environment and natural resources.

Finally, an unfortunate issue that penalizes Bosnia and Herzegovina heavily is the presence of landmines in some mountain areas, especially around Sarajevo, and along parts of the borders between the two entities. The territories that are being considered for the new national parks are not thought to have landmine problems.

As tourism has been identified as one of the priorities for the development of the country, a number of ecotourism and tourism programmes have been undertaken with the support of various donors. The following section lists some of the main projects.

Bosnia and Herzegovina, and Italy are cooperating to protect natural areas. They share experiences in promoting conservation and in valorizing natural and cultural resources in the Mediterranean basin and in particular in the Balkans.

The Japan International Cooperation Agency (JICA) is supporting a one-year programme to develop ecotourism through sustainable development. This programme will focus on two pilot areas: Velez Mountain including Nevesinje and Blagaj; and the canyon of the Pliva river with the villages of Jajce and Shipovo. The implementing partners are the Federation's Ministry of Physical Planning and Environment (Environment Sector) and Republika Srpska's Ministry of Physical Planning, Civil Engineering and Ecology (Ecology Sector).

The United States Agency for International Development (USAID) and the German technical cooperation agency Gesellschaft für Technische Zusammenarbeit GmbH (GTZ) have been supporting the tourism associations of the two entities to promote "Putting Bosnia and Herzegovina on the tourist map." Among other things, this has led to good cooperation in tourism between the entities and the publication of a joint tourism brochure. USAID is also supporting work on cultural and historical heritage and tourism, as well as a business development programme that focuses on tourism.

A project team of International Business Machines (IBM) business development consultants has put together a "cluster" of about 80 companies related to the tourist sector, including tourist board offices, national parks and restaurants. This cluster, which meets approximately once a month, examines the links among related sectors, including industry, transport and education, in the context of the policy, regulatory and institutional framework. Funding for the programme ended in December 2003, and the future of these cluster meetings was uncertain.

9.4 Environmental problems

Although relatively limited due to the sector's present low level of development, the tourism industry has an environmental impact mainly on the waste and waste-water management sectors. Future foreseeable impacts are related to the building of new hotels and tourism infrastructure in natural areas.

These impacts include:

- Production of solid waste to be adequately disposed of in sanitary landfills. This implies an efficient waste management service;
- Generation of liquid effluents that will have to be adequately treated before disposal into surface water bodies;
- Visual and structural impact of new buildings on pristine and protected areas; and
- Impact of increased traffic in newly created tourist areas.

Proper and efficient planning for the management of these infrastructure problems is essential to the development of a sustainable tourism industry in the country.

9.5   Policy objectives and management

Policy framework

There is no overall State policy for tourism, as tourism is a responsibility delegated to the entities.

Federation of Bosnia and Herzegovina

The Federation of Bosnia and Herzegovina has no strategy for the development of the tourist industry. It does, however, have a strategy for the development of its cultural heritage which includes the protection of national monuments and sites, but tourism aspects are not taken into account, due largely to the lack of contact between its Ministry of Culture and the Tourism Department of its Ministry of Trade.

During the preparations for the Poverty Reduction Strategy Paper or Mid-term Development Strategy of Bosnia and Herzegovina (2004-2007), adopted by the Council of Ministers on 5 February 2004, the Federation's Tourism Department drafted input that identified the objective of a possible tourism strategy as the sustainable development of the tourist economy with particular attention to increasing the use of local, rural products in order to stop migration from villages to towns. It also paid attention to upgrading the accommodation capacity and education and training of employees and managers in the tourist industry.

It noted that the current obstacles were the lack of a long-term tourism strategy for the country, the inadequate legal and institutional framework for the tourist sector, the lack of a long-term vision at all levels about the investment potential of the tourist

sector as well as the shortage of domestic capital to revitalize the tourist economy, insufficient and inadequate accommodation capacity, and the strict visa requirement for citizens from nearby countries such as Bulgaria, the Czech Republic, Hungary, Poland and Slovakia.

As a priority, the Tourism Department called for the development of a long-term strategy for tourist development in partnership with the private and non-governmental sector and the harmonization of regulations with EU standards, and the supervision of their implementation. It also proposed the adoption of economic instruments to support the tourist sector, such as tourist fees, residential [accommodation] taxes, and the use of funds from government budgets. This effort included an action plan, which defined objectives, parties responsible for implementation and deadlines for individual tasks.

Republika Srpska

There is a long-term tourism development strategy covering the years from 2002 to 2020. However, the Ministry of Trade and Tourism reports that its implementation is behind schedule because earmarked funds are not available and it is not a government priority.

The strategy includes objectives related to the refurbishment of hotel capacity. Reportedly, it identifies possible locations for ecotourism and village tourism. The work was conducted by local professors of the Economics Faculty. The Ministry of Physical Planning, Civil Engineering and Ecology was not involved.

The Ministry of Physical Planning, Civil Engineering and Ecology has asked the Government to draw up a strategy for the protection of the national parks and a master plan for their development and wants the Prime Minister to support the request. Reportedly, there is a proposal for the preparation of a master plan for the protection of national parks.

Natural reserves are endangered by logging facilities, of which there are nearly 900. The facilities endanger the woods and have a heavy impact on nearby rivers through their discharge of sawdust.

Although mentioned as one of the objectives of the tourism development strategy of Bosnia and Herzegovina, the development of local production related to the tourist sector, such as locally grown and possibly organic food and crafts, does not seem to be the object of any specific development effort.

In developing ecotourism and supporting local efforts, more support should be given to the production of local food and crafts. Efforts should also be made to organize cooperatives to help sustain local rural communities in their production of items such as fruit and vegetables, honey and flour. A survey of production capacities of rural communities may help in this regard.

Legislative framework

At present, no laws, draft laws or regulations address the sustainability of the tourism industry either in Bosnia and Herzegovina or in the entities.

In the Federation the only law related to tourism seems to be the 1996 Law on the Categorization of Hotels. Only one third of all hotels are categorized. This Law has now been brought before the Council of Ministers for adoption at the State level.

In Republika Srpska the Law on Tourism (Official Gazette RS 55/03) was adopted in July 2003 to regulate tourist organizations. The recently adopted Law on the Hotel Industry (Official Gazette RS 3/04) sets standards for hotels and tourist premises.

Economic instruments

There has been no financing for the national parks since the war. There are no entrance fees. Tourist guides estimate that before the war there were close to 50,000 visitors a year. Today the number is closer to 8,000.

Economic instruments do not seem to be used to support the development of sustainable tourism.

Institutional framework

At the State level

Tourism is not dealt with at State level. However, an effort is being made to establish a public, State tourist association to coordinate the development of the tourist industry in both entities.

At the entity level

The Ministry of Trade and Tourism in Republika Srpska and the Tourism Department in the Ministry of Trade of the Federation of Bosnia and Herzegovina are the institutional bodies directly responsible for tourist policies and legislation. Both have contributed a section on tourism to the Poverty Reduction Strategy Paper.

A number of other institutions also have responsibilities for sustainable tourism policy. These include the institutional bodies responsible for:
- Culture (sector of cultural heritage);
- Natural resources and environmental protection (national parks and protected areas; environmental impact studies of new tourist structures; protection and sustainable use of natural resources; identification of natural regions of significance for the country; and improvement, use and protection of forests and game);
- Spatial planning (for development planning issues); and
- Education (for education and training of operators, education of schoolchildren, and raising public awareness about the environment and ecotourism).

Interviews with representatives of these institutions revealed that there is virtually no coordination and no sharing of information or related activities among the ministries within the entities. Such a lack of coordination among institutions is a significant obstacle to coherent planning and implementation.

Education and capacity-building

There are no institutions to train people in the tourism sector. No training is given to workers of the tourist sector in environmental awareness and sustainable tourism, and there seem to be no specific environmental awareness programmes in primary and secondary school curricula.

Sustainable tourism indicators

The statistics on hotels and tourist numbers in both entities are unreliable due to the reportedly insufficient inspection network.

Important data for sustainable tourism development, such as the ratio of overnights to tourist arrivals, the ratio of overnights to residents, or the annual value of the trade in catering for residents, have never been collected. These are important indicators for monitoring the development of sustainable tourism.

9.6 Conclusions and recommendations

At the State level

Tourism is not dealt with at State level. However, an effort is being made to establish a State tourist association to coordinate the development of the tourist industry in both entities. The tourism strategy that is being finalized as a contribution to the State's development strategy is also an effort at State level to which the two competent ministries in the entities are contributing. Neither the State nor the entities have a policy or legislation on sustainable tourism.

Recommendation 9.1:
The State Ministry of Foreign Trade and Economic Relations in cooperation with the relevant entities' ministries and supported by international experts should:
(a) Coordinate the development of a State strategy for sustainable tourism. It should be made an integral part of the development strategy for tourism. This policy could provide a cohesive framework and ensure that sustainability criteria are consistently applied in all laws and regulations affecting tourism development.
(b) Develop adequate legislative tools for the sustainable development and management of the tourism sector. These tools should address the problem of unreliable statistics and the introduction of sustainable tourism indicators

At the entity level

Once a framework policy has been established, it is important to develop a general master plan for sustainable tourism and a series of individual master plans for specific sites. To provide baseline data for the master plan, it is important to make an inventory of all sites of interest (including sites with a potential for cultural heritage, rural tourism, river tourism, industrial heritage, nature tourism and spas). This can be done by the entities.

Recommendation 9.2:
(a) On the basis of the State strategy for sustainable tourism, the Ministry of Trade and Tourism in Republika Srpska and the Ministry of Trade in the Federation should develop local guidelines and regulations for tourism development and introduce eco-standards for tourist premises.

(b) A tourism master plan, also based on the overall policy for sustainable tourism, should be developed for both entities, to allow for appropriate economic, environmental, spatial and resource planning and the development of the necessary infrastructure in tourist areas.
(c) The competent bodies for tourism, in cooperation with the Ministries of Culture and the Environment Ministries, should make an inventory of all sites of tourist interest. As the sites are identified, individual management plans for their sustainable development should be prepared.

Although mentioned as one of the objectives of the tourism development strategy of Bosnia and Herzegovina, the development of local production related to the tourist sector such as locally grown and possibly organic food and crafts does not seem to be the object of any specific development effort.

Recommendation 9.3:
The competent authorities for tourism, in cooperation with local authorities, should undertake a survey of local products that could be supported and included in a sustainable tourism development plan.

There are no economic instruments for natural resources management or supporting the development of sustainable tourism.

Recommendation 9.4:
The responsible authorities should establish the following economic instruments to support sustainable tourism:
• *Entrance fees at national parks;*
• *An eco-tax on tourist infrastructure putting environmental pressure on nearby protected areas, to be paid by the owners (e.g. hotel owners); and*
• *Fiscal incentives for tourist premises that implement eco-standards, such as "green hotels" that save and protect resources such as water and energy. These could take the form of tax breaks or reduced licensing fees.*

There are no programmes to train people in the tourist sector. No training is given to workers of the tourist sector in environmental awareness and sustainable tourism, and there seem to be no specific environmental awareness programmes in primary and secondary school curricula.

<u>*Recommendation 9.5:*</u>

(a) The responsible authorities for tourism, in cooperation with the Ministries of Education, should introduce training programmes in tourism and sustainable tourism in the curricula of higher education institutions.

(b) The Environment Ministries in cooperation with the Ministries of Education should develop and introduce environmental awareness programmes in primary and secondary schools.

(c) The responsible authorities for tourism, in cooperation with the Environment Ministries, should carry out widespread campaigns to raise awareness of sustainable tourism particularly among hotel managers, tourist agencies, tourists and municipal authorities. The campaign should make use of workshops, community meetings, brochures and posters, and other media.

Figure 9.1: Tourism in Bosnia and Herzegovina

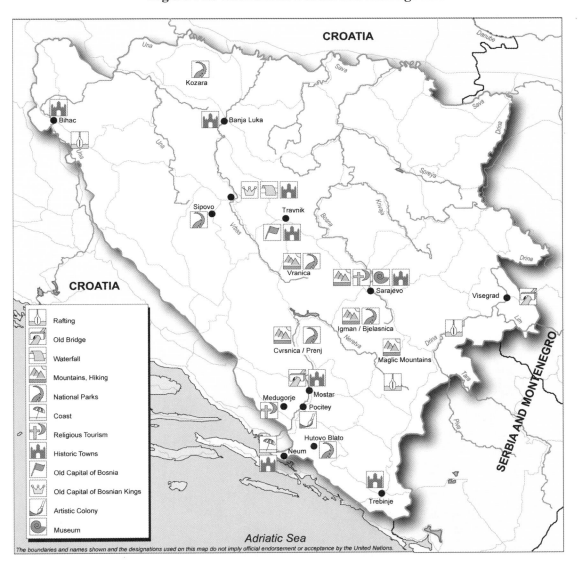

Chapter 10

AGRICULTURE AND ENVIRONMENT

10.1 Introduction

Bosnia and Herzegovina's gross domestic product (GDP) in 2001 was KM 10.233 billion, of which primary agricultural production represented 12%, i.e. KM 1.228 billion. In the same year, agriculture also accounted for 0.7% of the total consolidated budgets of the State, the entities and the cantons. In the overall foreign trade deficit, agricultural products represent a significant share at US$ 200 per capita (compared to US$ 73 in Croatia). Domestic food production covers only 35 to 40% of needs, which is much lower than before the war, when it accounted for about 60%. Bosnia and Herzegovina is not self-sufficient in any major agricultural product except potatoes. The country imports about three quarters of its total demand for milk and other dairy products, and the situation with beef and veal is similar. Since milk production acts as an engine for the development of all agriculture in Bosnia and Herzegovina, the reliance on imports has acted as a barrier for the development of the whole sector. Based on indicators of agricultural productivity, Bosnia and Herzegovina is at the bottom of the European scale. The age structure of the population working in agriculture has deteriorated, since young people seek better living conditions in towns and abroad.

The war also resulted in the loss of export markets, which are difficult to re-establish. In general, there are few resources to compete on international markets through subsidies. Bosnia and Herzegovina has signed bilateral free-trade agreements with some countries, but it has not succeeded in increasing its exports, largely due to non-customs-related measures, poor organization and the lack of export products. There is also a problem in meeting the requirements of international markets in food quality and standardsin the food and food-processing industry. The processing industry is weak, although in milk, meat and fruit and in the vegetable sector some progress has been made with the help of foreign capital.

The level of use of natural resources, particularly land, is the second important indicator of the situation in agriculture. In 2001, 50% of arable land in the Federation and 33% in Republika Srpska were unused, and arable land continues to shrink, which could lead to the total collapse of this sector. This is due to a number of factors, for example, the abandonment of agricultural land, pending issues related to its privatization, a lack of investment and poor organization.

The sector has been recovering very slowly. The country's environment is favourable for many types of agricultural production, but it is unlikely that conditions permit intensive, commodity-oriented production on a worldwide scale. More than 50% of the land is covered by forests.

Natural conditions in lowland areas are favourable for sustainable agricultural production and in some areas for market-based agriculture. The north was oriented to more intensive agriculture than the centre because of natural characteristics. Before the war, Bosnia and Herzegovina used to harvest up to 6 metric tons of grain per ha; the yield is now only about 2 tons. Only a fraction of agriculture is market-oriented; it acts more as a factor of social stability, particularly for the rural community. Even small farmers try to sell their products - mainly milk and meat. Experts estimated that a minimum of 5 head of cattle on a farm could provide enough income for one person (one job). The fact is, however, that though such a small herd may represent a substantial and relatively permanent source of income for a family, it cannot ensure a reasonable living standard on a family farm.

Most of the rest of the country is characterized by unfavourable environmental factors for agriculture, because of steep slopes, high altitude or karst (dry climate and shallow soil), and remoteness. Production is therefore limited, the range of suitable crops and animals is narrow, and even the plots are smaller and scattered due to the relief. In collaboration with the European network EUROMONTANA, experts have assessed the land. On the basis of 10 different environmental, technological and demographic criteria, about 57% could be considered as unfavourable for agriculture (mountainous, hilly, Mediterranean).

10.2 Conditions and activities in agriculture

Land use

There is no register of agricultural holdings in either entity, although some basic land data are collected, a soil map on a scale of 1:400,000 was completed in 2003, and agro-ecological zoning was carried out in the same year (by the Institute for Agropedology). In addition the Food and Agriculture Organization of the United Nations (FAO), in collaboration with the Institute for Agropedology in Sarajevo, the Agricultural Institute in Banja Luka and the Agronomic Institute of Mostar University, published some basic land use and soil data on a scale of 1:200,000.

The land-use structure changed after the war, with more land left unused. Furthermore, large areas have been devastated, arable land has been abandoned, large tracts of land are mined, and fires in recent years have burned thousands of hectares of agricultural land and forests. Although there are no exact data from land-use monitoring, estimates suggest that, on average, at least 50% of the agricultural land is underused or unmanaged. The intensive use of fertile soils (ploughed land planted with annual and permanent crops) and pastures, mainly in hilly and mountainous regions of the Federation, is growing. The situation in Republika Srpska appears to be slightly better.

The situation is the worst in areas that were abandoned by refugees who have not returned. About 200,000 hectares are mined, and it is estimated that it will take 40 years to clear all the mines in agricultural areas. Some 10,000 hectares are damaged by ore mining, and only 10% have been rehabilitated. In addition, 3 of the 14 investigated sites had been contaminated with depleted uranium (DU). Usually soil contamination is found up to 200 metres from the contamination point (where DU was used), and in these areas DU in drinking water and air was reported. Contamination with DU may cause more environmental and health problem in the future in these areas.

Soil quality

According to the former soil classification, which delimited the area on the basis of soil quality, slope and agricultural potential, the best categories of soils are in the valleys of the rivers Una, Sava, Vrbas, Bosna, Drina, Sana and Spreča. These valleys are suitable for sustainable crop production

(wheat, barley, soybean, corn), cattle breeding, orchards (plums, apples, pears), and vegetables, medicinal herbs and industrial crop production. In the highlands the agricultural land is of a poorer quality. This land is suitable for cattle breeding and complementary activities. The war has left it devastated, often with large strips of mined land. For environmental, economic and social reasons, it is necessary to revive the highlands. The Mediterranean region covers the southern Dinarides up to the Illyric-Mesian ecological-vegetation region. Karst fields, valleys and plains in this area cover about 170,000 hectares. Frequent floods prevent sustainable intensive agricultural production on about 40% of this land. Over 30% of the sub-Mediterranean area is under highland pastures. Both areas are suitable only for few crop and animal varieties due to the specific water and nutrition regime.

Erosion has endangered 89% of the land, and 10% is badly damaged by it. In general, land management was always very poor. The unfavourable relief, poor agricultural practices and the low level of farmers' knowledge cause large losses of land every year. There are some 20,000 ha of so-called "technological deserts," with only 1.5% of the destroyed land being recultivated. The deserts are the result of mining and some industrial activities.

Table 10.1: Regions damaged by surface excavations, 2002

(ha)

Region	Area
Total	12,839
Kreka	3,600
Ugljevik	1,879
Banoviæi	1,879
Ljubija	1,609
Durðevik	1,050
Kakanj	806
Zenica	850

Source: Mid-term Development Strategy (2004-2007).

Pasture

A large share of agricultural land is suitable for grassland only, both for environmental and for economic reasons. The consequence is that extensive animal husbandry, mainly sheep breeding, has developed in both entities, particularly in the hills and mountains. Although the system of nomadic pasture has almost vanished, it still exists in some parts. Shepherds move with their sheep from the centre of the country to the north. Mountain pasture has a long tradition in some rural communities, and is also linked to some traditional handicrafts, including the weaving of woollen carpets (*čilim*) and the knitting of socks, jackets and other traditional clothes. The survival of many mountainous regions still depends on this traditional approach, which could be a good basis for the development of farm tourism or other types of ecotourism.

Animal husbandry

Livestock production makes up about 50% of agricultural production and includes cattle, sheep, pigs, fisheries and bee-keeping. Poultry production depends mainly on foreign inputs. There is a large deficit of animal products (milk and other dairy products, veal), but there is a possibility for the export of sheep and related products. Up to three quarters of milk and dairy products on the market are imported. Although the current level of meat consumption is low, the production deficit of meat is huge. Only poultry and pork production have recently increased.

The meat-processing industry, especially beef and veal, depends on foreign raw materials and not on domestic production. The development of sheep-herding is not constrained by demand, and imported mutton is not competitive with domestic meat. Sheep-herding is very important in underdeveloped

hilly areas and in the mountains where pastures are extensively maintained and used in a traditional way. However, the consumption of mutton lags behind that of other types of meat. Intensive production of pork can be organized in the parts of the country where corn is produced. Fish farming has significant potential, thanks to natural resources and imported fish fodder. Fish production lacks modern facilities for the production and rearing of fish roe. Bee-keeping recovered relatively fast after the war and many people have made bee-keeping their primary occupation. The biggest problem is the standardization of honey quality. Poultry and egg production have been developed successfully, and they meet the needs of the population.

Crop production

Bosnia and Herzegovina is highly dependent on imported basic crops, i.e. all types of cereal, spring vegetables and fruit. The production of industrial crops (vegetable oil and sugar beet) is negligible. There are several reasons for the import dependency: unfavourable overall agricultural and economic environment, old technology, poor equipment, fragmented landownership, foreign competition, and low prices on the world market. According to the country's Mid-term Development Strategy (2004-2007), the emphasis during the next five years will be on activating land resources, increasing the level of production and meeting half the domestic needs.

Table 10.2: Animal production in 1990 and 1997

	1990	1997	Difference 1990 - 1997	Index 1997 = 100
A) Meat production in kgs				
1. Gross weight				
Cattle	71,920	30,880	-42,040	53.3
Sheep	25,323	6,410	-18,913	25.3
Pigs	68,496	25,170	-42,326	36.7
Poultry	16,504	8,440	-8,064	51.1
2. Net weight				
Cattle	37,918	16,060	-21,858	42.3
Sheep	12,914	3,240	-9,674	25.1
Pigs	53,426	19,030	-34,396	35.6
Poultry	11,552	5,880	-5,672	50.9
Other	7,700	3,500	-4,200	45.4
Total	123,510	47,710	-75,800	38.6
B) Milk in thousand litres				
Cows	854,906	355,706	-499,200	41.6
Sheep	13,460	6,597	-6,863	49.0
Total	868,366	362,303	-502,063	41.7
C) Eggs in thousands	406,747	250,500	-156,247	61.6
D) Wool in tons	1,628	735	-893	45.1

Source: Mid-term Development Strategy (2004-2007).

In the crop structure, cereals represent about 60%, of which about three quarters are corn. Vegetable production is highly labour-intensive and is carried out on smaller plots. The diversity of environmental conditions in the country enables the production of almost all types of vegetables. There is a high level of self-sufficiency in vegetable production, and processing and exporting of vegetables should be seen as the next step. Similarly, the production of fruit and wine can be organized on smaller plots, with a relatively high income per unit of area. The objective is to cover 90% of consumption demands in continental fruits by 2007. The production of berries is highly profitable and labour-intensive, and has export potential. Domestic producers must meet international standards, and they need to have a joint market strategy.

About 10% of arable land is used for the production of fodder crops, of which the different types of clover represent 75%. To optimize the resources, rationalize the production of milk and meat of grazing cattle and decrease the dependency on imported concentrated fodder, it is necessary to increase the amount of fodder crops sown on arable land.

Tobacco is grown on 4,800 hectares. It is a relatively labour-intensive crop, planted on small plots. Its production is subsidized by the State. Today, 80% fewer oil-producing crops are sown than before the war. This decline was caused by the discontinuation of production in the only vegetable oil production plant, in Brčko. In the northern plains, conditions for industrial crops are favourable. Their introduction would optimize a significant part of arable land, crop rotation could be extended, some of the imported vegetable oil could be replaced by domestic products and jobs would be created.

The share of domestic seed production is only 5-10% of the overall consumption of certified seed, although the consumption of certified seed is significantly lower than the actual needs for quality seed. This is one of the basic reasons for the low yields and the spreading of plant diseases and harmful organisms. With modern technology the crop yield could increase by 50%, particularly if irrigation facilities are reconstructed and properly used (200,000 ha).

Fisheries

The river Sava with its tributaries the Una, Vrbas, Ukrina, Bosna, Tinja and Drina as well as the river Neretva, which empties into the Adriatic Sea, are important for freshwater fishery. These could be further developed. Construction of hydropower plants on the rivers Neretva, Drina, Vrbas, Rama and Sana created many artificial lakes where fisheries could also be developed. Besides, the natural lakes offer favourable conditions for smaller fish farms.

Irrigation

The Assessment of Sustainable Development, prepared by Bosnia and Herzegovina for the World Summit on Sustainable Development (Johannesburg, South Africa, 2002), stresses the importance of irrigation for the future of agriculture. Irrigation would not only make it possible to get a higher yield from crops, but also to apply appropriate modern farming techniques that would not interfere with either the natural quality of the soil or the groundwater quality. The arable land area appropriate for intensive agriculture production is relatively small. Rainfall distribution is unfavourable, particularly in the region with a Mediterranean climate. About 15% of arable land in the world is irrigated, but in Bosnia and Herzegovina it is only about 0.65%. The precipitation from May to August in many regions is only 25% to 30% of the annual rainfall. Lack of water during the vegetation period is a key factor limiting the development of agriculture, particularly in the region close to the Adriatic Sea.

Many irrigation systems have been seriously damaged due to poor maintenance and the war. Only 4,630 hectares are irrigated in this region. There are some projects that are just beginning to reconstruct former irrigation systems, but the real problem is the establishment of economically viable irrigation networks that also address environmental impact. At present some farmers use water from freshwater sources without any system to control water quality and quantity. Improperly designed irrigation can cause significant environmental damage; it is important to put in place a good system of legislation, permitting, implementation of control mechanisms and field inspections.

Many hydrophilic soils are used as arable land, although they are not suitable for competitive agricultural production without proper reclamation measures. High moisture is the main limiting factor. Water surplus on arable land occurs as surface, subsurface and groundwater that fills surface soil layers. For efficient agriculture, it would be necessary to drain surface water and regulate (maintain) tolerable groundwater levels.

10.3 Organization of agriculture

Market agriculture used to exist mainly on relatively intensively used, State-owned agricultural holdings (cooperatives). Although neither the war nor recent changes in the ownership structure have necessarily resulted in better management, these holdings could be used for commodity-oriented agriculture, especially in crop production.

Cooperatives are traditional producer organizations in Bosnia and Herzegovina. There are 210 cooperatives, which have generally not yet adjusted to the management and business conditions required by an open market. There are three cooperatives' associations and one business cooperatives' association, regulated by the Federation's 1997 Law on Cooperatives and Republika Srpska's 1999 Law on Agricultural Cooperatives. These Laws are outdated and need to be replaced by legislation that reflects the current situation. A new framework law on cooperatives is being adopted in the Federation.

Some producer organizations are beginning to emerge in branches directly connected to the processing industry. For example, in the area of Banja Luka and Gradačac over 100 producers established their own "producer organization" for integrated fruit production. It provides technological advice to farmers and labels their products with a special "integrated production" label.

An additional problem is that the land registries have not been updated and do not reflect the actual situation. There are no official data on the number of landowners or the number of agricultural and mixed households.

10.4 Environmental concerns in agriculture

Agricultural pollution

Current agricultural data indicate that agriculture has not had a major negative impact on the environment as a result of intensive production, but this could change quickly with the development of the sector and production-oriented agriculture in the next years. Since there is no environmental monitoring of agriculture, any analysis of the situation is based only on estimates. In the main productive areas and in the river valleys the incorrect and excessive use of mineral fertilizers and pesticides is a threat. Nitrates from fertilizers are soluble, and could easily penetrate soils and directly pollute aquifers. Surface run-off could pollute rivers and other freshwaters. Agricultural inputs are not tested to see if they contain potentially toxic substances. Even before the war, pesticide use was a problem, being uncontrolled and excessive, reaching levels as high as 1 kg per hectare of cultivable area. During the war agrochemical inputs were drastically reduced. The land was able to recover from the overuse of pesticides, but agricultural redevelopment will bring back this risk.

The war also destroyed many of the laboratory facilities and equipment for food quality control (pesticides, mycotoxins and additives), so there is no longer any testing in this area either. Training in the application of pesticides and other protective agents (quantity, dosage, time of application, frequency) is inadequate and unsystematic.

During the war and since then, farmers have not been able to invest much, particularly in soil improvement. The use of mineral fertilizers and pesticides is on average still low; the real problem is that soils will become exhausted without additional nutrients. In addition, crop rotation has been limited to the main crops (for example: corn, grains, potato, some of industrial crops). This general situationis not even favourable for organic production, although there are areas that have not been used for many years and that could therefore be considered "clean".

Animal production could have a negative impact on the environment (point and non-point pollution) with nutrients leaching from animal waste disposal sites or from the improper use of animal waste. There is no evidence that building permits depend on farmers improving the storage capacities for animal waste, but even if they are this is not verified. This applies not only to bigger farms, but also to small family farms, which nearly always have a mixed structure (animals and some crops for subsistence). Non-point pollution from animal production is not an issue at the moment, as the average number of animals per farm (or per area) is low, but if this sector develops and animal numbers rise (which is supported by donors – particularly for refugees), this should be considered as a long-term threat and regulated by environmental legislation.

Agricultural land is encroached upon by urbanization and suffers other permanent losses.

The most endangered is the high-quality land, which comprises only 15% of the overall land area. Almost all infrastructure is concentrated on this land. It is estimated that more than 5,000 hectares are lost annually to make way for growing cities and new settlements.

Agro-biodiversity

Agricultural biodiversity is preserved in crop and animal production, sometimes even in the absence of organized and planned measures. The gene base of fruit trees was enriched for centuries during the Ottoman Empire, when consumption of fruit and juice increased. Beside rare natural fruit plants, there are several indigenous and traditional varieties of cherries, plums, pears and nuts, from which modern varieties have also been derived. Some typical traditional sorts are threatened by extinction because of diseases (e.g. *"požegača* plum attacked by the *"šarka" or "plum pox"* virus). Although new plant varieties are available for production, they generally do not taste as good and

they are not so suitable for traditional agricultural products.

There are some activities for ex situ protection, but there is no (at least not organized) in situ conservation. Biodiversity in animal breeding still exists partly because some indigenous breeds were kept on farms far from outside influence, and these breeds have been able to survive even in a simple environment (little feed, no exposure to animal diseases, geographically remote areas). There are some indigenous breeds in each category of animals. Republika Sprska alone provides some funds for the conservation of some indigenous animal breeds. Table 10.3 provides information on some of the indigenous and traditional animal species and breeds in Bosnia and Herzegovina.

The preservation of genetic resources in agriculture should be one of the most important long-term issues in Bosnia and Herzegovina's agriculture. The establishment of national or Balkan gene banks could preserve most of these vulnerable genetic resources before extinction.

Table 10.3: Indigenous animal species and breeds

Species	Breed	Description
Horse	Bosansko – brdski konj	The total number of animals is not known, but there is a farm in Rogatica where pure breds are kept. Horses of this type are found also on family holdings, but there is no breeding control.
Cattle	Gatačko govedo	The breed was introduced and selected centuries ago from so-called grey cattle *sivo govedo* and local *buša*. The cattle is not very demanding. It has a small shape and can survive even where grass is limited, as in Herzegovina. The pure breed is kept on a farm in Gacko.
Cattle	Buša	Is almost extinct. It is estimated that there could be 1,000-2,000 animals in the mountains. A serious study of the breed as well as gene protection are needed.
Sheep	Pramenka	The sheep is used for meat, milk and to a smaller extent for wool. It is still found in many places in the county (30,000 - 40,000 animals), although the type could be mixed with more productive foreign breeds. This type is still used for semi-nomadic pasturing. The sheep used to be moved every year from the area of Vlašič to the Pannonian plain (now in Serbia and Montenegro). It is still interesting because it is not demanding, and could be promoted as a part of a traditional lifestyle through ecotourism.
Dog	Tornjak	An indigenous breed, still found on Vlašči, Vranica and high mountains where it helps shepherds to protect sheep herds against wolves. Dog breeders association performs breeding control.
Trout	Lipan or Grayling	The endemic river trout is threatened with extinction, because of over fishing during the war, pollution and poaching. The fish farms of rainbow trout operate without proper infrastructure and control of their impact on river downstream (mixing with river trout and pollution of water with nutrients).

Source: Interviews in Bosnia and Herzegovina, November 2003.

Controlled agriculture and organic agriculture

In both entities some projects are geared towards improving crop quality and avoiding the potential negative impact of intensive agriculture on the environment. Systems of integrated and organic farming are developing with bilateral and multilateral assistance. Integrated fruit production started in Republika Srpska in the area of Banja Luka and Gradačac as a project financed by the German Gesellschaft für Technische Zusammenarbeit GmbH (GTZ) and the Swiss Agency for Development and Cooperation (SDC). The project includes 100 producers with 200 ha of orchards, who have established a producer organization. Producers use pesticides and fertilizers according to guidelines. Control is performed by two experts from the Agricultural Faculties in Sarajevo and Banja Luka, with substantial help from SDC and GTZ experts. Analyses of fruit are performed in laboratories in Germany. The project has also developed an integrated production trademark.

Organic agriculture began in 2000 and received support in 2001 with a project initiated by the non-governmental organization ECON with funding from Sweden. It includes six organic farming controllers who work in the field and six advisers who work with farmers on markets, technology and finances. Though there is no national legislation on organic farming, the project follows the guidelines set by the International Federation of Organic Agricultural Movements (IFOAM). Thirty-five farm holdings (individuals and producer organizations) already produce according to these standards.

The project has contributed to the organization of an association for organic farming certification and is helping to develop a system of certification for organic products. The trademark of a Swedish control organization, "KRAV", is used when organic products are exported to EU countries. The first certified organic products were wild plants (wild mushrooms, wild berries and medicinal plants), and some vegetables have now been added. The main target of the certification process is exports, but the organic farms are also trying to develop marketing in the country.

There appears to be considerable interest in expanding the production of organic foods, but the lack of legislation on organic farming and of data about contaminated soils and degraded land is a hurdle.

Genetically modified organisms

Republika Srpska is preparing a law on genetically modified organisms (GMOs), but there is no State law. It is important for GMOs to be regulated nationwide to ensure consistent application and an appropriate control of imports and exports. The main crops for which GMOs might be used in the near future are corn and soya. Bosnia and Herzegovina does not have a laboratory to perform GMO analyses. The law should regulate the marketing and labelling of GMO products, GMO seeds and GMO food and fodder products. This is important to preserve indigenous plant varieties and, more broadly, to protect consumers.

Erosion of agricultural land

According to the Assessment for Sustainable Development, before the war, about 5,200 hectares of farmland were lost annually, owing to construction, mining, flooding by man-made lakes and the construction of landfills. Losses are currently even higher due to the abandonment of agricultural activities and fires. According to statistical records, the losses for the past two years amounted to over 10,000 hectares a year on average. Furthermore, the expanse of karst in Herzegovina and western Bosnia and Herzegovina results from the misuse of sloping land (clear-cutting of forest, improper agricultural management).

Lijevče polje, Semberija and fertile farmland along the rivers Drina, Bosna, Vrbas, Sana, Spreča, Una, Sava and Neretva are endangered because of water erosion and the flooding of lowlands.

As a result of the recent war, the land in Bosnia and Herzegovina is also marked by hundreds of kilometres of trenches, innumerable concrete bunkers, and craters from shells, bombs and missiles. Many agricultural areas are mined, which at present prevents them from being managed and is a threat to people.

The issue of land protection and controlled land use is in general governed by the Laws on Physical Planning. Special importance in spatial plans should therefore be given to forests and other vegetation, agricultural land of high value or of specific use, areas endangered by erosion or floods, karst, flatlands, degraded forests, soils and vulnerable areas that require special protection.

Guidelines for the protection and use of forests and agricultural land are given in the entities' Laws on Forests and Laws on Agricultural Land. There are no special environmental charges or taxes on fertilizers, pesticides or other agrochemicals nor are there charges or taxes on land use with clear environmental relevance. Erosion is not directly addressed in these Laws. However, some articles define the action that should be taken to protect the land from harm. These include a construction ban in the protection zones, the obligatory deposition of humus land, afforestation, ground levelling and grass cover after certain land works (civil constructions, mining, tree cutting), and a ban on the discharge of harmful substances (e.g. pesticides, oil derivatives, radioactive material). The Laws do not prescribe a programme for the conservation of water and soil or measures to combat soil contamination, and there is no action plan to combat desertification and soil degradation.

Animal waste

The disposal of waste of animal origin, particularly carcasses and potentially dangerous animal parts, requires far more attention that it is now getting. The problem could otherwise have a serious negative influence on animal and public health as well as on the environment. A few of the bigger towns have rendering plants (Sarajevo, Mostar, Banja Luka), but their capacities are not sufficient. It is common practice to dump animal carcasses on municipal landfills. There is also no service to take care of animals killed on the road or in similar situations. This is a permanent health threat, as it could affect water, wild fauna and other resources. Urgent action in this respect is necessary.

Mines

Minefields are found throughout the country, particularly on State borders, the entities' borders, and on former front lines where battles took place during the war. The local inhabitants, particularly farmers, know the areas that might be mined, but there is no guarantee that an area is free of mines. So because of their lifestyle farmers are particularly exposed and vulnerable. The total area known or suspected to be dangerous is 2,145 km2, which constitutes 4.2% of the country. According to current estimates, the total suspect area is some 4,000 km2, that is, 8% of the country (according to some estimates up to 30% of agricultural land is

mined). A systematic inquiry in 2001 reduced the total suspect area by 50%.

Table 10.4: Priority mine-clearing of agricultural land

Priority demining area for agriculture/fishery (ha)	185,433
% on total	4
% on agricultural/fishery	31

Source: Food and Agriculture Organization of the United Nations, GCP/BIH/002/ITA.

Monitoring

Data on agriculture are not always based on actual measurements and studies. Statistics are collected slowly and the fact that the country does not have an agricultural census makes it particularly difficult. Nationwide data on agriculture are derived from a statistical survey, mainly based on the latest census, which was carried out in 1991. Post-war data are based on estimates, which are not necessarily reliable and sometimes contradictory.

10.5 The decision-making framework

Policies and strategies

Agriculture is one of the most important national sectors, not only from the economic point of view, but also from the point of food security, a stable rural society and the environment. There is no overall agricultural strategy, but for the Mid-term Development Strategy (2004-2007) agriculture is one of the priorities. The issues that it covers range from the legal and institutional framework, funding, science and education to land management, environmental impact, livestock production, plant production, industrial crops and ecological production.

The overriding objective given in the Mid-term Development Strategy is to redevelop the agricultural sector to its pre-war level, to strengthen its competitiveness and to take into account the challenges and difficulties stemming from international integration processes. The Strategy also seeks to:
- Strengthen human capacity and increase employment;
- Reform working and living conditions in the rural areas to enable the population to realize its economic, cultural and social potential;
- Improve and preserve the natural environment, while promoting sustainable and ecological agriculture;

- Decrease the country's dependence on the imports of agricultural products;
- Decrease the overall trade deficit; and
- Improve demographic coverage.

Privatization

In a country where agricultural land is scarce, policies that promote optimal land use are fundamental to the future of the agricultural sector. Current policy remains largely as it was before the war, with a strong emphasis on private landownership. Before the war, approximately 90% of agricultural land was owned by individual farmers, 6% by State farms and 4% was managed by farm cooperatives. Few agricultural producers have the capacity for commodity production. The average size of a farm is about 3.5 ha further divided into 7 or 8 separate parcels (plots). Such fragmentation has been under way for the past 50 years as a result of nationalization and agrarian reform, as well as inheritance legislation.

The current Law on Property Inheritance (from the former Yugoslavia) allows the successors to inherit a proportion of the real estate, or the land is split according to the will of the deceased owner. This Law also established a maximum size for private farms, at 10 ha of land. In the collectivization process, the best land was nationalized and became State property, and smaller plots (usually of worse quality) remained private. Denationalization (where the land is given to its previous owners) has started, but is still far from complete. Agricultural land is not yet privatized, while the privatization of agricultural enterprises has been formally but not always successfully finished. The number of owners is growing continuously and the size of the holdings is getting smaller. This fragmented structure impedes any serious production and management schemes in modern agriculture, and it is too optimistic to expect large-scale structural improvement in the next five years.

About 100,000 hectares of very good quality arable land remains in State ownership. The privatization process started in 1999, with the privatization of small and medium-sized businesses. Privatization is a prerequisite for future development, and it is expected that the State will facilitate and speed up the process. Private ownership, with its accountability, will also likely improve the environmental situation, in particular the identification of environmental damage and polluters.

The legal framework

Legislation currently regulating the sector is listed in table 10.5, together with the year of adoption (any by-laws are marked with "+").

Table 10.5: Agricultural legislation

Level	Law	Year	By-laws
State	Law on Veterinary Medicine	2002	-
	Law on Plant Health Protection	2003	
Federation	Law on Cooperatives	1997	+
	Law on Agricultural Land	1998	+
	Law on Medicines in Veterinary Medicine	1998	-
	Law on Waters	1998	-
	Law on Measures for the Improvement of Livestock Raising	1998	-
	Law on Recognition and Protection of Agricultural and Forest Plants	2000	-
	Law on Veterinary Medicine	2000	-
	Law on Seed and Plant Material for Agricultural Plants	2001	-
	Law on Tobacco	2002	-
Republika Srpska	Law on Brandy and Wine	1997	-
	Law on Tobacco	1997	-
	Law on the Agricultural Inspectorate	1997	-
	Law on Agricultural Land	1997	+
	Law on Plant Protection	1997	+
	Law on Seed and Seeding Material	1997	+
	Law on Measures for the Improvement of Livestock Raising	1998	+
	Law on Agricultural Cooperatives	1999	-
	Law on Procurement and Allocation of Resources for the Development of Agriculture and Rural Areas	2002	+

Source: Official Gazettes.

Although these laws establish the legal framework for agriculture, there are few regulations and by-laws and those that do exist remain largely unimplemented. In addition, some of the basic strategic laws are still missing; there is no State law on agriculture, agricultural land, animal production or forestry. But there is definitely positive evidence of State regulation in the veterinary and phyto-sanitary field, although this is not fully implemented either. In Republika Srpska a new law on agricultural land is being prepared. The law should accelerate the privatization of the agricultural sector and resolve several landownership issues as well as the long-term leasing of land. In the Federation, preparation of the legislation has been slower (as seen in the table).

The main problem is the fact that there are no nationwide strategic documents, particularly in agriculture, or they are still in the pipeline. While some are implemented as projects in the cantons or in institutes, the lack of coordination of all those activities is crucial at more central levels. But some subjects have been omitted at all levels: genetically modified organisms, the carbon cycle, many subjects that are the responsibility of the State according to worldwide conventions, or rural development, which should be directly influenced by the outcome of the Johannesburg Summit and other major conferences.

Institutional framework

There is no State ministry for agriculture, but there is a State Veterinary Office under the direct responsibility of the Ministry of Foreign Trade and Economic Relations (see box 10.1). This Ministry is responsible for some other agriculture-related activities as well, including exports, imports and responding to international markets. The State Veterinary Office has been preparing a new law on animal welfare, for possible adoption in 2004.

The Office seems to be working well, but there is one particular area that needs more attention, namely the disposal of animal waste, as discussed above.

Almost all agricultural responsibility lies with the two entities: the Federation's Ministry of Agriculture, Water Management and Forestry and Republika Srpska's Ministry of Agriculture, Forestry and Water Management. In addition, within the Federation, there are seven cantonal ministries of agriculture. In three cantons (Sarajevo, Gorazde and West Herzegovina) the agricultural sector is under the auspices of the economy ministries. There is a Department of Agriculture and Forestry in Brčko District. Inspection is the responsibility of the entities and the District.

All of these institutions need to be strengthened to meet the specific objectives of the Mid-term Development Strategy, particularly to be able to respond both to domestic and to international markets, to prepare a national policy, to monitor the environmental impact of agriculture and to establish databases to store and share this information; to prepare the necessary legislative and regulatory framework, and to manage natural resources.

Significant problems arise from the fragmented administrative structures, especially in the Federation, and from understaffing. Environmental issues are not incorporated into the structure. Cooperation among the ministries or institutions responsible for agriculture and the environment remains weak.

There are also differences in the way in which advisory services are organized. Republika Srpska has had its Agricultural Advisory Service (2-3 persons per region) since 2002, financed by its Ministry of Agriculture, Forestry and Water Management and this is a good basis on which to build. Advisory services are provided free of charge. There is no comparable system in the Federation, although some of the cantons have set up such services. There is also no public financing for advisory services in the Federation despite widespread agreement on the need for an effective extension service, and an acceptable institutional framework has yet to be developed. In both entities, the advisory services, as well as other public institutions in agriculture, are running out of funding for their future operations.

There is no formal State-wide body to coordinate agricultural activities or monitor the environmental impact of agriculture across the country. But at least two State laws have already been adopted: the Law on Cooperatives and the Law on Veterinary Medicine. They coordinate State action, and apply to both entities and to Brčko District. Unfortunately, without a State ministry of agriculture, implementation of these Laws is problematic.

Box 10.1: Veterinary Office

The Veterinary Office has been organized and staffed, but some of its responsibilities are still carried out by the entities (veterinary border control at nine border points). Its responsibilities also include those required by the Convention on International Trade in Endangered Species of Wild Fauna and Flora (CITES), with implementation by the entities.

Prevention control against animal diseases is based on the laws and regulations of the exporting country. Animals are imported only from EU member States or from countries with prevention control of at least EU standards. Two laboratories can perform analyses for BSE ("mad cow disease").

The Office also has important responsibilities towards consumers, particularly in ensuring a traceable system of animal products for human consumption. A decree requiring registration of animals was adopted in 2003 (Official Gazette BiH 28/2003).

Rural development is in its infancy, and no ministry has clear responsibility in this area, although the Ministry of Agriculture, Forestry and Water Management in Republika Srpska is considering establishing a department for rural development, which would play a coordinating role.

Financing

In the absence of agricultural legislation and multi-year programmes, yearly incentive packages were created, but they did not allow producers to have a long-term view for their production plans. In 2001, budgetary allocations for incentives to agricultural production amounted to about KM 20 million (about 0.7% of consolidated budgets). In Bosnia and Herzegovina, 1.5 to 2% of gross agricultural product is allocated to incentives, which is many times lower than in neighbouring countries and much less than estimated in the Mid-term Development Strategy. In order to achieve the Strategy's agricultural objectives it is estimated that at least 3% of budgets (of the State, the entities, the cantons and Brčko District) would be necessary in 2003-2007, as shown in the table below. There are two major types of State-funded agricultural support schemes, one is for milk and the other for tobacco production.

In 2002, Republika Srpska adopted its Law on Procurement and Allocation of Resources for the Development of Agriculture and Rural Areas, which stipulated that, in the future, at least 4% of its budgetary revenues would be allocated for agriculture. In 2004, the Rulebook on the Conditions and Procedure of the Agricultural Subsidies Allocation (Official Gazette RS 28/04), regulating the procedure and rates of financial subsidies for agricultural production, was adopted. In 2003, the Government approved an Agricultural Trust Fund of KM 22,665,900, of which 6,108,000 was designated for crop production, and 3,600,000

for livestock. However, in the 2003 budget, this fell short, the amount budgeted being only 2.35%.

In 2003, the Federation allocated KM 12 million to agricultural subsidies for animal, crop and vegetable production, fishery and bee-keeping, with the biggest share given to milk and tobacco production, and to investments in new orchards. Some cantons also provide small amounts from their budgets to agriculture. There is no support for non-production-oriented agriculture. There are no funds provided anywhere in the country directly to agriculture and the environment; funds are primarily meant to intensify production, boost yields and increase income.

Investments have till now been market-driven. Most foreign investment has been in the processing industry. There are some good examples of industrial processing of raw agricultural products (milk, fruit); most of these industries are connected to one or more international donors or foreign companies.

Within the framework of the reconstruction programme for Bosnia and Herzegovina, a number of projects focused on reviving agriculture. Donations and credits were used to revitalize and strengthen agriculture, but the results failed to meet expectations, in most part because the projects were conceived and managed with a "top-down" approach. Poor credit repayment rates are another reason for the current unfavourable policy towards farmers. Potential farmers, entrepreneurs and other investors do not have access to adequate and favourable credits. There has been no continuity of the action, and the results are therefore minor. In 2003, Republika Srpska began to subsidize interest rates (at the level of 6%) for agricultural credits from its budget. This measure slightly increased the availability of credits.

Table 10.6: Estimated agricultural incentives (2003-2007)

million KM

Budgets	2003	2004	2005	2006	2007
Total	40	60	80	100	120
Entities	35	53	70	88	105
Cantons	3	5	6	8	9
Brčko District	2	3	4	5	6

Source: Mid-term Development Strategy (2004-2007).

10.6   Conclusions and recommendations

Agriculture in Bosnia and Herzegovina is one of the most important sectors, but it faces many difficulties. The country used to be a supplier of raw materials; agricultural production was quite developed in some places. During and since the war the structure of the rural community changed dramatically. Thousands of people fled their homes and villages, leaving farms unattended. Many have still not returned. Normal country life was interrupted and traditional activities were changed. The situation is now calmer and becoming better organized, but it will take some time before the infrastructure can be rebuilt and daily life fully ordered.

In this post-war period, the lack of a national strategy for agriculture is a serious constraint. Such a strategy is needed for many purposes, such as improving agricultural practices, raising awareness of the links between agriculture and the environment, and developing agriculture-related activities in the rural areas, for example agro-tourism, ecotourism and handicrafts. A strategy could also support the integration of the environment with other sectors, and cooperation and coordination between the entities and Brčko District and within the Federation.

A national legal framework for agriculture is also important. A law on agriculture should be prepared just after adoption of the strategy and should also deal with environmental issues and the sustainable development of rural areas. Once the basic legislation has been adopted and implemented, public services and other activities connected to rural communities should be able to built on that.

From the strategy, Bosnia and Herzegovina should derive a programme to support the return of the rural population, to revive rural areas and employment opportunities for the rural population, to clear mines in the agricultural areas and to ensure the quality of the soil. In this regard, it is important to pay attention to areas that are now contaminated with chemical substances and to prohibit the use of

chemicals in areas where they might pollute sources of water supply, farming soil, forests or air.

Management structures for the rural areas need to be developed. This is an area that needs the close attention of the ministries in the entities and the cantons. Their task should be to integrate agricultural development and rural development. Small-scale production and marketing can be efficient only through well-organized farming cooperatives or producer organizations.

Institutional strengthening is needed at the State level, too. A State ministry or other body responsible for agriculture should be established, inter alia, to control the certification of imports and exports, promote the export of organic food, ensure the harmonization of procedures and standards of agricultural and food safety inspectorates throughout the country, establish guidelines for the preservation of agriculture biodiversity and prepare for the requirements of the European Union.

Recommendation 10.1:

(a) A State ministry for Agriculture should be established and should be responsible, inter alia, for preparing the State's agricultural policy, facilitating inter-sectoral coordination, developing certification and promoting exports, standardizing the inspectorates, protecting agricultural biodiversity and cooperating with international partners. If no new ministry is established, these functions should be delegated to the State Ministry of Foreign Trade and Economic Relations.

(b) As a matter of priority, the State ministry responsible for agriculture should prepare a strategy and action plan for sustainable agricultural development to clearly set targets for agricultural development, provide the means to achieve these targets, address the links between agriculture and other sectors, and identify measures to promote sustainable rural development.

(c) From this strategy and action plan, the State ministry responsible for agriculture should

derive a law on agriculture and sustainable development.

As indicated, it is important for the State to establish an overall national strategy and action plan and ensure the standardization of agriculture. Implementation, however, is likely to continue to take place in the entities and Brčko District, and local communities should have the possibility of initiating activities for rural development. This will require a strong administrative structure and the development of infrastructure in the rural areas.

In much of the country the land is less suitable for an agricultural production economy, but living in the countryside could be improved by additional craft activities and tourism. These have to become a substantial livelihood in the rural communities. Some municipalities are already thinking of developing their villages and towns and these initiatives should be supported.

Recommendation 10.2:
The Federation's Ministry of Agriculture, Water Management and Forestry, Republika Srpska's Ministry of Agriculture, Forestry and Water Management and the Government of Brčko District should prepare multi-year sustainable rural development programmes.

Environmental concerns in agriculture are far more likely to be taken into account if there are strong, functioning extension or advisory services for the farmers that address the technical, organizational and environmental aspects of agriculture.

Research projects in agriculture, whether national or foreign-funded, have to be coordinated and easily accessible to the public and to professionals. The results and reports have to be regularly presented and shared with farmers through well-run advisory service offices. The media should also inform the general public about sustainable agriculture. Consumers need to recognize the quality of domestic products, become acquainted with organic production and learn to trust products with special labels.

Recommendation 10.3:
The Federation's Ministry of Agriculture, Water Management and Forestry, Republika Srpska's Ministry of Agriculture, Forestry and Water Management and the Government of Brčko District should establish, strengthen and support public advisory services and promote their activities in order to improve the transfer of knowledge in

agriculture and to raise the rural population's awareness of environmental issues.

The huge variety of indigenous plant species and breeds could be lost by the introduction of foreign high-yield varieties. Farmers look for a higher income and therefore higher yields. Of course, some of these new crop varieties are better suited for intensive production with more fertilizers and other chemicals. On the other hand, farmers still keep traditional crop seeds, which are adapted to the specific local environmental conditions. If farmers were to replace their seeds with newly imported cultivars, the richness in traditional crops would be reduced, and farmers would be exposed to additional risks.

The situation in traditional animal husbandry is similar; there are still some unique breeds, which are preserved only because of traditional farming. For instance, in the high mountains indigenous sheep and dogs with their nomad shepherds form a traditional way of life with different animals and people depending on each other in a rough environment. If only one is excluded, the system will collapse.

In underdeveloped areas some autochthonous breeds are still kept on farms, but in limited numbers, and they could be lost in a few years' time. There are also many semi-wild crops, which could serve as a genetic source for biotechnology and genetic engineering in agriculture.

Unique genetic sources should be protected immediately to prevent the genetic erosion of vulnerable indigenous agricultural organisms.

Recommendation 10.4:
(a) The State Ministry of Foreign Trade and Economic Relations, or another appropriate State body, should establish clear guidelines for the preservation of agricultural biodiversity.
(b) The Federation's Ministry of Agriculture, Water Management and Forestry, Republika Srpska's Ministry of Agriculture, Forestry and Water Management and the Government of Brčko District with the entities' ministries for environment, in consultation with cantonal governments and local authorities, should jointly prepare actions plans for agro-biodiversity preservation and provide funds for the preservation of indigenous and traditional animal breeds and plant species within the framework of the Convention of Biological Diversity (See recommendation 8.1).

Organic farming is definitely a market niche for traditional farmers and can also have a positive impact on the environment. To develop this type of farming, it is necessary to have a strong legislative framework that ensures inspection and certification and protects plants that could be overexploited (e.g. wild medicinal plants and wild mushrooms).

Recommendation 10.5:
The State ministry responsible for Agriculture, in coordination with the Federation's Ministry of Agriculture, Water Management and Forestry, Republika Srpska's Ministry of Agriculture, Forestry and Water Management and the Government of Brčko District, should develop and adopt the necessary legislation to support and promote organic farming. In drafting this legislation, the relevant directives of the European Union should be taken into account.

Chapter 11

ENVIRONMENTAL CONCERNS IN THE ENERGY SECTOR

11.1 Introduction

The energy sector is traditionally very important to Bosnia and Herzegovina, which used to be a producer of energy and raw materials for the other parts of the former Yugoslavia. The sector may be divided into four subsectors:

* Power;
* Coal mining;
* Gas; and
* Oil and oil derivates.

The power and mining sectors are predominantly based on indigenous resources of hydropower and coal. Gas, oil and oil derivates are imported either as raw materials or in processed forms.

The power sector is one of the strong points in the development of Bosnia and Herzegovina. The country has a surplus of generation capacity based on coal and hydropower. This creates an opportunity for the export of power to neighbouring countries, which in most cases are short of electricity. Considerable investments have been made since the war in refurbishing and improving the technical facilities, such as generation plants and the transmission network. Furthermore, the country still has large untapped hydropower resources and coal reserves, which make the power sector a potentially growing export earner.

Coal, exclusively lignite and brown coal, is mined in opencast and subsurface mines, primarily from the Tuzla, Central Bosnia and Ugljevik and Gatacki basins. Current production, approximately 50-60% of its pre-war level, covers to a large extent the needs of the power generation sector, which was developed on the back of the mines. The remaining coal production is supplied to households and industry.

Natural gas is imported by pipeline from the Russian Federation via Ukraine, Hungary and Serbia and Montenegro. Natural gas distribution within Bosnia and Herzegovina is basically limited to the major consumption centres in the regions of Sarajevo and Zenica. Before the war much of the gas was used in industry, but since the war industrial consumption has declined and demand has shifted predominantly to the household and heating sectors.

Before the war, Bosnia and Herzegovina used to have a substantial processing capacity for imported crude oil. Today, refinery capacities have declined, and many of the refined products for transport, energy and industry are imported.

There are no reliable data on the use and production of energy. No institution consolidates energy-related data, and the data that are available are scattered and inconsistent.

The description of the sector and its subsectors below is therefore not a complete quantitative description. The numbers given are "snapshots" illustrating the situation; they do not give an exact and detailed picture.

11.2 Energy supply

Primary energy supply

The basic indigenous resources of primary energy are hydropower and coal (lignite and brown coal), constituting some 60% of total primary energy spent. Table 11.1 shows the primary energy balance for the country in 2000 and 2001.

Table 11.1: Primary energy balance

Resources	2000				2001			
	Total primary energy (PJ)	% of gross total	Indigenous production (PJ)	Import (PJ)	Total primary energy (PJ)	% of gross total	Indigenous production (PJ)	Import (PJ)
Total	209.7	100.0	125.5	84.2	231.2	100.0	137.2	94.0
Per cent of total			59.9	40.1			59.3	40.7
Coal	94.2	44.9	94.2	..	92.0	39.7	92.0	..
Natural gas	8.3	4.0	..	8.3	5.5	2.4	..	5.5
Crude oil	32.5	15.5	..	32.5	48.7	21.1	..	48.7
Refined petroleum products	50.4	24.0	10.0	40.4	56.8	24.5	20.0	36.8
Firewood	4.0	1.9	4.0	..	4.5	2.0	4.5	..
Other fuels	3.0	1.4	..	3.0	3.0	1.3	..	3.0
Hydroelectric energy	17.3	8.3	17.3	..	20.7	9.0	20.7	..

Source: Ministry of Foreign Trade and Economic Relations. 2003.

Consumption of energy has declined considerably since the beginning of the war. In 1991 average energy consumption was about 73 GJ/capita; in 2000 it had fallen to some 45 GJ/capita. The pre-war level was slightly above the world average (1991; 69 GJ/capita), but by 2000 this had fallen to well below the world average of 70 GJ/capita (developed countries had an average of 236 GJ/capita). The drop is attributed mainly to the sharp decline in industrial output and in general economic activity. The years after the conflict show a recovery, but considerable development is still required.

Coal

The coal reserves of Bosnia and Herzegovina are estimated at around 10 billion tons. They are mainly located in three basins: Tuzla, Central Bosnia, and Ugljevik and Gatacki. Only lignite and brown coal are extracted, and hereinafter coal refers exclusively to lignite and brown coal. Over 80% of current production comes from these basins. Mines are mainly developed for two purposes: supply of coal to the thermal power plants and supply for a broad market, including export. Coal production (see table 11.2) has declined since the war.

Coal is predominantly produced in opencast mines. Before the war two thirds of the coal in the Federation and 95% of the coal in Republika Srpska was produced in opencast mines. Most is used for power generation: in 1990 about 70% (ca. 11.2 million tons) and now around 80% (ca. 7 million tons).

The balance is used for domestic and industrial purposes and some is exported. Coal production is expected to remain at its current level, or slightly increase over the next 10-15 years. The sector is at the same time expected to be restructured to enable

production to be maintained, while decreasing the number of employees from 15,000-16,000 to about 3,500. This will require substantial investments in the modernization of the mining operations.

Table 11.2: Coal production

		million tons
	1990	2000
Total	12.0	8.8
Federation	8.0	5.5
Republika Srpska	4.0	3.3

Source: Mid-term Development Strategy, Annex IX. Energy Sector Priorities. December 2002.

Oil and oil derivatives

Bosnia and Herzegovina has no proven resources of oil or gas, even if research surveys before the war indicated promising deposits.

Its refinery capacity is located in Republika Srpska. It consists of one refinery for the processing of crude oil into various petroleum products, such as motor fuels and fuel oil, and another processing facility for the production of motor oils and special-purpose lubricants. Both processing facilities are operating at low capacity, ca. 25% of their pre-war level.

As the domestic processing capacity is insufficient, refined petroleum products are imported.

Natural gas

Natural gas is imported from the Russian Federation (Gazprom), via Ukraine, Hungary and Serbia and Montenegro, and distributed by four distributors, two in each entity. Distribution is relatively limited and stretches only from Zvornik, where gas enters from Serbia and Montenegro, to Sarajevo and Zenica. The main consumption centres are Sarajevo and the industrial works in Zenica. The system is designed for approximately 1 billion m³/year, and current leased transport capacity to the border is around 750 million m³/year. Before the war annual consumption was above 600 million m³, and rising. Now consumption is down to between 150 and 200 million m³, primarily owing to reduced industrial activity. The shift in gas consumption from industry to residential use has also led to considerable seasonal variations in gas consumption, which is resulting in a less-than-optimum use of the infrastructure. To address the problem, the country is taken steps to extend the capacities in the Stell Company Zenica and the Coke Factory Lukavac.

The development of a regional energy market in South-East Europe is expected to lead to the development of a natural gas supply system in Bosnia and Herzegovina, with the possibility of new supply routes and an extended distribution system.

<u>Alternative energy sources</u>

Bosnia and Herzegovina could use alternative energy sources. These are, except for hydropower and some biomass, not developed to any large extent. Furthermore, there are few reliable data and studies on their actual potential. Possible alternative sources are:

- Wind power: there are several locations with favourable wind conditions in the country. A survey of the potential for establishing wind farms is planned with international assistance. Preliminary estimates indicate a technical potential of wind power of up to 50 MW_{el} for the period up to 2020.

- As solar radiation in Bosnia and Herzegovina is among the highest in Europe, solar energy could provide a substantial input, for heating, hot water and power generation. No assessment of the overall solar energy potential is available.

- Geothermal energy is traditionally used for spas in the region. Use on a larger scale could substantially help the heating sector and possibly, depending on geological conditions, also power generation. On the basis of existing wells, the potential for home heating and similar, relatively low-temperature purposes has been assessed at 30-35 MW_{th}, while the potential for electricity generation is considerably lower. Private companies are currently investigating a possible commercial use for geothermal energy in the Sarajevo Region.

- Energy from biomass plays locally a large role in the form of firewood for heating and other domestic purposes, particularly in rural areas. However, the sector has a far bigger potential, as Bosnia and Herzegovina has a relatively developed forest industry, including sawmills and wood processing. Residues from industry and selected residues from forestry operations that today are dumped or burnt in the open are potentially an important energy source.

11.3   Energy conversion and use

Electricity

Currently, Bosnia and Herzegovina has three vertically integrated power utilities, which each have a monopoly in their distribution areas:
- Electricity Company of Bosnia and Herzegovina (Elektroprivreda Bosnia and Herzegovina, EPBiH);
- Electricity Company of the Croat Community Herzeg-Bosnia (Elektroprivreda Hrvatske Zajednice Herceg-Bosne, EPHZHB); and
- Electricity Company of Republika Srpska (Elektroprivreda Republike Srpske, EPRS).

Each company has its own generation, transmission and distribution facilities; the Common Electricity Coordination Centre (ZEKC), jointly owned by the three power utilities, coordinates dispatching and ensures the system's integrity.

In the former Yugoslavia, Bosnia and Herzegovina's power system was developed to supply power to other parts of the country, it therefore has strong links to neighbouring countries, as shown on figure 11.1. Furthermore, the country will, like all other countries in South-East Europe, be connected to the single European electricity market in 2005 or 2006 and intends to participate in supplying green electricity (through a green certificate system), generated by renewable energy sources, in accordance with EU Directive 2001/77/EC on renewables. This will encourage the country to improve its energy mix by developing domestic renewable energies, but it will also require new legal provisions that provide for green certification. At the moment, no such mechanism exists.

Figure 11.1: Map of Transmission system and generation facilities

Source: http://www.elektroprivreda.ba

Even though the transmission system is not fully rehabilitated, considerable power exchange is taking place in the region, as shown for instance on figure 11.2. The transmission system will be rehabilitated by the end of 2005.

Power production facilities comprise hydropower plants and thermal generation plants using local coal. Installed capacities are shown in table 11.3.

The division of production between hydropower and thermal generation varies from year to year depending on rainfall, with a potential of about 50% of current generation coming from hydro-sources. Table 11.4 shows the available production statistics.

The power plants as well as the transmission and distribution system were severely damaged during the war, as evidenced by the very low production rates. After the war, the World Bank, EBRD and bilateral financing institutions invested considerable sums into refurbishment and rehabilitation. Now the newer units of the thermal power plants are in relatively good operating condition, while the oldest units have, in principle, been retired. However, even the most modern units are fairly inefficient. The most efficient units, Ugljevik and Gacko, have heat rates of about 11,500 $kJ_{fuel}/kWh_{electricity}$, which corresponds to an electric efficiency of 31%. Large modern units may have electric efficiencies of 35-40%, even with the relatively low calorific value coal qualities at hand in Bosnia and Herzegovina. The current utilization levels of the thermal plants is relatively low compared to installed capacity; the produced energy corresponds to only between 3,500 and

4,000 hours of full-load operation, or some 50-60% of practicably possible production.

Hydropower generation, transmission and distribution have similarly been rehabilitated with assistance from the international community.

The final rehabilitation of the transmission systems will make it technically possible to increase power exports from Bosnia and Herzegovina. This is an opportunity for the country to boost its export earnings. It will also increase the pressure to better use the existing thermal generation capacities and to develop new capacity, in both thermal generation and hydropower.

Bosnia and Herzegovina has a large potential in both hydropower and thermal generation based on coal. The untapped hydropower potential is 6,000 MW above the generation capacity, i.e. more than 22,000 GWh a year. Several new hydropower projects have reached relatively advanced stages of design, and the power companies are looking for international financing for their realization. Some thermal generation projects based on local coal have also reached advanced planning stages.

Heating

The climate is in most parts of the country such that substantial home heating is required during wintertime. Home heating is for the most part done by individual stoves and boilers. In urban areas block heating systems for several buildings are also quite common. Some district heating systems exist, especially in Sarajevo, Banja Luka, Zenica and Tuzla. Electric heating is used as a supplement or in some cases the sole heating source, which increases pressure on power distribution.

The district heating system in Tuzla derives its heat from the Tuzla power plant, thereby being the sole example of an operational co-generation installation for domestic heating in Bosnia and Herzegovina. Before the war the Banja Luka district heating system used co-generation heat from a pulp and paper industry. The industry is now not operating, and district heating is supplied by heavy fuel oil (*mazut*) fired heat-only boilers. The Sarajevo district heating system uses natural gas in heat-only installations.

Figure 11.2: EPRS power exchange with neighbouring utilities 2002

Source: http://www.elektroprivreda-rs.com

Table 11.3: Power production facilities

Plant	Location	Thermal power plants				
		Gross capacity	Installed capacity	Technical minimum	Available capacity for energy	for steam
		M W	M W	M W	M W	M W
Total		**2,320**	**1,957**	**1,243**	**1,690**	**40**
Tuzla Total	**Federation**	**921**	**779**	**523**	**671**	**40**
Tuzla 1		40	32	16	19	10
Tuzla 2		40	32	16	13	16
Tuzla 3		118	100	56	77	14
Tuzla 4		235	200	145	182	..
Tuzla 5		235	200	145	182	..
Tuzla 6		253	215	145	198	..
Kakanj Total	**Federation**	**693**	**578**	**360**	**486**	**0**
Kakanj 1		40	32	18	25	..
Kakanj 2		40	32	18	25	..
Kakanj 3		40	32	18	25	..
Kakanj 4		40	32	18	23	..
Kakanj 5		125	110	55	84	..
Kakanj 6		138	110	55	96	..
Kakanj 7		270	230	178	208	..
Gacko	Republika Srpska	353	300	180	265	..
Ugljevik	Republika Srpska	353	300	180	268	..

Plant	Location	Hydroelectric plants			
		River	Plant type	Usable storage hm^3	Installed capacity MW
Total				2,043	2,064
Trebinje 1 100%	Republika Srpska	Trebisnjica	PA	1,100	2 X 54 + 1 X 60
Dubrovnik 100%	Republika Srpska	Trebisnjica	DA	9	2 X 108
Trebinje 2	Republika Srpska	Trebisnjica	P		1 X 8
Capljina	Federation	Trebisnjica	RHE	5	2 X 215
Rama	Federation	Rama	DA	466	2 X 80
Jablanica	Federation	Neretva	DA	288	3 X 25 + 3 X 30
Grabovica	Federation	Neretva	PA	5	2 X 58.5
Salakovac	Federation	Neretva	PA	16	3 X 70
Mostar	Federation	Neretva	PA	6	3 X 25
Jajce 1	Federation	Pliva	DP	2	2 X 30
Jajce 2	Federation	Vrbas	DP	2	3 X 10
Bocac	Republika Srpska	Vrbas	PA	43	2 X 55
Visegrad	Republika Srpska	Drina	PA	101	3 X 105

Sources : Elektroprivreda BiH. The Public Electric Power Company of Bosnia and Herzegovina. www.elektroprivreda.ba, 2003.

Note : P = run-of-river; DA = derivation storage; DP = derivation run-of-river; RHE = reversible; PA = storage.

Before the war district heating systems were established also in some smaller communities. Few have been restarted owing to war damage, and neglected maintenance.

Energy intensity and efficiency

Per capita energy consumption in Bosnia and Herzegovina is, as stated above, low, both compared to the world average and certainly in comparison to developed countries. Consumption of electricity is also below the world average: in 2000 it was 1,915 kWh/capita, while the world average was 2,243 kWh/capita and the OECD average 8,089 kWh/capita.

An indication of the overall efficiency of energy use is the energy intensity ratio of primary energy supply (in, for instance, tons of oil equivalent (TOE)) to GDP (in, for instance, US$), that is, how much energy is used to create one unit of GDP. Recent developments in Bosnia and Herzegovina and a comparison with other countries are shown in table 11.5.

Table 11.4: Total power production

GWh

	EPBiH		EPHZHB	EPRS		Total	
	HPP	**TPP**	**HPP**	**HPP**	**TPP**	**HPP**	**TPP**
1991	1,413	6,014	1,688	n/a	n/a	n/a	n/a
1992	1,069	2,160	n/a	n/a	n/a	n/a	n/a
1993	497	650	n/a	1,319	276	n/a	926
1994	716	550	n/a	2,299	164	n/a	714
1995	767	649	n/a	2,341	14	n/a	663
1996	1,124	1,127	n/a	2,893	1,077	n/a	2,204
1997	1,172	2,298	n/a	2,372	1,709	n/a	4,007
1998	1,264	2,740	n/a	2,026	2,290	n/a	5,030
1999	1,443	2,601	n/a	2,630	2,375	n/a	4,976
2000	1,275	3,420	n/a	2,213	2,182	n/a	5,602
2001	1,526	3,589	1,939	2,626	2,051	6,091	5,640
2002	1,233	4,307	n/a	n/a	n/a	n/a	n/a

Sources : Elektroprivreda BiH. The Public Electric Power Company of Bosnia and Herzegovina.
www.elektroprivreda.ba, www.elektroprivreda-rs.com, www.ephzhb.ba. 2003.
Note : HPP is hydro power plant and TPP is thermal power plant.

The relatively bad starting point in 1991 has been further worsened by low capacity utilization, damage from the war and neglected operations and maintenance. Generally, efficiency in energy generation as well as in end-use is low.

An example of end-use inefficiency is the reported 160 kWh/m^2 for domestic heating in the Sarajevo district heating system. The average in Western Europe would be 90-120 kWh/m^2 for similar climatic conditions.

It is worth noting that the efficiencies in comparable countries in the region, such as Croatia and Albania, have developed considerably more favourably than in Bosnia and Herzegovina. This may be partly explained by their better economic development, but may also be attributed to their faster development of institutions fostering energy efficiency and incentives to save energy. Furthermore, it is apparent that Republika Srpska uses energy considerably less efficiently than the Federation.

Table 11.5: Energy intensity

a) Energy intensity ratio

TOE per thousand "1995 US$" GDP

	1991	**1997**	**1998**	**1999**	**2000**	**2001**
Bosnia and Herzegovina	..	0.615	0.701	0.618	0.718	0.678
World average	0.326	0.308	0.304	0.301	0.297	0.295
European Union	0.167	0.158	0.157	0.153	0.149	0.15
Croatia	..	0.369	0.372	0.366	0.344	0.337
Albania	0.931	0.399	0.411	0.581	0.549	0.525

Source : International Energy Agency. http://www.iea.org. 2003.

b) Energy intensity ratio

TOE per thousand current US$ GDP

	1991	**1997**	**1998**	**1999**	**2000**	**2001**
Bosnia and Herzegovina	0.715	..	0.846	0.769	0.796	0.876
Federation of Bosnia and Herzegovina	..	..	0.661	0.564	0.577	0.667
Republika Srspska	..	..	1.363	1.358	1.446	1.486

Source : Federation's Ministry of Energy. Mining and Industry. 2003.

11.4   Environmental impacts from energy

Coal mining has a negative environmental impact: soil destruction as a result of opencast mining, landfilling of overburden and washing residue from the mines. Opencast mines alone are estimated to cover approximately 12,800 ha and waste from mining operations is estimated to occupy some 6,000 ha. Furthermore, effluent from the washing of coal and other mining operations as well as leaks from dumps are polluting water bodies and threatening groundwater, because effluent treatment plants are virtually non-existent.

The thermal generation plants are big polluters. The energy sector is at present the country's main air polluter. Table 11.6 shows that the energy sector in the Federation of Bosnia and Herzegovina emits between 65 and 90% of all SO_2, NO_x and CO_2 emissions to the atmosphere. Before the war, heavy industry, such as the chemical or steel industry, was a major air polluter. Many of these factories are today closed, which is why the thermal power generation can be assumed to be the biggest air polluter.

Similar data from Republika Srpska were not available, but it is assumed that the situation is largely the same as in the Federation.

As previously mentioned, a comprehensive modernization and refurbishment programme has been undertaken at a number of thermal generation plants with international financing. Some of the improvements brought about are:

- The Tuzla power plant has reduced total dust emissions to 20-25% of its pre-war levels, at unit 3 from 800 to 100 mg/Nm³ and at unit 4 to around 70 mg/Nm³;
- It has also cut the NO_x emissions from unit 3 to 400 mg/Nm³ and from unit 4 to some 350 mg/Nm³;
- Dust emissions at the Kakanj power plant have fallen to about 150 mg/Nm³; and

- Emissions are monitored continuously at the major production units.

Generally, the dust and NO_x emission values presented for the rehabilitated units are in line with current EU legislation for large combustion plants (Directive 2001/80/EC). Sulphur emissions have not been tackled so far. The local coal generally has a moderate sulphur content calculated by weight, but total sulphur emissions will nevertheless be substantial as much fuel is required due to its low calorific value and high ash content. Desulphurization equipment is planned for some generation plants, but funding may not be forthcoming.

Despite its efforts to cut emissions, the power generation sector continues to be the major source of air emissions. The best available estimates for air emissions in the Federation of Bosnia and Herzegovina are presented in table 11.7.

The energy sector supposedly refers primarily to power generation. Substantial emissions are likely from domestic heating (see the section on heating); therefore, total emissions are probably substantially higher than indicated. Even the levels presented here are high, considering the country's comparatively small energy sector. For the sake of comparison, the agreed 1998 SO_2 and NO_x emission ceilings for existing combustion plants in some EU countries with a population comparable to that of Bosnia and Herzegovina are presented in table 11.8.

In addition to the impact on ambient air, the power generation sector emits pollutants to water, mainly from the handling and treatment of ash and slag. These effluents have so far been discharged untreated into rivers. Now some plants have been modified to use a system of dry ash handling, which in addition to reducing the effluents facilitates the use of ash as a raw material in the cement industry. In recent years about 400 tons of ash from the Tuzla power plant has been used at the nearby Lukavac cement factory.

Table 11.6   Air emissions from the energy sector in the Federation of Bosnia and Herzegovina

% of total

	Actual			Estimated	
	1999	2000	2001	2002	2003
SO₂	89	89	89	88	89
NOₓ	69	70	69	69	70
CO₂	71	70	69	67	65

Source: Federation's Meteorological Institute. Pressure on the Environment, 2003.

Table 11.7: Air emissions in the Federation of Bosnia and Herzegovina

kilotons/year

	Actual			Estimated	
	1999	2000	2001	2002	2003
SO_2					
Energy sector	218.0	204.0	189.0	176.0	160.0
Industry	24.0	22.0	20.0	20.0	15.0
Transport	2.9	3.2	3.5	4.0	4.5
NO_x					
Energy sector	46.6	48.0	46.8	47.0	48.0
Industry	6.3	6.5	6.3	6.0	6.0
Transport	14	14	15	15	15
CO_2					
Energy sector	8,351	8,776	8,621	8,700	8,800
Industry	1,438	1,511	1,484	1,600	1,650
Transport	2,038	2,249	2,435	2,700	3,050
CO					
Energy sector	2.1	2.1	2.0	2.1	2.1
Industry	0.4	0.4	0.4	0.4	0.4
Transport	115.0	113.0	119.0	121.0	123.0

Source: Federation's Meteorological Institute. Pressure on the Environment, 2003.

The disposal of ash and slag is another major environmental concern related to the power sector. Ash and slag are estimated to occupy about 600 ha in total, and, even if no evidence has been found, leaks and effluent from these sites may threaten groundwater and surface water. Moreover, if improperly managed, this disposal may also create dust, which could become a local environmental and health problem.

The individual heating of houses and apartments uses mainly local fuels such as coal and firewood. Combustion is generally poor, generating substantial local emissions to air, which in wintertime create a considerable health problem. It is unclear if emissions from the heating sector are included in the available emission estimates (see table 11.7). The reported emissions from the energy sector supposedly relate mainly to power generation, and possibly also the larger district heating plants. Individual heating installations and small and medium-sized block heating plants probably also create emissions, which are largely unaccounted for in the statistics.

Existing hydropower plants have a relatively limited impact on the environment provided that they are properly maintained and operated. New hydropower developments may have considerable negative environmental consequences, including diverse effects on biodiversity and tourism. The damming of rivers for small and large-scale hydro

applications may have a significant environmental impact. Firstly, it affects the migration of fish and disrupts their spawning habits. Secondly, it leads to the flooding of valleys that often contain wilderness areas, residential areas or archeologically significant remains. Moreover, there are also concerns about the consequences of disrupting the natural flow of water downstream and disrupting the natural course of nature. On a more positive note, the reservoirs behind dams are valuable recreation areas and dams assist in flood control, thereby preventing economic hardship to local agriculture and municipalities. Bosnia and Herzegovina is now requiring an environmental impact assessment for all new hydropower projects.

Table 11.8: Emission ceilings 1998, for existing combustion plants in selected EU countries

kilotons/year

Country	SO_2	NO_x
Austria	36	11
Belgium	212	66
Denmark	141	81
Finland	68	48
Greece	320	70
Ireland	124	50
Portugal	270	64
Sweden	45	19

Source: European Union. Directive 2001/80/EC, Annexes I and II.

11.5   Policy objectives and management

The policy framework

There is no specific State energy policy or strategy. The Federation of Bosnia and Herzegovina did develop a framework for an energy sector strategy in 2002, but it has yet not been turned into an adoptable strategy.

The Federation's framework identifies important areas that could also serve as a basis for a nationwide strategy, including:

- Restructuring (all sectors) and regulatory changes;
- Integration of the energy market, between entities and regionally;
- Introduction of modern technology and efficiency improvements, including the encouragement of renewable energy sources and the co-generation of heat and power;
- Introduction of a commercial pricing policy excluding social considerations (leaving social support to other sectors); and
- Encouragement of foreign investments in the energy sector.

Republika Srpska has not yet developed a comparable draft energy strategy.

The latest State strategy for economic development and the recently adopted Mid-term Development Strategy emphasize that environmental protection and energy savings are important in the fight against poverty. The energy priorities in the Mid-term Development Strategy, which are broadly similar to those in the Federation's draft strategy discussed above, constitute a first step towards a national energy strategy.

The NEAP deals with the energy sector rather superficially; however, it proposes the following energy-efficiency (and thereby emission-reducing) measures:

- Development of a programme of stabilization and gradual decrease in the emission of greenhouse gases by improving energy efficiency through technology restructuring, better use of energy sources and increased use of renewable energy sources; and
- Preparation of a development strategy for the energy sector that would provide balanced consumption of domestic and foreign energy resources and maximize the use of renewable sources.

Neither the entities nor the State seem to have taken concrete steps to develop such programmes and strategies following the NEAP.

The Mid-term Development Strategy provides a good foundation for the development of an energy strategy for the country. This is to a certain extent also true for the NEAP, even if it does not focus on the fundamental problems of the sector, but rather on issues somewhat down the road. However, it is imperative for these high-level policy documents to be further developed into a concrete strategy for both entities that could guide society towards a sustainable, environmentally acceptable energy system.

Energy prices

Energy prices are traditionally set by the Governments of the entities and kept artificially low. Particularly the household sector is subsidized for social reasons. For example, natural gas is slightly cheaper for households than for large buyers. The district heating company in Sarajevo, which buys approximately 50% of the natural gas imported into Bosnia and Herzegovina, pays KM $0.42/m^3$, while individual consumers pay KM $0.41/m^3$. This pricing policy does not encourage a switch-over from individual heating to a centralized supply, which has a potential for higher efficiency, through, for instance, combined heat and power production.

The legal framework

The energy sector's legal framework, including rules and regulations, is largely inherited from the former Yugoslavia and needs to be modernized and adapted. There are no specific laws or legislation on energy efficiency and energy saving. The legal regulations as well as the tax policies in the civil engineering, construction and building industry do not encourage energy savings or its efficient use. So most reconstructed building and installations do not meet modern efficiency standards.

A set of laws governing the restructuring of the electricity sector has been adopted in both entities:

- Act on Electricity Transmission, System Regulator and Operator in Bosnia and Herzegovina (Official Gazette No. 7/02);
- Law establishing the company for the transmission of electric power in Bosnia and Herzegovina; and

- Law establishing an independent system operator for the transmission system of Bosnia and Herzegovina.

The above legislation has been developed to modernize the structure of the power sector, to break up the current monopolies and to transform the sector so that generation, transmission and distribution are open to competition. It also includes provisions regulating fair and equal access to the transmission system. The legislation does not specifically address environmental issues or efficiency; neither does it address technical issues related to the generation, distribution and use of electricity. A set of laws on the production and distribution of electricity exists for each entity. These do not seem to have been updated to meet modern standards.

To use legislation as a tool for improving efficiency, a set of appropriate by-laws and updated legislation in the entities on distribution and generation, regulating pricing for instance, is required. Furthermore, by-laws to apply the requirements of the Laws on Environmental Protection, the Laws on Air Protection and the Laws on Nature Protection to the energy sector are required, through, for example, emission standards. The country intends to join the single European electricity market, and thereby start trading in green electricity in the near future. Current legislation does not seem to have the appropriate mechanism, e.g. regulations for green certificates, to enable this.

The natural gas sector will be required to undergo a similar restructuring as the electricity sector when the country joins the European energy market.

The institutional framework

Overall State responsibility for energy issues rests with the Ministry of Foreign Trade and Economic Relations. Its energy responsibilities include:
- To develop a common legal and institutional framework for the sector;
- To establish the country's international electricity policy; and
- To coordinate and as far as practicable harmonize energy sector laws and regulations in the entities.

In the entities the responsibilities of the Federation's Ministry of Energy, Mining and Industry and Republika Srpska's Ministry of Economy, Energy and Development include legislation, tariffs, energy inspectorates and policies. They also manage and oversee the large public energy corporations, including the power companies and gas distribution;

Compared to the entities' Ministries, the State Ministry seems to have few resources, which is why coordination appears to be weak, with the electricity sector being an exception. The State Ministry has set up a separate Department for Energy, but it is partly staffed.

In accordance with the draft Law on Energy Efficiency, it is foreseen to establish an energy efficiency agency or centre.

11.6 Conclusions and recommendations

The energy sectors of the two entities are very similar and suffer from the same problems of inefficiency and environmental impact. Development would be improved by a coordinated approach from both entities. The recommendations below are therefore directed towards the Ministry of Foreign Trade and Economic Relations as a State coordinating body, as well as to the Ministry of Economy, Energy and Development in Republika Srpska and to the Ministry of Energy, Mining and Industry in the Federation of Bosnia and Herzegovina.

In addition to being damaged by the war, the energy sector in Bosnia and Herzegovina is suffering from large inefficiencies inherited from the former Yugoslavia. These include outdated, inefficient and polluting technology, a structure with large integrated companies that does not encourage an increase in competition and efficiency, and legislation that does not provide incentives to save energy and does not penalize polluters. Initiatives have begun, largely driven by pressure from international financing institutions, to restructure the power sector, including the unbundling of the large power companies and opening up the generation and distribution of power to foreign investors, who may be necessary to develop a capital-intensive infrastructure. This process has not really got off the ground for other important subsectors, such as coal mining, natural gas and heating.

Recommendation 11.1:
The State Ministry of Foreign Trade and Economic Relations, in coordination with the Federation's Ministry of Energy, Mining and Industry and Republika Srpska's Ministry of Economy, Energy and Development, should extend the restructuring and liberalization of the electricity sector initiated for the power sector to other parts of the energy sector.

Once the overall framework is established, stable and flexible rules for energy activities have to be set. These should:

- Encourage the co-generation of heat and power (CHP) where economically justified and create incentives for its development. Such incentives may include: that the power companies have to take power produced by CHP at a preferential rate; the introduction of green certificates for power and heat produced by CHP combined with a demand that power companies should include a certain percentage of "green electricity" in their production mix; and support to the development or rehabilitation of district heating schemes allowing for the introduction of CHP instead of individual heating.

- Encourage energy production from renewable energy sources, such as biomass, wind energy, solar energy, geothermal energy and small-scale hydropower, where economically justified and environmentally acceptable and create incentives for its development. The incentive can largely be similarly structured as for encouraging CHP.

- Encourage end-use energy efficiency by setting standards for efficiency, e.g. by energy labelling schemes.

- Set rules for the technical performance of energy installations, including emission standards.

Recommendation 11.2:
The State Ministry of Foreign Trade and Economic Relations, in coordination with the Federation's Ministry of Energy, Mining and Industry and Republika Srpska's Ministry of Economy, Energy and Development, should develop an energy policy and common energy legislation that encourages a more sustainable and economical energy system based on renewable energy sources, co-generation of heat and power and end-use energy efficiency, and that sets a well defined framework for the performance of energy activities.

The development and implementation of an energy policy, framework energy legislation and detailed

rules and regulations for its implementation are complex tasks that involve a large number of players in the sector. A structure has to be created to enable this to happen. This structure may include:

- An energy agency, under the Ministry of Foreign Trade and Economic Relations to:
  o Prepare a sustainable and concrete energy strategy;
  o Draft the legal and regulatory framework for approval by the relevant legislative bodies of the entities and the State; and
  o Oversee the implementation of the strategy, the legal framework and the regulations, including the development of energy-efficiency standards;

- Independent price regulators for the subsectors where it is necessary; and

- One or more energy centres, possibly with private sector participation, to assist in dissemination, advice and implementation of energy-efficient technologies.

Recommendation 11.3:
The State Ministry of Foreign Trade and Economic Relations should coordinate the activities of the entities' ministries of energy and other relevant environmental authorities in implementing the environmental management instruments such as Environmental Impact Assessment for proposed energy developments and integrated permits (IPPC) for industrial installation.

A prerequisite for sustainable development in the energy sector is the financial viability of the energy companies, so that they have resources to invest in new technology, efficiency improvements and environmental protection. This requires prices to reflect real production cost. The energy companies, in a commercial environment, cannot be expected to provide social subsidies, even if they are expected to behave in a socially conscientious way. Furthermore, the environmental impact of energy activities should be reflected in their price, which creates an incentive to reduce pollution.

Therefore, a liberalization of the pricing policy towards a market level, including appropriate pollution fees, has to be implemented. However, pollution fees should not be allowed to be fully passed on to the end-user, in order to create a further incentive for the producers to invest in clean technology and abatement equipment. Furthermore, a price increase from current levels to a full cost-recovery level may need to be phased in over several years to be socially acceptable.

Recommendation 11.4:
The State Ministry of Foreign Trade and Economic Relations, in coordination with the Federation's Ministry of Energy, Mining and Industry and Republika Srpska's Ministry of Economy, Energy and Development, should:
(a) Adjust energy prices gradually to reflect the real cost of production, including environmental impact, taking into account the UNECE Guidelines on Reforming Energy Pricing; and
(b) At the same time protect vulnerable consumer groups through needs-based social assistance programmes instead of through subsidized energy prices.

A liberalization of the energy sector and particularly a policy where the actual cost of production, including the environmental cost, is reflected in prices would potentially lead to unaffordable energy prices with the current production technology. The free and competitive European energy market will create further pressure on the energy producers, by increasing competition, e.g. through an extended gas supply network, and in terms of new business opportunities through an extended market for export of electricity.

To become competitive, both to be able to supply to the domestic market subject to competition and to be able to export, the energy companies have to improve efficiency. To supply electricity to increasingly environmentally conscientious buyers on the European market, the companies will have to prove that their environmental performance meets EU requirements. Furthermore, when Bosnia and Herzegovina enters the European electricity market, an opportunity for trading in green electricity will create new business opportunities for the companies.

These challenges and opportunities will require particularly the thermal power plants to improve their performance in terms of both efficiency and emissions. Furthermore, they will require new "green" power production capacity to be developed.

Recommendation 11.5:
The State Ministry of Foreign Trade and Economic Relations, in coordination with the Federation's Ministry of Energy, Mining and Industry and Republika Srpska's Ministry of Economy, Energy and Development, should:
(a) Encourage the further rehabilitation of the thermal power, industrial and heating sector to increase energy efficiency and seek to meet EU emission levels and climate change requirements; and
(b) Develop new green production capacity of heat and electricity.

Chapter 12

HUMAN HEALTH AND ENVIRONMENT

12.1 Overall health status

Population development

The war in Bosnia and Herzegovina has had an impact on the country's demographic and health situation, which will be felt for decades. There has been no census since 1991; the scale of the changes can, therefore, only be estimated. Different documents give various estimates of population developments and of the number of deaths during the war, ranging from 140,000 to more than 250,000 people. It is estimated that approximately 16,000 to 17,000 children died during the war and another 40,000 were wounded. Table 12.1 provides some estimates of the demographic changes in Bosnia and Herzegovina as a whole and in both

entities – the Federation of Bosnia and Herzegovina and Republika Srpska – as a consequence of the war.

According to the World Health Report, the estimated life expectancy in Bosnia and Herzegovina in 1999, 2000 and 2001 was 73.1, 72.6 and 72.8 years, respectively. This is in line with the Central and East European average (71.9, 72.7 and 72.8 in those same years), but below the EU average (77.9, 78.2 and 78.5 years). According to the same source, women in Bosnia and Herzegovina have a longer life expectancy than men: respectively 75.0, 76.2 and 76.4 in 1999-2001 against 71.2, 69.1 and 69.3.

Total fertility rate declined from 1.6 per 1000 in 1991 to 1.3 in 2001.

Table 12.1: Demographic changes – consequences of the war

	Bosnia and Herzegovina	Federation of Bosnia and Herzegovina	Republika Srpska
Population on 31 March 1991	4,377,033	2,783,711	1,593,322
Natural growth (+)	144,202	117,910	26,292
Return of refugees from abroad (+)	373,400	346,140	27,260
Dead, missing and higher wartime mortality (-)	269,810	149,860	119,950
Expelled by force (refugees) (-)	1,168,000	735,000	433,000
Voluntary emigration after Dayton (-)	92,000	64,400	27,600
Population on 31 March 2001	3,364,825	2,298,501	1,066,324
Demographic structure in percentage of total			
1991	100	63.6	36.4
2001	100	68.3	31.7

Source: UNDP. Human Development Report. Bosnia and Herzegovina 2002.

Table 12.2: Demographic indicators, 1991-2001

Indicators	1991	1996	1997	1998	1999	2000	2001
Mid-year population	4,518,000	3,524,000	3,784,000	3,655,000	3,746,000	3,774,000	3,755,000
% of population aged 65+ years	6	..	..	..	11	..	9.6 (est)
Birth rate (per 1000 population)	14	..	13	12	11	10	10
Crude death rate (per 1000 population)	7	..	..	..	..	..	8
Life expectancy of women (in years)	76	..	..	..	75	76	74.9 (est)
Life expectancy of men (in years)	70	..	..	..	71	69	69.3 (est)
% of urban population	..	..	42	42	43	43	43
Average population density per square km	..	69	74	71	73	74	73

Source: WHO. Health For All Database; UNDP Bosnia and Herzegovina, June 2003 Human Development Report/Millennium Development Goals.

Infant mortality decreased from 24.7 per 1,000 live births in 1993 to 15.0 in 2000, which was higher than the Central and East European average of 15.8 and 11.2, and approximately three times the EU average of 6.5 and 4.9 in the same years.

Development of selected causes of death

The variation in leading causes of death in 2001 is summarized in table 12.3. For both entities the leading causes of death and their magnitude are similar to those in the EU and Central and Eastern Europe, namely diseases of the circulatory system, malignant neoplasms, external causes and diseases of the digestive system. The leading causes of death are diseases of the circulatory system, 54.1% and 53.6 % of all deaths respectively in the Federation and in Republika Srpska. This is in line with the data for Central and Eastern Europe, but higher than the EU average, where in 1998, the percentage was 39%.

It should be noted that even though the World Health Organization (WHO) recommends the exclusive use of specific mortality rates standardized by gender and age, the mortality indicators are not standardized.

The number of people injured in traffic accidents per 100,000 inhabitants in 1991 was 243. This rate shows an increasing trend between 1991 and 2000. In the Federation the rates were 285, 319 and 318

per 100,000 in 1998, 1999 and 2000. In Republika Srpska they were 229, 251 and 267 per 100,000 inhabitants.

Trends in morbidity

The incidence of tuberculosis in 2000 was 65.7 per 100,000 population, and had not changed significantly over the previous decade. These rates are higher than the average rates in Central and Eastern Europe and EU, where in 2000 they were 49.3 and 10.6 respectively.

A significant share of the 10 leading infectious diseases are transmitted by water and food. In 1998-2000 there was a decreasing trend in epidemics of communicable diseases transmitted by water and food in Republika Srpska. In 1998 there were 28 such epidemics, of which 23 were of diseases transmitted by water and food (trichinellosis, salmonellosis, food poisoning, intestinal bacterial infections, enterocolitis, shigellosis, hepatitis A). The micro-organisms that caused most of the epidemics were confirmed through laboratory tests. In 1999 there were 25 epidemics, of which 18 were caused by infected water and food, and in 2000 there were only 9 epidemics of communicable diseases transmitted by water and food. After peaking in 1986 at 199.9 per 100,000, the reported incidence of hepatitis A plunged to 11.24 in 1999.

Table 12.3: Five leading causes of death in 2001, all ages

	Federation of Bosnia and Herzegovina		Republika Srpska		EU average (1998)	CEE* average (1998)
	Number	% of total	Number	% of total	% of total	% of total
Diseases of the circulatory system	9,133	54.1	7,195	53.6	39.0	57.0
Malignant neoplasms	3,066	18.1	2,256	16.8	27.0	20.0
Symptoms signs and ill-defined conditions	964	5.7	2,067	15.2	0.0	0.0
External causes	615	3.6	663	4.9	6.0	7.0
Diseases of the digestive system	492	2.9	335	2.5	5.0	5.0
All causes	16,891	100.0	12,469	100.0	100.0	100.0

Sources : Republika Srpska Institute for Statistics. Demographic Statistics, 2003; Federation of Bosnia and Herzegovina. Public Health Institute, Health Statistics Annual, 2002.
Note : * CEE = Central and East Europe

Table 12.4: Incidence of tuberculosis and hepatitis A, 1999, 2000 and 2001
per 100,000 population

	Tuberculosis			Hepatitis A			
	BiH	CEE	EU	BiH	FBiH	CEE	EU
1999	78.0	48.5	12.3	11.2	18.9	42.9	5.6
2000	65.6	47.7	11.6	..	69.0	46.9	4.7
2001	65.7	49.3	10.6	..	31.7	42.5	4.8

Sources: WHO. Health For All Database; Federation of Bosnia and Herzegovina. Public Health Institute, Health Statistics Annual, 2002.
Note : BiH = Bosnia and Herzegovina, CEE = Central and Eastern Europe, EU = European Union.

12.2 Environmental conditions associated with health risks

Ambient and indoor air pollution

Bosnia and Herzegovina was one of the most polluted parts of the former Yugoslavia and was responsible for 32% of its total air pollution. The biggest polluter was industry, including the steel industry in Zenica, thermal power plants in Kakanj, Tuzla, Ugljevik and Gacko, the cement factory in Kakanj and Tuzla, the wood-processing industry in Doboj and Maglaj, the acetylene, chlorine and chloricacid factory in Jajce; and the chemical, detergent and fertilizer industry in Tuzla. In 1988/89, the steel factory in Zenica produced 73,000 metric tons of SO_2 and 20,000 metric tons of dust; 90 organic substances were found in the atmosphere. In Kakanj, the annual SO_2 emission was 84,194 metric tons. Currently few of the industrial plants are working, so pollution is much lower than before the war. However, as industries are rehabilitated and restart production, industrial air pollution may take off too.

In Republika Srpska, air quality differs from one area to another. Cities with industrial and power plants, such as Banja Luka, Bijeljina, Ugljevik and Gacko, have poorer air quality than rural areas. In 2000, the median yearly concentration of SO_2 varied from 14 to 17 g/m^3 at seven locations in Banja Luka, and the highest median monthly concentration varied between 23 and 52 g/m^3. The average median yearly soot concentration varied from 8 to 22 g/m^3, while the highest median monthly concentration was between 37 and 90 g/m^3.

No information was available on the contribution of transport to air pollution. It can only be guessed that the increase in traffic is contributing substantially to air pollution and its health effects.

In both entities, the most significant indoor air pollutant is tobacco smoke (75-80% of the population over 18 smokes). The people of Bosnia and Herzegovina were among the leading cigarette consumers in 2000, with an annual consumption of 6 billion units, or four-five cigarettes per person per day. Special attention should be given to the effects of environmental tobacco smoke because the incidence of acute respiratory infections in children whose parents smoke at home is higher than in other children. The Health Behaviour in School-Aged Children Survey, conducted in the Federation in 2002, revealed that 20.8% of schoolchildren have

a smoking history. The proportion is higher in boys (25.3%) than in girls (16.3%). A similar survey was conducted in Republika Srpska, and the results showed that up to 26.8% of school-aged children have tried to smoke tobacco at least once. The results of a survey conducted in Republika Srpska in 2002 show that 33.6% of the total adult population (44% of the men and 24.2% of the women) smoke daily. The survey found that 15.2% of individuals are exposed to environmental tobacco smoke for more that five hours a day at the workplace.

A study of 6,000 inhabitants of the Banja Luka area published in 1997 found a high correlation between SO_2, soot and humidity, and bronchitis, pharingitis, laringitis and infections of the upper respiratory tract. The study related the seasonal variation in air pollution to respiratory diseases. Another study has shown the increase in hospital admissions due to bronchitis, asthma and cancer.

Drinking water

Water supply in Bosnia and Herzegovina depends mainly on groundwater – 89% of overall sources of water supply, against 10.2% from rivers and 0.8% from natural lakes and artificial reservoirs.

In the Federation the population is supplied with drinking water from 78 central (public) water-supply systems, 742 local water-supply systems, about 10,000 cisterns, and between 18,000 and 22,000 other individual local water-supply facilities (e.g. wells, water springs, open springs). About 50% of the population is supplied with drinking water from central water-supply systems. During the war about 45% of water-supply systems were destroyed. Massive population movements during and after the war made it even more difficult to deliver basic water services. Leakage wastes up to an estimated 70% of the total running water. This leads to a high risk of secondary water contamination. All water-supply systems have considerable losses (25-60%), which appears to be a result of war damage.

In Republika Srpska 48% of the population is supplied with drinking water from public municipal water pipeline systems, while 35.6% are supplied from local water pipeline systems and the rest are supplied from other water plants, deep and shallow drilled wells, dug wells, springs and tanks. The sanitary conditions of 28 out of the 57 municipal pipeline systems are unsatisfactory. Aeration is performed only in two pipeline systems, sedimentation in five systems, coagulation in two, filtration in ten, chlorination in four and disinfection in 37. Purification and disinfection of local pipeline systems are performed only occasionally and are in any case of low quality and without any control.

Water pollution caused by human activity reduces the amount of safe drinking water that is available and exposes the population to microbiological and chemical contamination. Unsafe drinking water can be a significant carrier of water-borne infectious diseases such as enterocolitis or hepatitis A, and can cause severe diarrhoeal infections and other health problems. Drinking water can also be tainted with chemical, physical and radiological contaminants with harmful effects on human health. Continuing and regular laboratory testing of water is ensured for only 55% of the population in the Federation. Only 32% of the urban population is supplied with safe, treated drinking water. Some 42% of laboratory-tested water samples are unsafe. Microbiological analyses show that 32.5% of all water samples are unsafe. It is likely that significantly less than 32% of the rural population is supplied with safe drinking water.

In 2000 microbiological analyses of 10,496 samples were conducted in public health laboratories; 2,212 (21.1%) did not meet the standards. The most frequent anomalies were the total number of bacteria, E. coli, coliform, faecal coliform and faecal streptococcus, which by number exceeded prescribed standards. Chemical analyses were conducted on 7,421 samples; 1,337 (18.2%) did not meet the standards, predominantly due to the increased levels of potassium permanganate,

nitrites, nitrates and iron. Data for previous years are shown in table 12.5. They indicate a decreasing trend for the percentage of samples that fail to meet standards.

In the country as a whole the number of epidemics of water-borne diarrhoea and hepatitis A is growing. For example, in 1991, there were 1,875 cases of hepatitis A and 3,411 cases of diarrhoea. In 1993, the number of cases of hepatitis A increased to 7,421 and of diarrhoea to 21,937. Initially these outbreaks were water-borne, but because of poor sanitary conditions and a shortage of water the epidemics continued to be spread by human contact.

In the Federation in 1998 three epidemics of water-borne diarrhoea were reported with 183 cases. In 1999, there was one epidemic with 105 cases. In 2000, no outbreak was registered. In 1998, one water-borne epidemic of viral hepatitis A with five cases was reported. In 1999, there were six epidemics with 48 cases. In 2000, there were three epidemics with 549 cases.

In Republika Srpska epidemics where the carrier is conveyed by drinking water are rare. They tend to be seasonal and occur mostly in smaller water-supply plants, which are not constantly supervised by public health institutions. Microbial water examinations are carried out in most municipalities, while basic physico-chemical examinations are undertaken on request. In 1998 there were 28 epidemics of water-borne or food-borne diseases. In 1999 there were 25 and in 2000 only 9 epidemics of communicable diseases transmitted by infected water or food.

Table 12.5: Laboratory-tested drinking water samples

	Chemical analyses			Microbiological analyses		
	Number	Unsatisfactory		Number	Unsatisfactory	
		Number	%		Number	%
Federation of Bosnia and Herzegovina						
1998	2,464	929	37.7	4,529	1,173	25.9
1999	3,040	976	32.1	5,054	1,102	21.8
2000	3,940	1,005	25.5	6,974	1,318	18.9
Republika Srpska						
1998	1,831	258	14.1	2,380	538	22.6
1999	2,077	245	11.8	2,638	484	18.3
2000	3,481	332	9.5	4,522	892	19.7

Source: Public Health Institute of Federation of Bosnia and Herzegovina and Public Health Institute of Republika Srpska. 2003.

Food safety

As a result of the collapse of State institutions caused by the war, microbiological contamination of food and food-borne diseases are major problems. The control of food contamination carried out before the war by authorized State institutions was virtually abandoned, which led to more microbiologically contaminated food being available on the market. In 2000 the incidence of food infections was 38.3 per 100,000, making it the ninth leading infectious disease. There were 16 outbreaks of intestinal infectious diseases and 4 outbreaks of food poisoning. In the Federation, in 1999 and 2000, there were 306 and 366 cases of salmonellosis, all of serotype S.Enteritidis. In Republika Srpska, in the same years, there were 254 and 118 cases of salmonellosis, all of serotype S.Enteritidis. In 2000, intestinal infectious diseases were the second leading infectious diseases, with a rate of 11.6% of total infectious and parasitic morbidity.

In the Federation the incidence of microbiological food-borne diseases is declining. In 1998 the incidence was 43.6 per 100,000 with 959 cases, then the rate declined to 34.7 per 100,000 with 845 cases.

In Republika Srpska in 2000 the most commonly registered food-borne diseases were: food poisoning – 38.3 per 100,000; salmonellosis – 13.1/100,000; and hepatitis A 8.8/100,000. As mentioned above, in 1998 there were 28 epidemics of communicable diseases transmitted by infected water or food; in 1999 there were 25 and in 2000 the number fell to 9. In most cases the causes were confirmed through laboratory tests. The most frequent causes were salmonella and staphylococcus toxin as well as parasitoses such as trichinosis. In the past three years cases of some rare diseases have been registered, including brucellosis (only in 2000), echinococcosis, trichinellosis and anthrax.

It should be mentioned that diseases caused by chemically contaminated food are not monitored. The number of well-equipped laboratories for the control of food safety is insufficient. Only five of the Federation's ten cantons have equipped laboratories in their public health institutes. In addition, control is carried out by the laboratories of some research and university institutions, like the Faculty of Veterinary Sciences and the Faculty of Natural Sciences, or by the laboratories of food companies. In Republika Srpska physico-chemical and microbial analyses of food are performed in the laboratories of the public health institutes in Banja Luka, Doboj, Zvornik, Srbinje, Trebinje and Sarajevo. In the Federation, in 2000, laboratory examination of samples from food production processes showed that 11.1% of samples did not meet the microbiological standards and 17.7% did not meet physico-chemical standards. The equipment of the laboratories is inadequate and insufficient. Chemical laboratories use simple instrumental technology so they monitor only basic chemical parameters. It is still not possible to perform specific analyses of additives, mycotoxins, antibiotics, hormones, vitamins, dioxins and heavy metals.

Table 12.6: Food analyses samples

	Physico-chemical analyses			Microbial analyses		
	Number	Unsatisfactory		Number	Unsatisfactory	
		Number	%		Number	%
Federation of Bosnia and Herzegovina						
1998	..	..	18.1	..	..	12.3
1999	..	..	16.6	..	..	13.3
2000	..	..	17.7	..	..	11.7
Republika Srpska						
1998	2,286	253	11.0	3,927	537	13.7
1999	2,418	270	11.1	3,225	547	16.9
2000	2,647	398	15.0	5,243	528	10.1

Sources : Public Health Institute of Republika Srpska, Banja Luka, Report, 1998/1999/2000. Public Health Institute of Federation of Bosnia and Herzegovina, Report, 1998/1999/2000.

There is no State body responsible for food safety. Responsibility is divided among the entities' ministries. In Republika Srpska the responsibilities are divided among the Ministry of Health and Social Welfare, the Ministry of Agriculture, Forestry and Water Management, the Ministry of Economy, Energy and Development, and the Ministry of Trade and Tourism. In the Federation of Bosnia and Herzegovina they are divided among the Ministry of Health, the Ministry of Agriculture, Water Management and Forestry, the Ministry of Energy, Mining and Industry, and the Ministry of Trade.

The Law on the Safety of Food and Consumer Goods (Official Gazette SFRJ 53/1002) was adopted before 1991. It does not define the roles and responsibilities of the authorities working in the area of food safety and food quality. Bosnia and Herzegovina is not represented on the Codex Alimentarius Commission. The responsibilities are divided as follows: the Ministries of Agriculture are responsible for veterinary and phyto-sanitary control, the Ministries of Health for sanitary control and the Ministries of Trade for market inspection. In Republika Srpska food-processing facilities are inspected by the Department for Inspection Services. Health inspectors monitor food quality in markets and shops, except for fresh meat, which is monitored by veterinary inspectors. The health inspectorate within the Ministry of Health and Social Welfare of Republika Srpska monitors food imports, whereas food quality control is in the hands of the market inspectorate within the Ministry of Trade and Tourism. Local food production meets only 37-40% of demand; only 3% is produced in the State-owned sector. About 60% of food is imported, in many cases through informal channels. The control of imported food is still inadequate, so large quantities of imported food reach the end-consumers without any control or examination. In general, hazard analysis and critical control point (HACCP) systems are not implemented in food-processing establishments.

Waste and soil contamination

Owing to the increase in waste and inadequate waste management, waste is becoming a major environmental and health problem. Large quantities of waste are being dumped illegally, which represents a threat to the groundwater that is used for the water supply to the population. There is no treatment of waste water or liquid waste. Medical waste is not separated from other waste. Current methods of waste disposal cause direct

contamination of groundwater, food and air. Contamination from waste may contaminate water and food and cause intestinal infectious diseases (typhus, diarrhoea, dysentery and hepatitis) and many other diseases, too.

The country has a specific waste problem with expired drugs and chemicals. Large amounts of medicines and surgical material were sent to Bosnia and Herzegovina as humanitarian aid and now represent a big environmental problem.

Other risks related to the war are landmines, other kinds of unexploded ordinance and soil contaminated with depleted uranium.

Noise

Studies of the Institute of Hygiene of the Medical Faculty in Sarajevo showed that the health of people living in noisy streets was much more affected by various disorders than the health of those who lived in quiet areas. One in four people who lived in noisy urban areas experienced disturbance of their normal sleep pattern, while one in five reported that annoyance from various noise sources disturbed their normal daily activities. People who lived in noisy areas had a higher incidence of hypertension and neurotic symptoms, such as wet palms and tremor.

Currently, increased noise in urban areas is mainly due to increased road traffic and other noise pollution sources such as industry. Noise levels are not monitored and there are no studies of the effect of increased noise pollution due to road traffic intensification; it is therefore impossible to analyse the effects of noise on the health and psycho-physical abilities of the population. The limited measurements in Banja Luka have shown a variation of noise levels between 56.9 and 63.9 dB. On Sundays and at nights between 10 p.m. and 6 a.m., the levels vary between 53.8 to 58.7 dB (legal level for residential areas is 40 dB). Noise and vibration at the workplace are measured only occasionally, so no reliable data are available to assess their effect on human health.

Ionizing radiation

Ionizing radiation has not been systematically monitored during the past ten years. Sources of radiation are X-ray machines, lightning rods with radioactive isotopes, fire alarms and defectoscopes. The Federation has about 400 X-ray machines in the health care sector, 3 defectoscopes for industrial radiography, about 50-60 radioisotopes in industry, 5 nuclear medicine facilities with their own waste disposal, 290 radioactive lightening rods, and 15,000-20,000 smoke detectors in workplaces and homes. Republika Srpska has an estimated 250 radiographic devices in hospitals and primary health care centres (*Dom zdravlja*), and 215 radioactive lightning rods. These lightening rods are a potential health hazard because they are gamma emitters, with Co60 isotopes with a standard activity of 3.7 to 7.4 GB or with Eu152 and 154, which have a half-life of 13 years. During the war several radioactive lightning rods and large ionizing fire detectors in factory halls were damaged or destroyed. When the debris was removed, all radioactive material from ionizing fire detectors was dispersed without control and removed together with the construction waste.

In the Federation, the institutions which control ionizing radiation and work in radiation protection are the Administration Office for Protection from Radiation and for Radiation Safety, the Institute of Radiology of the Veterinary School in Sarajevo and the Meteorological Institute. The leading institution is the Public Health Institute, which assesses the radioactive contamination of air, soil, rivers, lakes and sea, as well as solid and liquid precipitation from the atmosphere, drinking water, and humans and animals. It also measures the occupational exposures of professionals working with radiation sources in health care and industry. The data show that levels of occupational exposure do not fully comply with domestic and international standards. Radiation protection for patients exposed to ionizing radiation in diagnostics or therapy does not meet the requirements and standards either.

Depleted uranium

A specific problem in Bosnia and Herzegovina is contamination with depleted uranium (DU). To estimate the consequences for the environment and health, the United Nations Environment Programme (UNEP) studied 14 sites targeted with DU weapons and issued a report "Depleted uranium in Bosnia and Herzegovina. Post-Conflict Environmental Assessment". Its objectives were: to examine the possible risks from any remaining DU contamination of soil, water, air and biota, as well as from solid pieces of DU; to compare the measurements with those published by various experts/expert groups; to gain an overview of the storage of radioactive waste and sources, as well as radioactive waste management within the country in general; and, finally, to obtain an indication of the current level of any existing health databases, both in general and specifically with respect to people who were thought to have been exposed to DU during the conflict. The report is based on data collected by an international team of experts on 12-24 October 2002. Their measurements revealed the presence of contamination points and pieces of DU at three sites – the Hadzici tank repair facility, the Hadzici ammunition storage area and the Han Pijesak barracks. DU contamination of the air was found at two different sites, including inside two buildings. Some of these buildings are currently in use, and UNEP recommends their "precautionary decontamination" to avoid any unnecessary human exposure.

The air contamination is due to the re-suspension of DU particles from penetrators or other contamination points due to wind or human action. The report records the first instance of DU contamination of groundwater. When contamination is found, UNEP recommends the use of alternative water sources and the continuation of water sampling and measurements for several years. The recorded contamination levels, however, are very low and do not present immediate radioactive or toxic risks for the environment or human health.

Landmines

Landmines are one of most serious problems facing Bosnia and Herzegovina. There are minefields throughout the country, particularly on the State borders, the entities' borders and on former front lines where battles took place. Minefields have a great impact on the population's health and influence everyday activities. Bosnia and Herzegovina is the most heavily mined country in Europe. According to the Bosnia and Herzegovina Mine Action Centre there are 10,000 minefields with 670,000 mines in the country: 70% of minefields are in the Federation. Around Sarajevo alone, there are about 1,500 minefields. The most dangerous areas are Gornji and Donji Vakuf, the area around Travnik, Zenica, Mostar and Tuzla, where many landmines were planted.

Figure 12.1: Map of Landmines

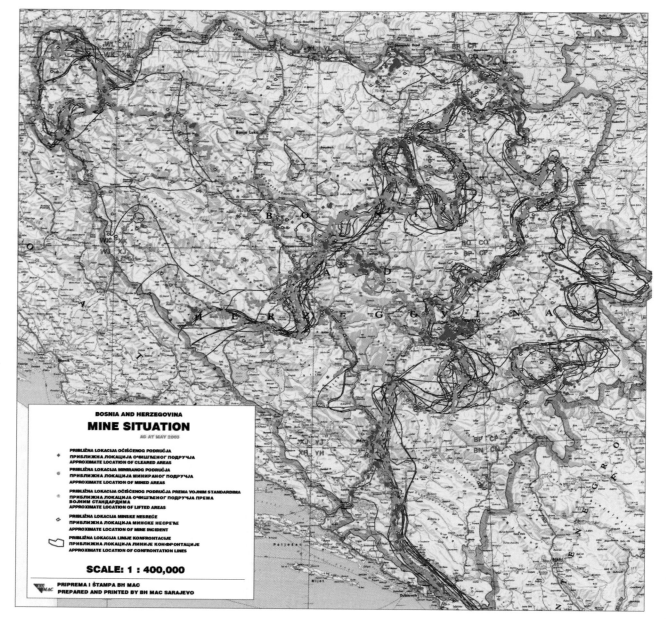

Source: Bosnia and Herzegovina, Mine Action Centre.
Disclaimer: The boundaries and names shown on this map do not imply official endorsement or acceptance by the United Nations.

According to the International Committee of the Red Cross, between the beginning of the war in 1992 and the end of 2001, mines alone killed 4,798 people, 28% of whom were killed after the war had ended. Although the situation has improved, in the two-year period from 1998 to 2000 alone, there were 125 accidents in the Federation, in which 71 people were killed and 113 injured (85 serious and 28 minor injuries).

In Republika Srpska 4,679 minefields have been registered. The largest number of accidents was recorded in 1996, but it has been decreasing ever

since. According to the Bosnia and Herzegovina Mine Action Centre, between 1996 and 2001, 344 accidents were registered, with 130 fatalities, 232 serious injuries and 94 minor injuries, in Republika Srpska. According to the International Committee of the Red Cross, the mine accident rate fell from an average of more than 50 a month in 1996 to fewer than 10 a month in 1999. Data for 2002 show that there were 72 mine accidents with 26 fatalities and 46 injuries in Bosnia and Herzegovina. The victims were: 26.3% children up to 18 years of age, 36.1% up to 39 years of age, 30.5% 40-60 years of age and 6.9% over 60 years of age. Of the total number, 6.94% were displaced persons, 18.05% returnees, and 75.01% local people.

The most endangered population are returnees and in rural areas, in particular, farmers, children, forestry and construction workers. Most accidents happen while victims are working in the fields or in forests, or among children playing, during mine-clearing operations, or when victims are fishing, driving, or visiting their pre-war homes. After the war, four out of five victims were civilians (the percentage of civilian victims rose from 21% during the war to 78% after the war). The remaining minefields are one of the main barriers to the return of refugees and the development of agriculture.

12.3 Environmental health policy and management

Policy framework

The National Environmental Action Plan (NEAP) was prepared jointly by the two entities, and adopted by their Governments and Assemblies. It provides detailed analyses of the country's environmental problems, and sets environmental protection and institutional development goals. Among the priorities are water and waste-water management, waste management, public health, and mine-clearing.

There are separate National Environmental Health Action Plans for the two entities.

The Federation of Bosnia and Herzegovina's National Environmental Health Action Plan was developed by its Public Health Institute, its Ministry of Health and its Ministry of Physical Planning and Environment, with the support of its Ministry of Agriculture, Water Management and Forestry. It has not yet been adopted.

Republika Srpska's National Environmental Health Action Plan is the result of the joint work of its Public Health Institute, its Ministry of Health and Social Welfare and its Ministry of Physical Planning, Civil Engineering and Ecology, with the support of its Ministry of Agriculture, Forestry and Water Management and its Ministry of Transport and Communications. It was adopted in December 2002 (Official Gazette January 2003).

Both NEHAPs have the same objectives: to provide the best possible mechanism for setting health and environment priorities; to lay the regulatory and institutional basis for public health reform; to mobilize all external resources for reconstructing the infrastructure in public health and environmental health; to serve as a coordinating mechanism for public services and authorities; to inform the public and enable the public to participate in environmental health decision-making.

Legal framework

In accordance with the Federation's Constitution, responsibility for environmental protection and health – health care, environmental policy, communication and traffic infrastructure, use of natural resources – is divided between the Federation and the ten cantons. Recently, several laws with implications for environmental health have been adopted (Official Gazette F BiH 33/2003). They provide a general legislative basis for the protection of public health from the effects of environmental pollution: The framework laws are:

- The Law on Air Protection;
- The Law on Water Protection; and
- The Law on Waste Management.

According to article 35 of Republika Srpska's Constitution, each individual has the right to a healthy environment. Republika Srpska has several environmental health laws:

- Law on Air Protection (Official Gazette RS 53/2002);
- Law on Water Protection (Official Gazette RS 53/2002);
- Law on Waste Management (Official Gazette RS 53/2002);
- Law on Radiation Protection and Radiation Safety (Official Gazette RS 52/2001). According to this Law, the Department of Radiation Protection of the Ministry of Health and Social Welfare is responsible for notifying, licensing and registering the use of ionizing radiation;
- Law on Sanitary Inspection (Official Gazette RS 14/1994); and
- Law on Water (Official Gazette RS 10/1998). Its paragraph 51 states that the Ministry of Health and Social Welfare is responsible for setting quality standards for drinking water and for controlling drinking water quality. Sanitary-hygienic control of the quality drinking water, and control of water supply system is under

responsibility of the Department of Health Inspection and Sanitary Control of the Ministry of Health and Social Welfare. In the municipalities, this is the responsibility of the health inspectorates of the departments of inspections.

In 2003 Regulations on hygienic quality of drinking water (Standards on drinking water) (Official Gazette RS 40/2003), and Regulations on sanitary protection of watershed zones of drinking water (Official Gazette RS 7/2003) were approved.

Institutional framework

There are no State institutions dealing with or responsible for environmental health issues, such as monitoring, inspection or reporting. These responsibilities are dealt with by the two entities.

In the Federation, responsibilities for environmental protection policy, health care, communication and transport infrastructure, tourism and the use of natural resources are divided between the Federation and the cantons. The health system is decentralized, with a central Ministry of Health and ten cantonal health ministries, responsible for health care in the cantons. The most important institution dealing with environmental health is the Federation's Public Health Institute. There are also cantonal public health institutes, which report directly to the cantonal authorities.

The environmental health activities of the Federation's Ministry of Health include the development of protective measures against the effects of environmental pollution (contamination of air, water, soil, food) on human health, radiation protection and protection against the harmful effects of noise and vibrations. It also carries out surveillance of the health and epidemiological situation of the population both at home and at work, and if necessary takes appropriate protective measures. Within the Ministry of Health, there is an agency for radiation protection.

According to the Federation's 1997 Law on Health Protection, the Public Health Institute's environmental tasks include: monitoring the safety of drinking water, water supply, food and consumer goods; public-health-related microbiological activities; and monitoring and analysing environmental impact (air, soil, noise) on public health. The Institute is entitled to propose measures for developing plans and programmes to protect health against the harmful effects of pollution, including measures for the protection, improvement and promotion of the living and working environment, and sanitary conditions in human settlements. Its Department of Health Statistics is responsible for collecting and reporting health-related data and statistics. The Institute also assists the cantonal public health institutes in their activities.

Table 12.7: Republika Srpska standards for drinking-water quality (2003) compared to WHO Water Quality Guidelines

Indicator	RS maximum permitted level	WHO Guidelines
Total coliforms	0.0 mg/l	0.0 mg/l
Faecal coliforms	0.0 mg/l	0.0 mg/l
Boron	0.3 mg/l	0.3 mg/l
Cadmium	0.003 mg/l	0.003 mg/l
Molubdenum	0.07 mg/l	0.07 mg/l
Arsenic	**0.01 mg/l**	**0.005 mg/l**
Nickel	0.02 mg/l	0.02 mg/l
NO3	50.0 mg/l	50.0 mg/l
NO2	**0.03 mg/l**	**3.0 mg/l**
Mercury	0.001 mg/l	0.001 mg/l
Lead	0.01 mg/l	0.01 mg/l
Selenium	0.01 mg/l	0.01 mg/l
Fluoride	**1.2 mg/l**	**1.5 mg/l**
Chromium	0.05 mg/l	0.05 mg/l
Manganese	**0.05 mg/l**	**0.5 mg/l**
Cu	2.0 mg/l	2.0 mg/l
Chlorine	200 mg/l	
Zinc	3.0 mg/l	3.0 mg/l

Source: WHO and Republika Srpska, 2003.
Note: Differing standards boldfaced

Figure 12.2: Structure of the Public Health Institute of the Federation of Bosnia and Herzegovina

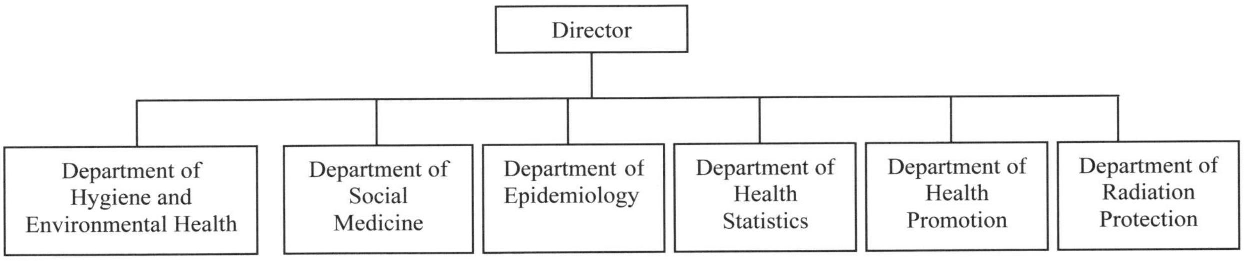

Department of Hygiene and Environmental Health	Department of Social Medicine	Department of Epidemiology	Department of Health Statistics	Department of Health Promotion	Department of Radiation Protection

(Organizational chart: Director at top, connected to six departments: Department of Hygiene and Environmental Health, Department of Social Medicine, Department of Epidemiology, Department of Health Statistics, Department of Health Promotion, Department of Radiation Protection)

In addition to the Ministry of Health and the Public Health Institute, there are also other institutions with environmental health responsibilities.

The Federation's Ministry of Physical Planning and Environment has administrative and other duties related to the use of natural resources (water, forests, mines, minerals, agricultural soil) environmental protection, and coordination of research, planning, financing and monitoring of the environment. The Ministry of Agriculture, Water Management and Forestry has administrative and other duties related to the management of agriculture, forests, water and soil conservation. The Meteorological Institute analyses air emissions and carries out basic 24-hour monitoring of SO_2 and black smoke. The Faculty of Veterinary Sciences, together with its institute and services, contributes by taking care of animal health with the aim of protecting human health. The Agropedology Institute performs soil investigations. The departments of hydrology, hydrogeology and hydrodynamics of the Technical Faculty monitor water quality.

In Republika Srpska, the Government, together with its ministries and other institutions, supports a comprehensive approach to preventing impacts on health and the environment. The health system is centralized, with planning, regulations and management functions held by the Ministry of Health and Social Welfare. According to article 22 of the 1999 Law on Health Protection (amended in 2001 and 2002), the central health institution for environmental health is the Public Health Institute. It also has regional branches (Banja Luka, Doboj, Srpsko Sarajevo, Trebinje, Srbinje and Zvornik).

The environmental health activities of the Ministry of Health and Social Welfare include: measures to protect human health from harmful environmental factors, such as pollution, chemical, physical or biological contaminants in water, air, food, articles of general use and drugs; measures to preserve and improve health conditions at home and at work; measures to protect the population from the harmful effects of ionizing radiation, noise and vibrations; control of the health and epidemiological situation in homes and at work, taking measures when necessary; production and sale of drugs, toxins and hallucinogens; sanitary inspections. There is also a regulatory body for protection from ionizing radiation and radiation safety within the Ministry.

The Public Health Institute is a professional and scientific institution. It provides support to health professionals who work to improve environmental conditions. According to the Law on Health Protection, its main environmental health tasks are: to monitor, study and evaluate the quality and safety of drinking water and water supplies, the safety of food and articles of general use; and to monitor, analyse and evaluate the impact of environmental hazards (soil, water, air, noise, etc.) on the health of the population.

There are other institutions dealing with environmental health, such as the Institute of Environmental Care and Ecology, the Institute of Veterinary Medicine, the Agropedological Institute, the School of Chemical Engineering, the School of Agriculture, the School of Forestry, the public company "Srpske Sume", the Faculty of Science and Mathematics, the Institute for Urbanism, the Hydro-Meteorology Institute, and the Directorate for Water. The Ministry of Health and Social Welfare has a health inspectorate, which is part of Republika Srpska's surveillance system, together with the veterinary, agricultural and market inspectorates. Local inspections are organized by the municipalities.

Figure 12.3: Organizational structure of Republika Srpska's Public Health Institute

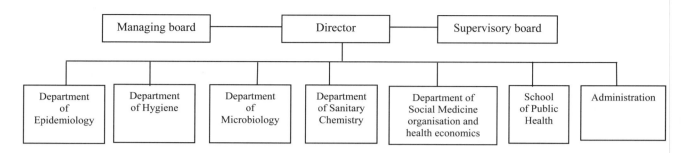

The Institute of Occupational Medicine monitors occupational hazards and occupational diseases, suggests and implements measures for the protection and improvement of employees' health, develops standards and regulations in occupational health and follows up the implementation of specific occupational health programmes.

In Brčko District, within the Government, there is a Department of Health, Public Safety and Community Services, and a Health Inspectorate. Among the responsibilities of the Inspectorate are the monitoring of drinking water, air and food.

Environmental health information systems

An integrated environmental health information system is needed to establish links between environmental conditions, population exposures and human health. A comprehensive monitoring system is needed to collect the relevant indicators regularly and consistently. The collected data have to be of sufficient quality and quantity to link them to health effects and to establish causal relationship. Before the war Bosnia and Herzegovina had an operational environment and food safety monitoring system, but it was damaged during the war.

Bosnia and Herzegovina faces many environmental and environmental health problems. The main obstacles to progress are the destruction of the information system, the inadequate equipment of laboratories performing environmental analyses, the lack of qualified staff and the lack of accurate indicators.

At present there is no regular monitoring. Organized air quality monitoring takes place only in Sarajevo and Banja Luka. There is some regular monitoring of air, water and food in Sarajevo, Zenica, Tuzla, Mostar, and Bihac. The cantonal public health institutes conduct monitoring and

send quarterly reports to the Public Health Institute in Sarajevo. However, sampling coverage and monitoring are insufficient. For the rest of the country there are some measurements that can give the total air pollution load. There is no effective legislation to regulate air emissions and air quality, and there is no effective framework for environmental licensing either. In Republika Srpska the regional public health institutes currently verify the safety of food and drinking water, but the scope and sampling are not comprehensive. The capacities and abilities for regular microbiological and physico-chemical analyses of food and water are inadequate. There are great difficulties especially in identifying certain microbiological parameters. There is no unified information system to enable public health institutes to share data and set up a unified database. Public health institutes collect data on mortality and morbidity, but do not link them to data on exposures to environmental risk factors.

In 2000-2002, the European Union's Phare Programme conducted a project to provide technical assistance in public and environmental health. One of its objectives was to improve the health status of Bosnia and Herzegovina's population by supporting efficient and sustainable public and environmental health functions, and by making the network of public health institutes stronger. Throughout the project, the equipment needs (laboratory and information) of the public health institutes were assessed, and training and technical support were developed. This will improve the scope and quality of their environmental health work.

12.4 Conclusions and recommendations

According to general health indices, the health of Bosnia and Herzegovina's population is worse than that of the population of the EU countries, but comparable to that of the population of Central and

East European countries. However, the health statistics system has difficulties in defining the size of the population and other basic demographic indicators. Underreporting and under diagnosis of diseases and incomplete registration of demographic indicators influence the quality of health statistics. These problems are also the result of the recent war. Health statistics are reported separately for the two entities. Only basic health indicators are reported State-wide to WHO. Most of the currently available health data are estimates; they therefore do not fully reflect the real situation. There is a lack of studies investigating the influence of environmental conditions on the health of the population.

The prerequisite for adequate environmental health policy, i.e. rational monitoring and evaluation, is the creation of an accurate database. Currently, there are no quality data on environmental pollution. This makes it impossible to estimate individual and population-wide exposure and subsequently leads to difficulties in linking health data to environmental exposure data and establishing a causal relationship between exposure and disease. The identification and registration of sources of contamination could contribute to assessing their risks for environmental health. A comprehensive monitoring system is needed, with regular and consistent collection of relevant indicators. In most cases the quality of air, drinking water and food is assessed on request. Such sampling coverage and monitoring are insufficient. The capacities and abilities for regular microbiological and physico-chemical analyses of food and water are inadequate.

Recommendation 12.1:
The Federation's Ministry of Health and its Public Health Institute, Republika Srpska's Ministry of Health and Social Welfare and its Public Health Institute, and the Government of Brčko District should work closely with the Ministries responsible for developing comprehensive monitoring systems for air quality, drinking water quality, waste and hazardous waste disposal, ionizing radiation sources, food production and distribution chain from primary producer to consumer, in order to:
(a) Develop an environmental health information system;
(b) Collect health statistics data;
(c) Promote epidemiological studies on environmental health-related issues; and
(d) Create a register of all ionizing radiation sources.

The National Environmental Action Plan (NEAP) was prepared jointly by the two entities and adopted by their Governments and Assemblies in 2003. This plan provides detailed analyses of the country's environmental problems, and sets environmental protection and institutional development goals. The National Environmental Health Action Plan (NEHAP) of Republika Srpska was adopted in December 2002; that of the Federation has been drawn up, but not yet adopted.

Recommendation 12.2:
(a) The Government of the Federation should speed up the adoption of its NEHAP.
(b) Both Governments have to develop an operational plan for the implementation of NEHAP.

Industrial production and technology led to an increase in production, distribution, storage and preparation of food. This increases the risk of microbiological and chemical contamination of food. In Bosnia and Herzegovina war damaged the system of food production and trade, as well as the system of food control and surveillance. Diseases caused by microbiological or chemically contaminated food remain a major concern and a top environmental health priority. Currently there is no national body responsible for food safety. Responsibilities for food safety are divided between the entities' institutions; the entities' food laws were adopted before 1992. No secondary laws for the new veterinary law, plant protection law and quality control law have yet been developed. Generally, hazard analysis and critical control point systems are not implemented for food production in either public or private food-processing establishments.

Recommendation 12.3:
All Ministries which currently have responsibilities for food safety, i.e. Republika Srpska's Ministry of Health and Social Welfare, its Ministry of Agriculture, Forestry and Water Management, its Ministry of Economy, Energy and Development, and its Ministry of Trade and Tourism, and the Federation's Ministry of Health, its Ministry of Agriculture, Water Management and Forestry, its Ministry of Energy, Mining and Industry, and its Ministry of Trade, should:
(a) Develop a common national food safety strategy within the framework of the organization of the Ministerial Conference on Food and Nutrition in 2006;
(b) Establish a State-level body responsible for food safety;

(c) Prepare a new State food safety law that meets the requirements of the European Union;

(d) Develop secondary legislation in the area of veterinary, phyto-sanitary and food quality control;

(e) Implement hazard analysis and critical control point (HACCP) systems in the food industry;

(f) Establish a State register of food manufacturers; and

(g) Identify an organization to participate in the Codex Alimentarius Commission.

The development of an integrated approach to environmental health management requires close cooperation between both entities, and within entities, close cooperation between ministries, professional and public institutions dealing with environmental health. Cooperation is needed in particular in environmental health monitoring, the sharing of information, environmental health assessment, and planning of activities. The development of the NEAP and NEHAPs represents

an opportunity for looking at environmental health from a cross-sectoral perspective. They identify priorities and areas for action on the basis of a broad consensus of the different sectors and agencies involved. However, there is much potential for more cooperation among the Federation of Bosnia and Herzegovina, Republika Srpska and Brčko District and for joint implementation of activities.

Recommendation 12.4:
The Federation's Ministry of Health and its Ministry of Physical Planning and Environment, Republika Srpska's Ministry of Health and Social Welfare and its Ministry of Physical Planning, Civil Engineering and Ecology, and Brčko District's Department of Health, Public Safety and Community Services should together establish mechanisms for closer collaboration in the development of an integrated approach to environmental health management and the development of effective procedures to carry out environmental health impact assessment.

ANNEXES

ANNEX I

SELECTED REGIONAL AND GLOBAL ENVIRONMENTAL AGREEMENTS

Worldwide agreements		Bosnia and Herzegovina	
Year		Year	Status
1951	(ROME) International Plant Protection Convention	30.7.2003	Ad
1971	(RAMSAR) Convention on Wetlands of International Importance especially as Waterfowl Habitat	1.3.1992	Ra
1982	(MONTEGO BAY) Convention on the Law of the Sea	12.1.1994	Su
1985	(VIENNA) Convention for the Protection of the Ozone Layer	6.3.1992	Su
	1987 (MONTREAL) Protocol on Substances that Deplete the Ozone Layer	6.3.1992	Su
	1990 (LONDON) Amendment to Protocol	11.8.2003	Ac
	1992 (COPENHAGEN) Amendment to Protocol	11.8.2003	Ac
	1997 (MONTREAL) Amendment to Protocol	11.8.2003	Ac
1989	(BASEL) Convention on the Control of Transboundary Movements of Hazardous Wastes and their Disposal	16.3.2001	Ac
1992	(RIO) Convention on Biological Diversity	26.8.2002	Ac
	2000 (CARTAGENA) Protocol on Biosafety		
1992	(NEW YORK) Framework Convention on Climate Change	7.9.2000	Ac
	1997 (KYOTO) Protocol		
1994	(PARIS) Convention to Combat Desertification	26.8.2002	Ac

Ac = Accession; Ad = Adherence; De = denounced; Si = Signed; Su = Succession; Ra = Ratified.

Year	Regional and subregional agreements	Bosnia and Herzegovina	
		Year	Status
1976	(BARCELONA) Convention for the Protection of the Mediterranean Sea against Pollution	1.3.1992	Su
	1976 (BARCELONA) Protocol for the Prevention of Pollution of the Mediterranean Sea by Dumping from Ships and Aircraft (amended in 1995)	1.3.1992	Su
	1976 (BARCELONA) Protocol concerning Cooperation in Combating Pollution of the Mediterranean Sea by Oil and other Harmful Substances in	1.3.1992	Su
	1980 (ATHENS) Protocol for the protection of the Mediterranean Sea against Pollution from Land-based Sources (amended in 1996)	22.10.1994	Su
	1982 (GENEVA) Protocol concerning Mediterranean Specially Protected Areas is replaced by	22.10.1994	Su
1979	(GENEVA) Convention on Long-range Transboundary Air Pollution	6.3.1992	Su
	1984 (GENEVA) Protocol - Financing of Co-operative Programme (EMEP)	6.3.1992	Su
1991	(ESPOO) Convention on Environmental Impact Assessment in a Transboundary Context		
	2003 (KIEV) Protocol on Strategic Environmental Assessment	21.5.2003	Si
1992	(HELSINKI) Convention on the Protection and Use of Transboundary Waters and International Lakes		
	2003 (KIEV) Protocol on Civil Liability and Compensation for Damage Caused by the Transboundary Effects of Industrial Accidents on	21.5.2003	Si
1998	(AARHUS) Convention on Access to Information, Public Participation in Decision-making and Access to Justice in Environmental Matters		
	(KIEV) Protocol on Pollutant Release and Transfer Register	21.5.2003	Si

Ac = Accession; Ad = Adherence; De = denounced; Si = Signed; Su = Succession; Ra = Ratified.

ANNEX II

SELECTED ECONOMIC AND ENVIRONMENTAL DATA

Bosnia and Herzegovina: Selected economic data

A. Entity Federation of BiH

	1999	2001	2003
TOTAL AREA (1 000 km^2) *1)	26.11	26.11	26.11
POPULATION			
Total population, (1 000 000 inh.)-estimation *1)	2.298	2.312	2.323
% change (1999-2003)	..	..	1.11
population density, (inh./km^2)	88.00	88.56	88.98
GROSS DOMESTIC PRODUCT *1)			
GDP, (billion US$)	3.35	3.33	4.74
% change (1999-2003)	..	..	41.68
per capita, (US$ 1000/cap.)	1.19	1.18	1.68
INDUSTRY *1)			
Manufacturing industry (% of GDP)	10.63	11.80	11.99
Industrial production % change (1999-2003)	..	..	..
AGRICULTURE *1)			
Agriculture, hunting and forestry (% of GDP)	9.18	7.18	6.48
ENERGY SUPPLY *2)			
Total supply, (M toe)	3.57	4.80	..
% change (1999-2003)	..	..	..
Energy intensity, (Toe/US$ 1000)	..	..	..
% change (1999-2003)	..	..	..
Structure of energy supply, (%)			
Solid fuels	55.00	58.00	..
Oil	27.00	28.00	..
Gas	5.00	5.00	..
Nuclear	..	..	..
Hydro, etc.	13.00	9.00	..
ROAD TRANSPORT *1)			
Road traffic volumes			
billion veh.-km	..	..	..
% change (1999-2003)	..	..	..
per capita (1 000 veh.-km/cap.)	..	..	..
Road vehicle stock			
10 000 vehicles (registered motor vechicles)	41.68	42.66	42.95
% change (1999-2003)	..	..	3.05
per capita (veh./100 inh.)	18.14	18.45	18.48

Bosnia and Herzegovina: Selected economic data
(continued)

B. Entity Republika Srpska

	1999	2001	2003
TOTAL AREA (1 000 km2) *3)	24.60	24.60	24.60
POPULATION *3)			
Total population, (1 000 000 inh.)-estimation	1.41	1.45	1.4635
% change (1999-2003)	..	..	3.83
Population density, (inh./km^2)	57.00	59.00	59.00
AGRICULTURE			
Value added in agriculture (% of GDP)	23.40	19.00	13.60

Sources:

* 1) Institut of Statisticks, Federation BiH
* 2) Ministry of Foreign Trade and Economic Relations BiH
* 3) Survey Institute, Republika Srpska

Bosnia and Herzegovina: Selected environmental data

A. Entity Federation of BiH

	1999	2001	2003
LAND *1)			
Total area (1 000 km^2)	26.1	26.1	26.1
Major protected areas (% of total area)	..	..	2.5
Nitrogenous fertilizer use (t/km^2 arable land)	..	..	..
FOREST *2)			
Forest area (% of land area)	..	44.6	..
Forest harvest (1000 m^3)	2,599.0	2,800.0	2,880.0
Tropical wood imports (US$/cap.)	..	..	..
THREATENED SPECIES *1)			
Mammals (% of species known)	..	..	..
Birds (% of species known)	30.0	30.0	30.0
Fish (% of species known)	11.8	11.8	11.8
WATER			
Water withdrawl (million m^3/year)	..	..	..
Fish catches (% of world catches)	..	..	..
Public waste water treatment	..	..	..
(% of population served)	..	98.4	..
Purified waste water (1000 m^3)	..	2,277.0	..
AIR			
Emissions of sulphur oxides (kg/cap.)	..	..	..
" (kg/US$ 1000 GDP)	..	..	..
Emissions of nitrogen oxides (kg/cap.)	..	..	..
" (kg/US$ 1000 GDP)	..	..	..
Emissions of carbon dioxide (kg/cap.)	..	..	..
" (kg/US$ 1000 GDP)	..	..	..
WASTE GENERATED			
Industrial waste (kg/US$ 1000 GDP)	..	..	..
Municipal waste (kg/cap.)	..	..	..
Nuclear waste (ton/M toe of TPES)	..	..	..
NOISE			
Population exposed to leq>65dB (A)-mil inh.	..	..	..

B. Entity Republika Srpska

	1999	2001	2003
LAND *3)			
Total area (1 000 km^2)	24.6	24.6	24.6
Nitrogenous fertilizer use (t/km^2 arable land)	0.3	0.3	0.2
Protected area (National parks)	..	..	128.0
FOREST *3)			
Forest area (% of land area)	43.2	43.7	44.0

Sources:

* 1) Institut of Statisticks, Federation BiH
* 2) FAO
* 3) Land Registar, Republika Srpska

SOURCES

Personal authors

1.   Danojevic, D. and O. Slipicevic. Environmental Health Priorities, Health Policy and Poverty Reduction. Draft Report. Banja Luka, Sarajevo, 2002.

2.   Grujic, L. Centar za promociju civilnog druπtva (Civil Society Promotion Center). Environment in Bosnia and Herzegovina 2002. Sarajevo 2002.

3.   Health Care System in Transition: Bosnia and Herzegovina. By J. Cain et al. in Cain, J. and E. Jakubowski eds. Copenhagen, European Observatory on Health Care Systems, 4 (7) 2002.

4   Manenti, A. World Health Organization. Regional Office for Europe. Decentralised Co-operation a New Tool for Conflict Situations. The experience of WHO in Bosnia and Herzegovina: A case study. 1999.

5   Miller, D. PA Consulting. Memorandum. Water Usage for Hydro Power Plants in BiH. 16 July 2003.

6   Milorad, B. Survey of Correlation between Air Pollution, Meteorological Conditions and Health Consequences among Population of Banja Luka. Master's Thesis. University of Banja Luka, Medical Faculty. Banja Luka, 1997.

7   Pöschl, J. The Vienna Institute for International Economic Studies (WIIW). The Economic Situation in Bosnia-Herzegovina. Vienna, April 2002.

8   Prepared by Cryan, S. and H. Peifer. EEA. EIONET Priority Data Flows 2002.Sixth Progress Report to the Management Board. Copenhagen, June 2003.

9   Rudez, M. and B. Jaksic. Report on the Current Legal Structures and Resources Available to the Environmental Protection Agencies and Inspectorates in Bosnia and Herzegovina. April 2002

10   Thompson, S. Office of High Representative Legal Department. Legal Discussion Brief. Shared Competencies Over Natural Resources Within the Federation of BiH. June 2001.

11   Thompson, S. Office of High Representative. Legal Discussion Brief. Forestry and the Federation of BiH. April 2003.

12   Water Supply and Drinking Water Quality of Republic of Srpska. International congress "Health for All" – Health Perspective in 21st century. By D. Danoevic et al. Banja Luka, June 4-8, 2003.

Material from Bosnia and Herzegovina

13   Bosna-S Services Company. Bosnia and Herzegovina Environmental Infrastructure Project. Environmental Assessment and Management Plan. Sarajevo, March 2002.

14   Bosnia and Herzegovina Mine Action Center. Report on Mine Action in Bosnia and Herzegovina in 2002. Sarajevo 2003.

15   Bosnia and Herzegovina. Act on Transmission of Electric Power, Regulator and System Operator of Bosnia and Herzegovina. January 5, 2002.

16   Bosnia and Herzegovina. Assessment of Sustainable Development in Bosnia and Herzegovina. The Report of B&H for the World Summit on Sustainable Development (WSSD). Sarajevo, Banja Luka, Mostar, June 2002.

17   Bosnia and Herzegovina. Constitution of Bosnia and Herzegovina 1995.

18   Bosnia and Herzegovina. Federal Office of Statistics. 2002 Statistical Yearbook. Sarajevo, 2002.

19   Bosnia and Herzegovina. Law on Ministries and other Bodies of Administration of Bosnia and Herzegovina. 4th February 2003 and 13 February 2003.

20   Bosnia and Herzegovina. National Environmental Action Plan (NEAP). Thematic document No. 01. Issues Related to Preservation of Clean Air in Bosnia and Herzegovina. Bosnia and Herzegovina, April 2002.

21   Bosnia and Herzegovina. National Environmental Action Plan (NEAP). Thematic document No. 02. Integrated Water Resources Management. Bosnia and Herzegovina, April 2002.

22   Bosnia and Herzegovina. National Environmental Action Plan (NEAP). Thematic document No. 03. Protection, Use and Management of Soil. Bosnia and Herzegovina, April 2002.

23   Bosnia and Herzegovina. National Environmental Action Plan (NEAP). Thematic document No. 04. Forest Management. Bosnia and Herzegovina, April 2002.

24   Bosnia and Herzegovina. National Environmental Action Plan (NEAP). Thematic document No. 05. Waste Management. Bosnia and Herzegovina, April 2002.

25   Bosnia and Herzegovina. National Environmental Action Plan (NEAP). Thematic document No. 06. Integral Spatial Management. Bosnia and Herzegovina, April 2002.

26   Bosnia and Herzegovina. National Environmental Action Plan (NEAP). Thematic document No. 07. Economy and Environment. Bosnia and Herzegovina, April 2002.

27   Bosnia and Herzegovina. National Environmental Action Plan (NEAP). Thematic document No. 08. Biodiversity and Protection of Natural and Cultural Heritage. Bosnia and Herzegovina, April 2002.

28   Bosnia and Herzegovina. National Environmental Action Plan (NEAP). Thematic document No. 09. Public Health, Demographic Structure and Social Issues. Bosnia and Herzegovina, April 2002.

29   Bosnia and Herzegovina. National Environmental Action Plan (NEAP). Thematic document No. 10. Legal and Institutional framework of Environmental management. Bosnia and Herzegovina, April 2002.

30   Bosnia and Herzegovina. National Environmental Action Plan (NEAP). Bosnia and Herzegovina. March 2003.

31   Bosnia and Herzegovina. Statistical Bulletin 1. National Accounts – Gross Domestic Product for Bosnia and Herzegovina. 1996 –2001. Sarajevo, January 2003.

32   Bosnia and Herzegovina. Statistical Bulletin 2. Demography. Sarajevo, February 2003.

33   Bosnia and Herzegovina. Statistical Bulletin 3. Sarajevo, July 2003.

34   Centar za Ekologiju i Prirodne Resurse Prirodno-Matematičkog Fakulteta Univerziteta u Sarajevu. Evaluacija Prirodnih Vrijednosti Životne Sredine u Brčko Distriktu. Sarajevo, August 2002.

35   Center for Environmentally Sustainable Development. Regional Action Plan for Mine Water Pollution Control. Sarajevo, 2003.

36   Centre for Ecology and Natural Resources at the Faculty of Science. Evaluation of Natural Values of the Environment in Brčko District, BiH. 2003.

37   Citizens' Guide to the Institutions of Government of Bosnia and Herzegovina. June 2002.

38   Concil of Ministers BiH. Poverty Reduction Strategy Paper PRSP Sector Priorities: Environment and Water Resources Management, Version II, Sarajevo, November 2003.

39   Council of Ministers BiH, Government of FBiH, Government of RS. The Action Plan for the Implementation of Priority Reforms. August 1st, 2003 – March 1st, 2004. Sarajevo, July 29th, 2003.

40   Federal Ministry of Health. Strategic Plan for Health System Reform in the Federation of Bosnia and Herzegovina. Sarajevo, 2000.

41   Federal Office of Statistics, Agency for Statistics of Bosnia and Herzegovina and The Republika Srpska Institute for Statistics. Living Standard Measurement Survey (LSMS). Sarajevo 2001.

42   Federation of Bosnia and Herzegovina. Framework Law on Environmental Protection.

43   Federation of Bosnia and Herzegovina. Law on Air.

44   Federation of Bosnia and Herzegovina. Law on Nature Protection.

45   Federation of Bosnia and Herzegovina. Law on Waste Management.

46   Federation of Bosnia and Herzegovina. Law on Water protection.

47   Glasnik newsletter. April - June 2003.

48   Glasnik SMP 2/2002 – Official gazette – Institute for Standardization, Metrology and Intellectual Property of Bosnia and Herzegovina.

49   Institute for Protection of Cultural-Historical and Natural Heritage of FbiH. Study on the Influence of Forestry on Biologically Sensitive Areas in BiH, 2002.

50   Institute for Urbanism of Republic Srpska. Solid Waste Management Study for Banja Luka Region. July 2002.

51   Institute of Public Health of Federation of Bosnia and Herzegovina. Health Statistics Annual. Federation of Bosnia and Herzegovina. 2001. Sarajevo, 2002.

52   Institute of Public Health of Federation of Bosnia and Herzegovina. Network, capacities and function of health system in Federation of Bosnia and Herzegovina in 1998. Sarajevo, 2000.

53   Institute of Public Health of Federation of Bosnia and Herzegovina. Network, capacities and function of health system in Federation of Bosnia and Herzegovina in 1999. Sarajevo, 2000.

54   Ministry of Health of the Federation of Bosnia and Herzegovina, Public Health Institute of the Federation of Bosnia and Herzegovina. National Environmental Health Action Plan for Federation of Bosnia and Herzegovina. Draft. 1999.

55   National Environmental Health Action Plan for Republic of Srpska. Draft. December 2001.

56   Public Health and Disease Control. Strategic Plan for the Institute of Public Health of the Republic of Srpska. Proposal. Basic Health Project. Banja Luka, 2003.

57   Public Health Institute of the Federation of Bosnia and Herzegovina. Health Behaviour in School-Aged Children Survey: Federation of Bosnia and Herzegovina. Sarajevo-Mostar, 2002.

58   Republika Srpska. Constitution of Republika Srpska.

59   Republika Srpska. Institute for Statistics. Demographic Statistics. Statistical Bulletin No.4. Banja Luka 2001.

60   Republika Srpska. Institute for Statistics. Demographic Statistics. Statistical Bulletin No.5. Banja Luka 2002.

61   Republika Srpska. Institute for Statistics. Demographic Statistics. Statistical Bulletin No.6. Banja Luka 2003.

62   Republika Srpska. Ministry of Health and Social Affairs of the Republika Srpska. Strategic Plan for Health System Reform and Reconstruction 1997-2000. May 1997.

63   Svjetlost and Institute of Public Health of Bosnia and Herzegovina. Health and Social Consequences of the War in Bosnia and Herzegovina. Rehabilitation Proposal. Fourth Edition. 1996.

64   Working Groups FBiH/RS Development Strategy BiH – PRSP Annex IV Health Care. December 2002.

65   Working Groups FBiH/RS Development Strategy BiH – PRSP Annex VII Environment. December 2002.

Regional and international institutions

66   Commission of the European Communities. Commission Staff Working paper. Bosnia and Herzegovina. Stabilisation and Association Report. Brussels, April 4, 2002.

67   EBRD. Strategy for Bosnia and Herzegovina. April 2003.

68   Economist Intelligence Unit. Country Profile 2003. Bosnia and Hercegovina. United Kingdom, 2003.

69   Economist Intelligence Unit. Country Report, October 2003. Bosnia and Hercegovina. United Kingdom, October 2003.

70   EPOS Health Consultants. Health Behaviour in School-Aged Children in the Republic of Srpska. 2003

71   EPOS Health Consultants. Health Status, Health Needs, and Utilization of Health Care Services of the Population in the Republic of Srpska. 2003

72   European Commission. External Relations Directorate General. Bosnia and Herzegovina. Country Strategy Paper 2002-2006.

73   European Commission. External Relations Directorate General. CARDS Assistance Programme to the western Balkans. Regional Strategy Paper 2002-2006.

74   Eurostat and UN Economic Commission for Europe. A Global Assessment of the Statistical System of Bosnia and Herzegovina. June 2003.

75   GEF Pipeline Entry. Project Concept. Integrated Ecosystem Management of the Neretva and Trebisjnica River Basin. June 12, 2003.

76   ICG. International Crisis Group. Bosnia Brcko: Getting in, getting on and getting out. Sarajevo, Brussels, June 2003.

77   ICG. International Crisis Group. Bosnia's Alliance for (Smallish) Change. Sarajevo, Brussels, August 2002.

78   ICG. International Crisis Group. Implementing equality: The "Constituent Peoples" Decision in Bosnia & Herzegovina. Sarajevo, Brussels, April 2002.

79   ICG. International Crisis Group. Policing the Police in Bosnia: A further Reform Agenda. Sarajevo, Brussels, May 2002.

80   ICG. International Crisis Group. The Continuing Challenge of refugee Return in Bosnia & Herzegovina. Sarajevo, Brussels, December 2002.

81   International Monetary Fund. Bosnia and Herzegovina. IMF Country Report No. 03 / 4. First Review Under the Stand-By Arrangement and Request for Waiver of performance Criteria. January 2003.

82   Italian Ministry of Environment and Territory/REC Preparation of Draft Framework Environmental Law and Feasibility Study as Precondition for the Environmental Protection Agency in Bosnia and Herzegovina – Working Materials. Sarajevo, 2003.

83   Joint Declaration. For the Collaboration Between Italy and Bosnia Herzegovina in the Field of Natural Protected Areas for the Conservation of Nature and Sustainable Development. Sarajevo 25th July 2003.

84   Mediterranean Environmental Technical Assistance Program (METAP)/World Bank. Urgent Strengthening of Environmental Institutions in Bosnia and Herzegovina. Report on Section 1 Institutional Reorganization Plan – Final Findings. Sarajevo, 2003.

85   Office of the High Representative. OHR Mission Implementation Statement. January 30, 2003.

86   Official Gazette of Republic of Srpska. Privatization in RS. Book of Regulations. Banja Luka 2000.

87   Regional Environmental Center for Central and Eastern Europe. Basic Considerations for Environmental Approximation for the Non-governmental Sector in Bosnia and Herzegovina. July 2003.

88   Regional Environmental Center for Central and Eastern Europe. Country office in Bosnia & Herzegovina. Country Report. Bosnia & Herzegovina within Strategic Environmental Analysis of Albania, Bosnia & Herzegovina, Kosovo and Macedonia. June 2000.

89   Regional Environmental Center for Central and Eastern Europe. Environmental Enforcement and Compliance in south Eastern Europe. Hungary, Szentendre, February 2002.

90   Regional Environmental Center for Central and Eastern Europe. Environmental Financing in Central and Eastern Europe. 1996-2001. Hungary, Szentendre, May 2003.

91   Regional Environmental Center for Central and Eastern Europe. REReP. The Regional Environmental Reconstruction Program for South Eastern Europe (REReP) Building a Better Environment for the Future. Ed. Braswell Jennifer. Szentendre, Hungary, October 2000.

92   Regional Environmental Center for Central and Eastern Europe. REReP. The Regional Environmental Reconstruction Programme for South Eastern Europe. Snapshots of Environmental Information Systems in South Eastern Europe. Current Progress and Future Priorities. Ed. Jerome Simpson. Szentendre, Hungary. August 2003.

93   Regional Environmental Center for Central and Eastern Europe. The Regional Environmental Reconstruction Programme for South Eastern Europe. Model for a Successful Assistance Mechanism. Szentendre, Hungary. 2003.

94   Regional Environmental Center for Central and Eastern Europe. Training Manual for Environmental Inspectorates in South Eastern Europe.Hungary, Szentendre, 2003.

95   Regional Environmental Center. Presentation of Current State in Environmental Field in Bosnia and Herzegovina with Emphasis on Necessary Legislation and BiH EPA – Basis for Development of Project TORs –Working Materials.

96   Regional Environmental Reconstruction Programme (REReP). Strengthening National Environmental Protection Agencies and their Inspectorates in South Eastern Europe through the Creation of a Regional "Balkan Environmental Regulation Compliance Enforcement Network" (BERCEN). Sarajevo, August 2002.

97   UNDP Bosnia and Herzegovina. Bosnia and Herzegovina Human Development Report/ Millennium Development Goals 2003. June 2003.

98   UNDP. Early Warning System. Bosnia and Herzegovina. Annual Report. 2002.

99   UNDP. Early Warning System. Bosnia and Herzegovina. Quarterly Report January – March 2003.

100   UNDP. Human Development Report 2002. Bosnia and Herzegovina.

101   UNDP. Human Development Report 2003. Millennium Development Goals in Bosnia and Herzegovina 2015. June 2003.

102   UNDP. Independent Bureau for Humanitarian Issues. Human Development Report Bosnia and Herzegovina 2000 Youth. 2000.

103   UNDP; BiH Ministry of Foreign Trade and Economic Relations; RS Ministry of Economic Relations and Coordination; FBiH Ministry of Finance. International Assistance to BiH, 1996-2002. A tentative analysis: Who is doing what, where. 2003.

104   UNEP. Depleted Uranium in Bosnia and Herzegovina. Post-Conflict Environmental Assessment. March 2003.

105   UNEP. Priority Actions Programme. Sustainability of SAP MED. Pilot Project Implementation Plan. Implementation of Economic Instruments for Sustainable Operation of Wastewater Utilities in the Mediterranean Region of Bosnia and Herzegovina. Split, May 2002.

106   UNICEF. Republika Srpska Multiple Indicator Cluster Survey 2000.

107   UNIDO. National Ozone Unit. National Phase-out Plane for Bosnia and Herzegovina NPP-BiH

108   United Nations Environment Programme. Depleted Uranium in Bosnia and Herzegovina. Post-Conflict Environmental Assessment. 2003.

109   United Nations. Second country cooperation framework for Bosnia and Herzegovina 2001-2003. DP/CCF/BIH/2. 17 November 2000.

110   World Bank. Project Appraisal Document on a Proposed Credit for a Solid Waste management Project. Report No: 23929-BIH. May 23, 2003.

111   World Health Organization et al. Guidelines for Safe Disposal of Unwanted Pharmaceuticals in and after Emergencies. March 1999.

Internet addresses:

Ministries and government institutions

State institutions

112	Bosnia and Herzegovina Mine Action Centre	http://www.bhmac.org/
113	Central Bank of Bosnia and Herzegovina	http://www.cbbh.gov.ba/
114	Communication Regulatory Agency	http://www.cra.ba/
115	Constitutional Court of Bosnia and Herzegovina	http://www.ccbh.ba/
116	Department of Civil Aviation	http://www.bhdca.gov.ba/
117	Federal Meteorological Office	http://www.fmzbih.com.ba/
118	Federal Mine Action Centre	http://www.bhmac.org/fed/
119	Federal Ministry of Finance	http://www.fmf.gov.ba/
120	Federal Ministry of Physical Planning and Environment	http://www.grida.no/enrin/htmls/bosnia/soe/html/
121	Federal Ministry of Social Affairs, Displaced Persons and Refugees	http://www.fmsa.gov.ba/
122	Federal Ministry of Transport and Communication	http://www.fmpik.gov.ba/
123	Foreign Investment Promotion Agency	http://www.fipa.gov.ba/
124	Ministry of Foreign Affairs	http://www.mvp.gov.ba/Index_eng.htm
125	News Agency of Bosnia and Herzegovina	http://www.bihpress.ba/
126	Office of the Human Rights Ombudsperson	http://www.ohro.ba/
127	Radio Television of Bosnia and Herzegovina	http://www.rtvbih.ba/

The Federation of Bosnia and Herzegovina

128	Agency for Privatization in the Federation of Bosnia and Herzegovina	http://www.apf.com.ba/
129	Federation of BiH	http://www.fbihvlada.gov.ba/
130	Government of the Federation of Bosnia and Herzegovina	http://www.fbihvlada.gov.ba/
131	Institution of the Ombudsmen of the Federation of Bosnia and Herzegovina	http://www.bihfedomb.org/
132	Investment Bank of the Federation of Bosnia and Herzegovina	http://www.ibf-bih.com/
133	Parliament of the Federation of Bosnia and Herzegovina	http://www.parlamentfbih.gov.ba/
134	Securities Commission of the Federation of Bosnia and Herzegovina	http://www.komvp.gov.ba/

Republika Srpska

135	Commission for Real Property Claims of Displaced Persons and Refugees	http://www.crpc.org.ba/
136	Constitutional Court	http://www.ustavnisud.org/
137	Directorate for Privatization	http://www.rsprivatizacija.com/
138	Government of the Serbian Republic	http://www.vladars.net/
139	Office of the High Representative in Bosnia and Herzegovina	http://www.ohr.int/
140	Radio Television of the Serbian Republic	http://www.rtrs-bl.com/
141	Republican Customs Service	http://www.rucrs.com/
142	Republican Office of the Public Prosecutor	http://www.tuzilastvo-rs.org/

Political parties

143	Croatian Christian Democratic Union of Bosnia and Herzegovina	http://www.posluh.hr/hkdu-bih/
144	Croatian Democratic Community of Bosnia and Herzegovina	http://www.hdzbih.org/
145	Croatian Peasants Party of Bosnia and Herzegovina	http://www.hssbih.com.ba/
146	Liberal Democratic Party	http://www.liberali.ba/

147	Party of Democratic Action	http://www.sda.ba/
148	Party of Independent Socialdemocrats of the Republic of Srpska	http://snsd.tripod.com/
149	Serbian Democratic Party	http://www.sds-rs.org/
150	Serbian Party of the Serbian Republic	http://www.srpskastranka-rs.org/
151	Social Democratic Party of Bosnia and Herzegovina	http://www.sdp-bih.net/

Other internet sites

152	Atlapedia	http://www.atlapedia.com/online/countries/bosnia.htm
153	CIA Factbook	http://www.cia.gov/cia/publications/factbook/geos/bk.html
154	Foreign Investment Promotion Agency	http://www.fipa.gov.ba/
155	Governments on the Web	http://www.gksoft.com/govt/en/ba.html
156	Grida: BiH SOE 1998	http://www.grida.no/enrin/htmls/bosnia/soe/html/
157	Grida: BiH Environment in 2002	http://grida.no/enrin/htmls/bosnia/bosnia2002/
158	International Finance Center	http://biz.yahoo.com/ifc/ba/
159	Japan International Cooperation Agency	http://www.jica.go.jp/english/index.html
160	OSCE Mission to Bosnia	http://www.oscebih.org/oscebih_eng.asp
161	Soros English Language Program	http://www.soros.org/spelt/bih.html
162	Sustainability of SAP MED. Report on the Meeting on Implementation/ Evaluation of Pilot Projects, and Proposals for National Action Plans. Split, March 28 - 29, 2003.	http://www.pap-thecoastcentre.org/Split-EI.doc
163	Tias, Tilburg University, the Netherlands	http://timer.kub.nl/country.statistics/countrystats_bosnia.html
164	UN Agenda 21	http://www.un.org/esa/agenda21/natlinfo/
165	UN Cartographic Section	http://www.un.org/Depts/Cartographic/map/profile/bosnia.pdf
166	UNDP Human Development Report 2002	http://www.undp.org/hdr2002/
167	UNDP Office in BiH	http://www.undp.ba/onews.asp
168	UNEP Depleted Uranium	http://postconflict.unep.ch/publications/BiH_DU_report.pdf
169	UNEP Country Profile	http://www.unep.net/profile/index.cfm
170	USAID Country Profile	http://www.usaid.gov/regions/europe_eurasia/countries/ba/index.html
171	Web site of Heidelberg Cement Group	http://www.heidelbergcement.cz/cee/index.php?idp=42
172	Wikipedia	http://www.wikipedia.org/wiki/Bosnia_and_Herzegovina
173	World Bank	http://www.worldbank.org.ba/
174	World Health Organization. European Health For All Database. (HFA-DB).	http://hfadb.who.dk/hfa/
175	World travel guide	http://www.travel-guide.com/data/bih/bih500.asp

Conventions and PRogrammes

Global conventions

176	Convention concerning the Protection of the World Cultural and Natural Heritage (World Heritage Convention)	http://whc.unesco.org/nwhc/pages/doc/main.htm
177	Convention on Biological Diversity	http://www.biodiv.org/default.aspx
178	Convention on Fishing and Conservation of Living Resources of the High Seas	http://sedac.ciesin.org/entri/texts/high.seas.fishing.living.resources.1958.html
179	Convention on International Trade in Endangered Species of Wild Fauna and Flora (CITES)	http://www.cites.org
180	Convention on the Control of Trans-boundary Movements of Hazardous Waste and their Disposal (Basel Convention)	http://www.basel.int
181	Convention on the Conservation of Migratory Species of Wild Animals	http://www.wcmc.org.uk/cms/
182	Convention on Wetlands of International Importance especially as Waterfowl Habitat (Ramsar Convention)	http://www.ramsar.org/
183	Convention to combat Desertification in countries experiencing serious drought and/or desertification, particularly in Africa	http://www.unccd.int/main.php
184	International Maritime Organisation Convention	http://www.imo.org
185	International Plant Protection Convention	http://www.ippc.int/IPP/En/default.htm

| 186 | United Nations Framework Convention on Climate Change (UNFCCC) | http://unfccc.int/resource/convkp.html |
| 187 | Vienna Convention for the Protection of the Ozone Layer | http://www.unep.org/ozone/index.asp |

Regional conventions

188	Convention on Long-range Trans-boundary Air Pollution	http://www.unece.org/env/lrtap/lrtap_h1.htm
189	Protocol to Abate Acidification, Eutrophication and Ground-level Ozone	http://www.unece.org/env/lrtap/multi_h1.htm
190	Protocol on Persistent Organic Pollutants (POPs)	http://www.unece.org/env/lrtap/pops_h1.htm
191	Protocol on Heavy Metals	http://www.unece.org/env/lrtap/hm_h1.htm
192	Protocol on Further Reduction of Sulphur Emissions	http://www.unece.org/env/lrtap/fsulf_h1.htm
193	Protocol concerning the Control of Emissions of Volatile Organic Compounds	http://www.unece.org/env/lrtap/vola_h1.htm
194	Protocol concerning the Control of Emissions of Nitrogen Oxides	http://www.unece.org/env/lrtap/nitr_h1.htm
195	Protocol on the Reduction of Sulphur Emissions	http://www.unece.org/env/lrtap/sulf_h1.htm
196	EMEP Protocol	http://www.unece.org/env/lrtap/emep_h1.htm
197	Convention on Environmental Impact Assessment in a Trans-boundary Context	http://www.unece.org/env/eia/convratif.html
198	Protocol on Strategic Environmental Assessment (Kiev, 2003)	http://www.unece.org/env/eia/protocol_status.html
199	Convention on the Trans-boundary Effects of Industrial Accidents	http://www.unece.org/env/teia/signat.htm
200	Convention on Persistent Organic Pollutants (POPs)	http://www.pops.int/
201	Convention on Access to Information, Public Participation in Decision-making and Access to Justice in Environmental Matters	http://www.unece.org/env/pp/ctreaty.htm
202	Protocol on Pollutant Release and Transfer Registers	http://www.unece.org/env/pp/cprotocol.htm
203	Convention on the Protection and Use of Trans-boundary Watercourses and International Lakes	http://www.unece.org/env/water/status/lega_wc.htm
204	Protocol on Water and Health	http://www.unece.org/env/water/status/lega_wh.htm
205	Protocol on Civil Liability	http://www.unece.org/env/civil-liability/status_cl.html
206	Convention for the Protection of the Marine Environment and the Coastal Region of the Mediterranean	http://www.unepmap.org/
207	Convention on cooperation for the protection and sustainable use of the Danube river	http://ksh.fgg.uni-lj.si/danube/envconv/ http://www.rec.org/danubepcu/sign.html

Other Regional or International Agreements

| 208 | Global Environment Facility | http://www.gefweb.org/ |